Metropolitan College of NY
Library - 7th Floor
60 West Street
New York, NY 10006

FOCUS ON CIVILIZATIONS AND CULTURES

VIRTUAL CIVILIZATION IN THE 21ST CENTURY

Focus on Civilizations and Cultures

Additional books in this series can be found on Nova's website under the Series tab.

Additional e-books in this series can be found on Nova's website under the e-book tab.

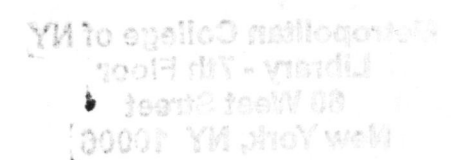

FOCUS ON CIVILIZATIONS AND CULTURES

HM
851
.V567
2016

VIRTUAL CIVILIZATION IN THE 21ST CENTURY

ANDREW TARGOWSKI
EDITOR

New York

Metropolitan College of NY
Library - 7th Floor
60 West Street
New York, NY 10006

Copyright © 2015 by Nova Science Publishers, Inc.

All rights reserved. No part of this book may be reproduced, stored in a retrieval system or transmitted in any form or by any means: electronic, electrostatic, magnetic, tape, mechanical photocopying, recording or otherwise without the written permission of the Publisher.

For permission to use material from this book please contact us: nova.main@novapublishers.com

NOTICE TO THE READER

The Publisher has taken reasonable care in the preparation of this book, but makes no expressed or implied warranty of any kind and assumes no responsibility for any errors or omissions. No liability is assumed for incidental or consequential damages in connection with or arising out of information contained in this book. The Publisher shall not be liable for any special, consequential, or exemplary damages resulting, in whole or in part, from the readers' use of, or reliance upon, this material. Any parts of this book based on government reports are so indicated and copyright is claimed for those parts to the extent applicable to compilations of such works.

Independent verification should be sought for any data, advice or recommendations contained in this book. In addition, no responsibility is assumed by the publisher for any injury and/or damage to persons or property arising from any methods, products, instructions, ideas or otherwise contained in this publication.

This publication is designed to provide accurate and authoritative information with regard to the subject matter covered herein. It is sold with the clear understanding that the Publisher is not engaged in rendering legal or any other professional services. If legal or any other expert assistance is required, the services of a competent person should be sought. FROM A DECLARATION OF PARTICIPANTS JOINTLY ADOPTED BY A COMMITTEE OF THE AMERICAN BAR ASSOCIATION AND A COMMITTEE OF PUBLISHERS.

Additional color graphics may be available in the e-book version of this book.

Library of Congress Cataloging-in-Publication Data

ISBN: 978-1-63463-261-4

Published by Nova Science Publishers, Inc. † New York

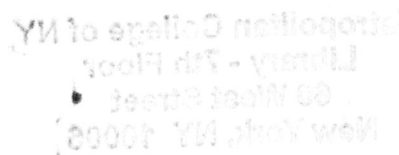

Contents

Foreword		vii
	Andrew Targowski	
Part I. Civilizing Virtual Society		1
Chapter 1	From Information Wave to Virtual Civilization *Andrew Targowski*	3
Chapter 2	Society of Virtual Civilization *Muhammad A. Razi*	27
Part II. Civilizing Virtual Culture		43
Chapter 3	Religion of Virtual Civilization *Andrew Targowski*	45
Chapter 4	Culture of Virtual Civilization *Kuanchin Chen*	55
Chapter 5	The Virtual Divide As One of Civilization's Divides *Andrew Targowski*	73
Part III. Civilizing Virtual Infrastructure		103
Chapter 6	Virtual and Augmented Reality Technology Development *William Tepfenhart*	105
Chapter 7	Virtuality and Reality of Civilization *Andrew Targowski*	121

Part IV. The Future of Virtual Civilization   **153**

Chapter 8   The Future of Virtual Civilization   **155**
Andrew Targowski

Afterword   **169**
Andrew Targowski

Editor Contact Information   **177**

Index   **179**

FOREWORD

Andrew Targowski[*]
Western Michigan University, US
President Emeritus of the International Society
For the Comparative Study of Civilizations (2007-2013)

In the 21st century the "real-space" of the world civilization gained the virtual space known as cyberspace. Cyberspace is a product of information technology exemplified by the Internet as the world system of information highways (INFOSTRADAS) which forms a digital space containing all sorts of files and communication exchanges practiced in online and real-time modes. These files comprise cyberspace (Figure F.1).

Because of the Internet and digital interactions, cyberspace is more active than real space (Figure F.2).

For the first time in 6,000 years of human civilization, society has become a quantum society, which at the same time can be real and virtual one. The virtual society is invisible for those who do not use networking computers. Even for those who do use them, cyberspace access requires some sort of commercial transactions-oriented activities (ex. on Amazon or eBay and others), searching on Google or Yahoo or communicating as a member of one of social networks, e.g., Facebook, Twitter, LinkedIn, and others (Figure F.3).

---

[*] andrew.targowski@wmich.edu

Figure F.1. The Internet creates cyberspace through the world system of information highways [in augmented reality (AR)].

Figure F.2. Cyberspace is more active than the real space, which is illustrated in augmented virtuality (AV).

Figure F.3. Social networks have experienced rapid growth almost everywhere on the Earth. (Photo: ncmedsoc.org).

This book recognizes the development of the Earth's space in the following scopes of mixed reality (MR) (Figure F.4):

- Real environment (RE) – a digital model of the real environment, which looks real, but is made by computers.
- Augmented reality (AR) – a live copy and view of a physical, real-world environment whose elements are augmented by computer-generated sensory input such as sound, video, graphics or GPS data (Figure F.1).
- Augmented virtuality (AV) – a virtual model of the real environment with an inserted real image of the reality (Figure F.2).
- Virtual environment (VE) - a virtual environment in real-time created by 3D computer graphics. This approach usually requires laborious modeling and expensive special purpose rendering hardware.

This book evaluates the phenomenon of the virtuality is it a temporary technological phantom or it is going to stay forever? Is it a new technological wave of civilization or is it even a new civilization (Chapter 1)? Since it is a new civilization its virtual society will be characterized (Chapter 2). If this is a new civilization what is its religion (since every civilization is characterized by a religion) (Chapter 3)? Also its culture will be analyzed too (Chapter 4). As a new civilization, virtual society will promote certain ways of practicing daily life. These new ways will be characterized and evaluated (Chapter 5).

Some trends of the virtual technology will be evaluated (Chapter 6). Is the virtuality a positive tool which will enhance the quality of our lives or will provide stronger inequality among skillful and unskillful users of it? So far the digital divide worsened peoples' well-being at the lowest social strata. Can virtuality improve those people's well-being or will it worsen (Chapter 7)?

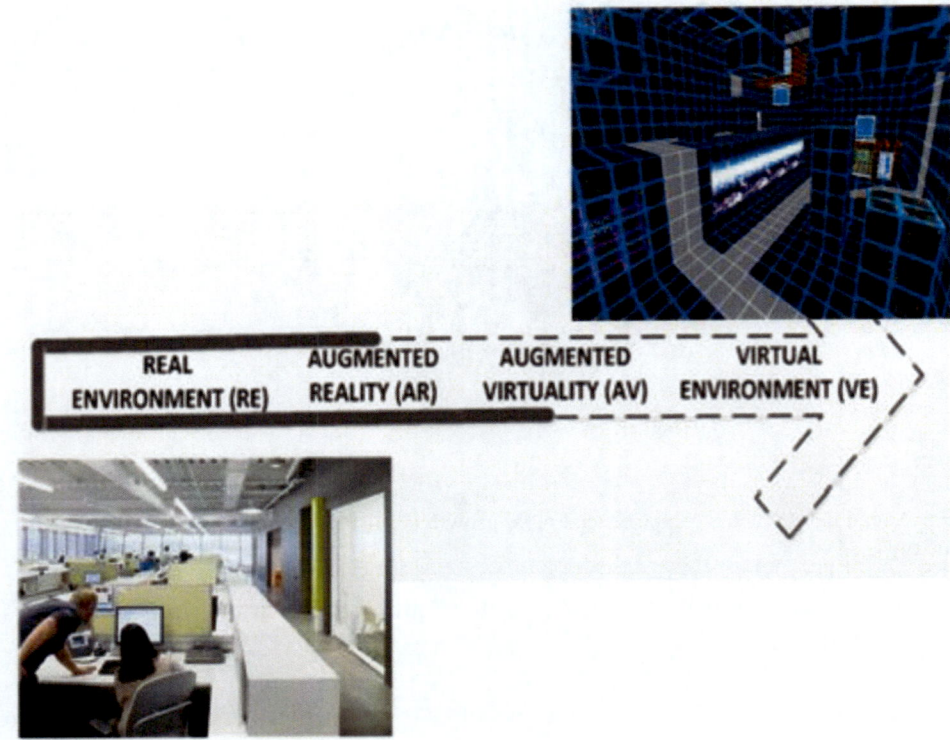

Figure F.4. The Mixed Reality (MR) - information technology-driven.

What is the future of the virtuality? As a new landscape of civilization its development will be predicted within the framework of several possible futures of real civilization which are seen today. However, *a la* science fiction, future will also be sketched, reminding us that when we deal with technology, particularly information technology, so called science fiction predictions usually take place in our real lives.

It looks as though the prediction of science fiction is that the political class world-wide is losing touch with the reality of citizens, and that social networks can evolve into virtual nations and even into a global virtual nation. There is only one condition in which the marketed-oriented social networks should evolve into citizens-owned networks: in order to secure independence of thinking and acting. Is it possible that something in the virtual landscape can be organized at such a large-scale and last if it is not for profit?

This kind a prediction of the architecture of cyberspace and realspace development in the context of the contemporary civilizations such ones as African, Chinese, Japanese, Hindu, Buddhist, Western, Eastern, Islamic, and Global will be evaluated in Chapter 8.

It will also be discussed that how we develop and behave in the Virtual Civilization will define our civilization's success in the 21st century. Will this civilization enhance the real civilization or will it leave many of us behind in a divided environment created by the rising virtuality.

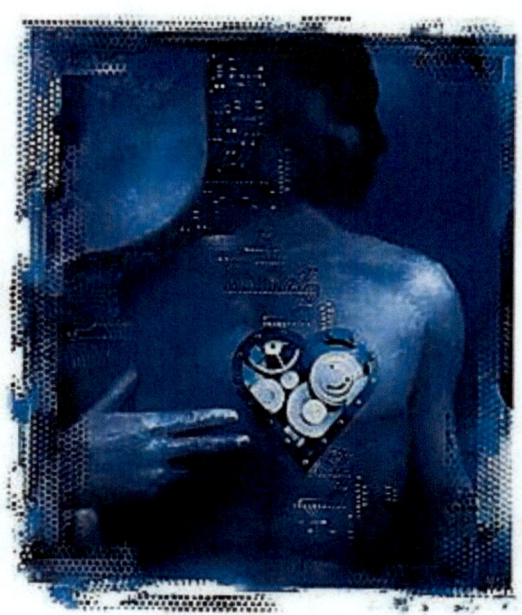

Figure F.5. Will humans be real, virtual, or combination of both? (Photo: schwartztronica.wordpress.com).

This book's ambition is to provide insights into how virtual technology is transforming our economy and society, a process that has just begun a few years ago. As massive applications of virtuality radically reshape our current real civilization, we need to develop new social and business goals, and strategies and public policies that can perhaps amplify our human abilities for the sake of civilization sustainability. It is important to see that every person is able to secure a vital and sustainable life style in these times of technological superiority and uncontrollable progress which seems largely for the sake of technology and not its users.

Part I. Civilizing Virtual Society

In: Virtual Civilization in the 21st Century
Editor: Andrew Targowski

ISBN: 978-1-63463-261-4
© 2015 Nova Science Publishers, Inc.

Chapter 1

FROM INFORMATION WAVE TO VIRTUAL CIVILIZATION

Andrew Targowski
Western Michigan University, US
President Emeritus of the International Society
For the Comparative Study of Civilizations (2007-2013)

ABSTRACT

The *purpose* of this investigation is to define the central contents and issues of the rise and development of Virtual Civilization. The *methodology* is based on an interdisciplinary big-picture view of the Virtual Civilization's elements of development and their interdependency. Among the *findings* are: Virtual Civilization has infrastructural characteristics, a world-wide unlimited, socially constructed work and leisure space in cyberspace, and it can last centuries/millennia - as long as info-communication technology is operational. *Practical implications:* The mission of Virtual Civilization is to control the public policy of real civilizations in order to secure the common good in real societies. *Social implication:* The quest for the common good by virtual society may limit or even replace representative democracy by direct democracy which, while positively solving some problems, may eventually trigger permanent political chaos in real civilizations. *Originality:* This investigation, by providing an interdisciplinary and civilizational approach at the big-picture level defined several crucial repercussions of Virtual Civilization, which is evolving in our times and offers a golden opportunity for the well-being of humankind.

INTRODUCTION

The purpose of this investigation is to evaluate the development of civilization since its beginnings 6,000 years ago (4,000 BC) in order to define the rise of the Virtual Civilization in the 21st century.

The English historian Arnold Toynbee (1889-1975) published his greatest work in the twelve-volume *A Study of History* [(1934-61) (1995)], where he compared the history of twenty six different civilizations and argued that each follows a similar pattern of evolution through a cyclical pattern of growth, maturity, and decay. He believed that societies thrive best in response to challenges and that a society's most important task is to create a religion. He stressed religious and philosophical factors as guiding civilizations.

There is only one world civilization, yet there are about 26 main autonomous civilizations that have developed in the last 6,000 years. Perhaps, if one included satellite civilizations (cultures), this number could possibly reach about 100 or even more. However, for the clarity of this synthesis we would like to limit the scope to the foremost 26 autonomous civilizations.

The world civilization as a continuum never dies—it only evolves from one stage to another. This evolution takes place through the life cycle of autonomous civilizations. At the very beginning of human civilization, there were several successful formations of living processes that could be considered autonomous civilizations. They took place in different parts of the world and, and there were about eight cases. The first autonomous civilization was the Mesopotamian Civilization (including Sumerian), which emerged in the valley of the Euphrates-Tigris rivers in the Middle East, about 4,000 B.C. In the Far-East, the first autonomous civilizations rose inland: Indus (Harrappan) about 2,500 B.C. and Sinic about 1,500. In Africa the initial civilization was the Berberic-Carthagean Civilization 600 B.C. and, in South America early autonomous civilizations included the Andean Civilization that emerged about 1500 B.C.. In Central America the first autonomous civilization was the Meso-American Civilization which rose 1000 BC. Both civilizations fell about 1600 AD.

Autonomous civilizations rose in response to physical challenges of nature (ecosystem). Humans began to organize themselves into a society, which provided exchangeable and specialized services, such as food hunting, food production, house building, road construction, transportation, health care, entertainment, and so forth. These services and growing human communication led towards the formation of cities. These types of autonomous civilizations we will call societal civilizations.

In addition to the environmental challenges, the societal civilization as a whole has been threatened by its own internal structure involving power, wealth creation, beliefs enforcement, family formation, leadership, and so forth. As societal civilizations evolved into more complex entities, they were managed by cultural manipulation. These types of autonomous civilizations we will refer to as cultural civilizations. By culture, we understand a value-driven patterned behavior of a human entity.

Ever since religion was transformed from beliefs in magic to beliefs in poly-gods and then to a mono-god, cultural civilization has applied religion as the main tool of cultural control. Religious and military forces were the foundations of the power apparatus that maintained the society as a governed entity. These forces civilized society and moved it into higher levels of organization. Among cultural civilizations one can recognize about 16 cases, such as the Egyptian Civilization 3100 B.C., the Minoan 2700 B.C., the Mycean Civilization 1500 B.C., the Sinic Civilization 1500 B.C., the Hellenic Civilization 750 B.C., the Canaanite Civilization 1100 B.C., the Hindu Civilization 600 B.C., the Roman Civilization 31 B.C., the Eastern Civilization 350 A.D., the Hellenistic Civilization 323 B.C., the Buddhist Civilization 600 A.D., the Ethiopian Civilization 400 A.D., the Sub-Saharan Civilization 800 A.D., the Western Civilization 800 A.D., the Islamic Civilization 1300 A.D. and the Maghrebian Civilization 1000 A.D. Cultural civilization evolves into a civilization with challenges generated by intra and inter-civilizational issues of war and peace. These types of issues have been managed by technological means of domination. Such civilizations we will call infrastructural civilizations.

Infrastructural civilization's purpose is to expand spheres of influence with the means of technology. Technology drives the development of infrastructural civilizations. The prime target of technological applications has been the military which supports the main values of a given civilization. By-products of militaristic applications of technology affect the civilian part of its infrastructure. Among eight infrastructural civilizations one can recognize the Sinic Civilization 1500 B.C., the Hindu Civilization 600 B.C., the Japanese Civilization 650 A.D., the Western Civilization 800 A.D., the Eastern Civilization 350 A.D., the Buddhist Civilization 600 A.D., the Islamic Civilization 1300 A.D., and the African Civilization 1847 A.D (after the Berlin Treaty).

By the end of the 2nd Millennium, infrastructural civilizations had become civilizations responsible for world hemisphere influence and domination. Hence, Western Civilization dominates the Western Hemisphere, Eastern and Hindu rule the Eastern Hemisphere, the Islamic Civilization rules the Near and Middle East Hemisphere and some parts of the Far East Hemisphere, the Japanese Civilization governs some parts of the Far East Hemisphere, the Chinese Civilization influences the majority of the Far East Hemisphere, and the Buddhist civilization influences a small part of the Far East Hemisphere.

The process of evolving civilizations at the end of the 20th century is depicted in Figure 1.1 according to the kinds of challenges they face and their responses.

According to a composite definition of a civilization (Targowski 2009b), it is characterized by the following important attributes:

1. Large society
   - Specializing in labor
   - Self-differentiating
   - Sharing the same knowledge system
2. Space and Time
   - Autonomous fuzzy reification
   - Distinguished and extended area or period of time
   - Reification not a part of a larger entity

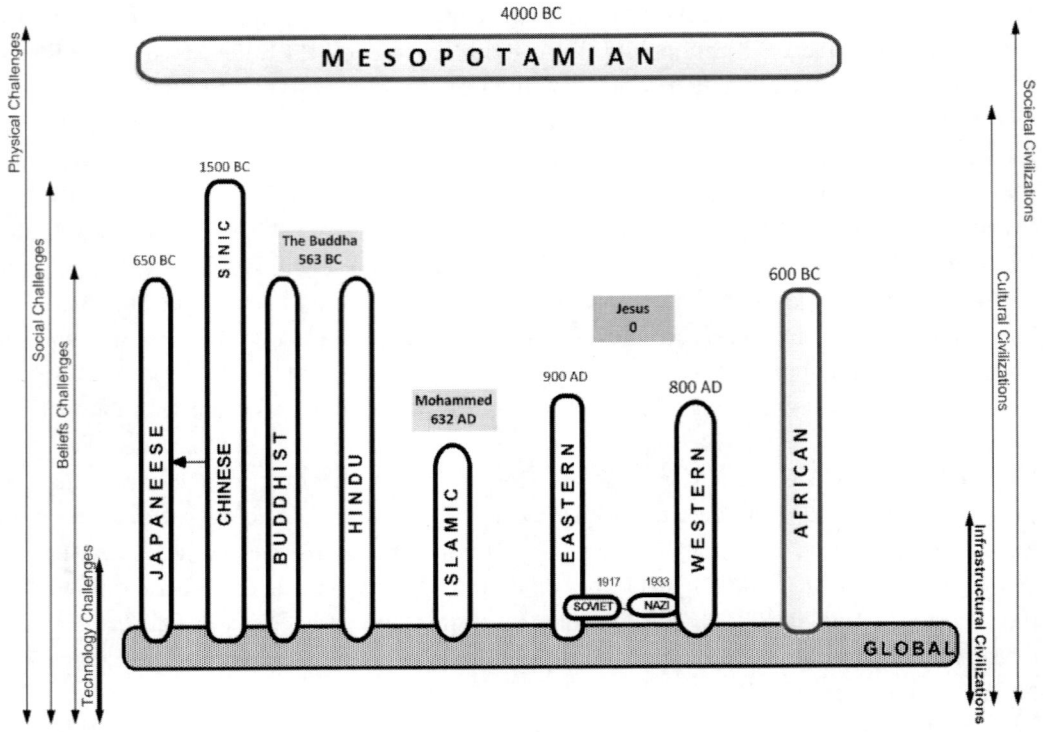

Figure 1.1. The Process of Evolving Civilizations at the End of the 20th Century.

- 3. Cultural system, values and symbol-driven
  - Communication driven (e.g.: literate and electronic media)
  - Religion, wealth and power driven
- 4. Infrastructural system, technology-driven by first at least one of the following:
  - Urban infrastructure
  - Agricultural Infrastructure
  - Other infrastructures (Industrial, Information and so forth)
- 5. Cycle-driven
  - Rising, growing, declining, and falling over time

Based on these attributes, the composite definition of civilization is as follows:

Civilization is a large society living in an autonomous, fuzzy reification (invisible-visible) which is not a part of larger one and exists over an extended period of time. It specializes in labor and differentiates from other civilizations by developing its own advanced cultural system driven by communication, religion, wealth, power, and sharing the same knowledge/wisdom system within complex urban, agricultural infrastructures, and others such as industrial and information ones. It also progresses in a cycle or cycles of rising, growing, declining and falling.

A graphic model of civilization is illustrated in Figure 1.2.

Figure 1.2. A Model of Civilization.

A short definition of a civilization can be as follows:

A civilization is a complex of compatibly interactive entities of society, culture(s) and infrastructure in a large frame of territory and time, usually embracing several nations and centuries/millennia.

Civilizations are dynamic and rise, grow, decline and disappear or transform into other ones. Usually the developmental process of civilization can be divided in states (feudal systems, state systems, and imperial systems) (Melko 1969). However, in the study of the history of political or technological developments, the time categories are usually considered as "ages," "eras," and "waves."

By an "ages" one can understand a dominant technology or political system applied in practice at a certain time, although a given technology/political system is sooner or later replaced by the next "age" of progressive or regressive solutions. An "era" is a synonym for "age" but implies a long "age." Also an "era" can be replaced by the next "era" of a progressive or regressive solution.

A "wave" is associated with the production, processing, or trade of a kind of food, good, or information related to a new technology or new rules. It has a very strong impact upon the *modus operandi* of a society. It is not replaceable, but is impacted by the next wave of technology.

AGES, ERAS, AND WAVES OF CIVILIZATION

Man has survived longer than stronger animals because he has had an important advantage: a *brain* driven by information-communication. With a brain, mankind has been able to learn, communicate, and develop a structure of consciousness. At first, the *nose* was the most important organ for the archaic, nomadic hunters. Then, about 200,000 years ago, the human information system began "upgrading" human consciousness through emotions and rituals, and the *ear* became the most important organ for those hunters. Their ears developed an appreciation for music and dance. That was the first advanced pattern of human cultural behavior. About 10,000 years ago, *consciousness* became mythical and 2-dimensional, with some appreciation for the natural tempo of events.

Mankind started farming, dreaming of a better social order for its members, and creating myths through symbolic imagination and *language*-driven communication. At this time, then, the *mouth* became the most important organ. Around 5000 BC, the Egyptian calendar, regulated by the Sun and Moon in 360 days (12 months of 30 days each), became the first organized information system (IS) device that supported man's survival and development. About 1000 years later, the Sumerians developed writing and organizational patterns for "civilized" cities. About 2,500 BC, the structure of consciousness became *mental* and 3-dimensional, with a sense of abstract time, cultural curiosity for science and art, dogma, rules, and laws. The first knowledge centers appeared in Egypt, where written literature lamented about the meaning of life using papyrus and collecting them in the first World's Library in Alexandria. The manufacturing of objects and the production of food (bread, beer) took place. Thus, the *eye* became the most important organ for the awakened man with volition and reflection about himself and the world (Simpson 1992).

For extended periods of time, the evolution of the Earth was understood as being regulated by a relationship between nature's internal forces such as gravity, atomic dynamics, time, and space dynamics. Today, the problem of life on Earth has become a puzzle based upon relationships (info-communication) among people and their level of *cognition*, and communicating this through *information-knowledge* systems.

The tool in achieving this role is *knowledge*, disseminated first by books and now by computers and their networks. Mediated communication has a long story. The invention of the printing press by Johann Gutenberg in 1454 boosted the spread of knowledge. This has become the most significant invention to separate written print from the spoken world. Printing soon became a means of disseminating and intensifying intellectual endeavors. Before Gutenberg, each volume was handwritten, often by monks. In the 15th century, a book was as costly and as rare as jewels.

Before the printing press, scientists would take long trips merely to familiarize themselves with the content of a certain book. The enlightened ruler Carl IV of Luxembourg collected 114 volumes, while the French king Carl V, amassed as many as 900. Then, printing houses began to print hundreds of books (2-3). By the year 1500, within 50 years of the invention of the German press,[1] 30,000 reasonably priced books were in circulation. The satire of Erasmus of Rotterdam appeared during his lifetime in 27 editions. Print was steering thoughts and ideas in millions of people, inspiring them to speed, simplify and strengthen the work of the mind.

(Photo: Library of Congress, www.loc.gov)

Figure 1.3. The Gutenberg Press modernized civilization for the next 500+ years.

The printed alphabet in book form, which was the first "computer terminal," became an absorber and transformer of civilization. New media such as letters and printed books altered the ration between our senses and changed the mental (information processing) process. Print made a split between the head and heart which has become a trauma, affecting Western Civilization up to the present (McLuhan 1962). It created government regulations, but it also inspired individualism and opposition to ideology, science, and art. Science and technology began to develop at an accelerated pace. Airplanes, cars, telegraphs, telephones, typewriters, phonographs, movies, radios, televisions, weapons, computers, automation, and telecommunications modernized human life and its story. Human consciousness has become integral and 4-dimentional (free from space and time), allowing us to enjoy learning, loving, wholeness, and wisdom for the community and ourselves. The nervous system has now become the most crucial organ, developing a "meta-sense." We are better at understanding rather than explaining the purpose and rules of our existence through education and research.

American physicist John Wheeler has formulated the Theory of the Participatory Universe. In this theory, observers are central to the nature of physical reality and matter is ultimately relegated to the mind. Wheeler sees the Universe as a gigantic "information processing" system with a yet-undermined output, and he has coined the phrase "IT from

---

[1] One must mention that woodblock printing of written characters was known in China by A.D. 350. Ceramic movable type was in use in China about A.D. 1040. The Koreans invented print in the 5th century; however, it was not applied widely and became unknown for others outside of Korea.

BIT," meaning every "thing" – a particle, a field of force, or even space-time itself - all is ultimately manifested to us through "bits" of information.

The curriculum of the Human Story driven by science, technology and info-communication is illustrated in Figure 2-4. This model tries to establish some relationships between the Political, Labor, and Intellectual Perspectives in the modern history of civilization. This period began in the Renaissance with a rebirth of learning following the darkness of the medieval period. The modern times started in 1453 when Constantinople fell to the Ottoman Turks. Many scholars who fled from the Byzantine Empire were fleeing westward for safety – (some are still fleeing). Their learning spread rapidly with the development of printing in Europe (1454). This boosted the questioning of established ideas regarding religion (Reformation), art, and science. When scholarship began to develop independently of the church, the human rather than divine in life and art was emphasized; the well rounded, informed individual (for example, Leonardo da Vinci) become the ideal. Certain (only major) "ages," and "eras" and "waves" (not exclusive) which influence the role of information (and vice-versa) will be characterized as follows:

1. The Modernity Era (1454-1814) – transition from the Middle Ages to early modernity.
2. The Science Age (1500-1800) – the rise of theoretical sciences and modern technology (maritime).
3. The Revolution Age (1685-1917) – The English, American, French, and Bolshevik Revolutions.
4. The Modern Era (1814-1914) – the Industrial Revolution (the engine, electricity, and the factory system).
5. The Control Revolution (since 19th century) – telegraphs, punched cards, typewriters, Transatlantic cable, telephones, cash registers, adding machines, motion pictures, wireless telegraphs and radios.
6. The Modernity Era (1914-1990s)-technological innovations of the 19th century were applied on a large scale during peace and war times.
7. The Electronic Age (1940s--) – computers and transistors were invented.
8. The Computer Age (1950s-1980s) – main-frames, minis, personals, and computer networks.
9. The Information Age (1980s--) – application systems such as management information systems (MIS) and e-commerce.
10. The Telecommunication Age (1960s--) – Satellites, break-down of AT&T.
11. The Communication Age (1983--) – the Internet, e-mail, mobile communication and smartphones.
12. The Next Globalization Wave (1990s---) – world-wide-web and global economy.
13. The Virtualization Age (2000s--) – virtual organizations and social networks.
14. The Internet of Things (2010s--) – info-communication among devises-sensor controlled.

15. Post-Modernization Era (1990s--) – from economic growth towards sustainability and from materialism towards subjective well-being as the leading ideas, but not applied on a large scale in the world societies.

Civilization began about 4000 BCE, meaning it is 6000 years old. However, modern civilization is about 500 years old, as it is characterized by 15 ages, eras, and waves.

To establish more synthesized periods of civilization development, one must see them in terms of waves.

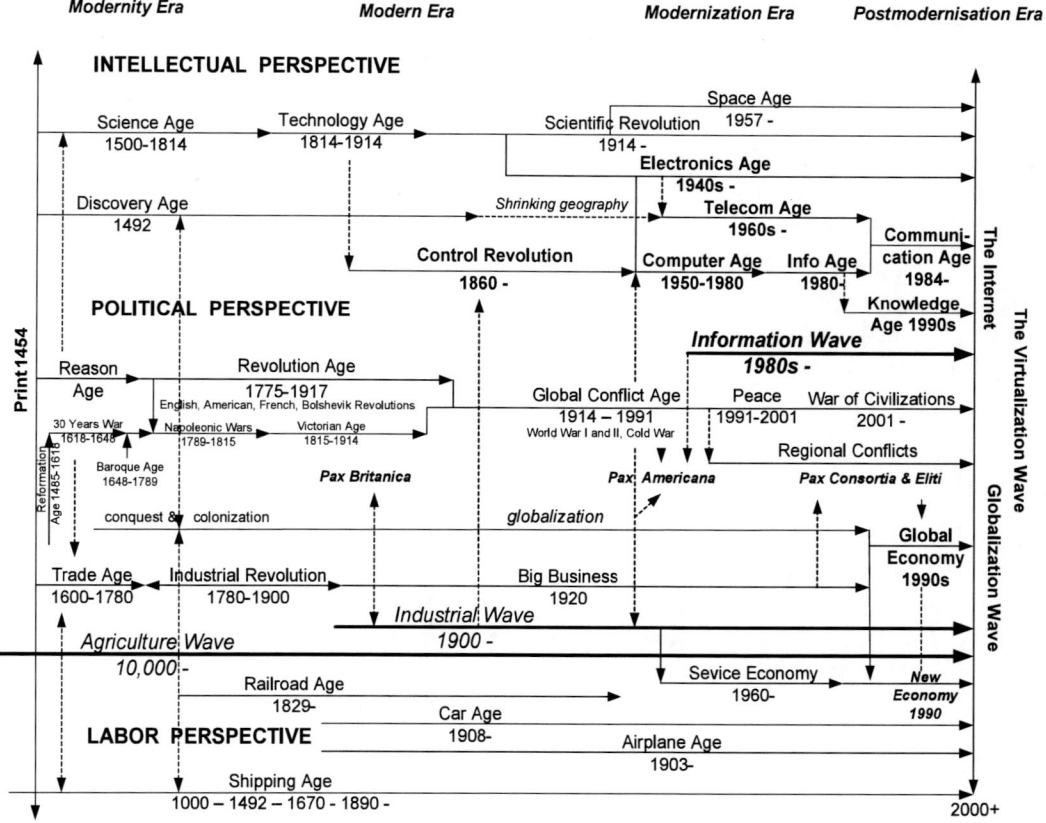

Figure 1.4. A Set of Civilization Ages, Eras, and Waves in the last 500+ Years.

Most of the writing on waves of civilization was done by Alvin Toffler (1980) who recognized three waves: First Wave (Agriculture Wave), Second Wave (Industrial Wave) and the Third Wave (Information Wave). However, one can note additional waves in the development of humankind, which number at least seven in total:

0. Settlers Wave (9,000 BCE - 7,000 BCE)
I. Agriculture Wave (7,000 BCE+)
II. Industrial Wave (1800+)

III. Information Wave (1980+)
IV. Globalization Wave (1990+)
V. Virtualization Waves (2000+)
VI. Communicating Things Wave (2010+)

The Zero Wave – Settlers Wave – This wave transformed hunters and farmers into settlers, who organized the first villages in the Middle East and stabilized their lives around animal domestication and food production, which after 5,000 years of wealth accumulation led to the rise of the first civilization in 4,000 BCE. It is interesting to notice that after 9,000 years (7,000 BCE-2,000) mankind is moving again and has become a "global hunter" for profit and jobs, while the Fourth Wave, Globalization, took off in the 1990s through the global infrastructures of info-communication and transportation networks.

The First Wave – the Agriculture Wave – began in 7,000 BCE and will remain active as long as food is needed, which means that it will be active as long as humankind is alive. The Second Wave – the rise of the Industrial Wave – is about 200 years old. It minimized human's physical effort through mechanization and freed up time for education, which led to the Scientific Revolution and invention of aircrafts and computers. The latter has led to the Third Wave, the Information Wave, and its magic tool, the Internet. The airplane and Internet have increased human global mobility, which has triggered the Fourth Wave – The Globalization Wave.

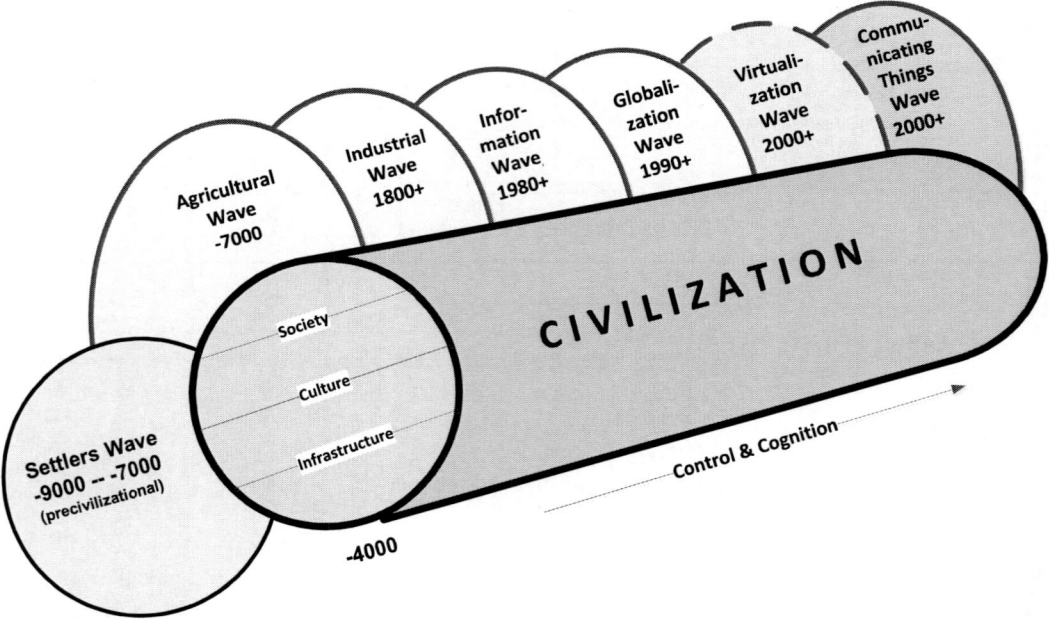

Figure 1.5. Civilization Waves.

The waves of civilization are shown in Figure 2-5. Each wave has its own set of civilization tools, which primarily support control processes by elites over their clients. The main control solutions for each wave are shown in this figure. It is important to notice that none of these waves replace the wave that precedes it. For example, information cannot replace food, steel or plastic; it can only improve their creation and utilization.

Each civilization wave is not disappearing (with the exception to a certain degree being the Settlers Wave, which is a de facto pre-civilization wave). Perhaps each new wave takes the place of leadership in civilization development and selects the best talent to work for it. Furthermore, each wave perpetuates other waves, as is shown in Figure 2-4. Current job trends, which focus on outsourcing computing to India, contradict earlier assessments that the millennial American workforce would be heavily focused in computing. In the twenty-first century it is even possible to outsource computer programming to India, thousands miles away from headquarters, similarly to how manufactured goods are outsourced to China.

THE RISE OF THE INFORMATION WAVE

As the Industrial Wave declines and the Control Revolution rises, the Information Wave rises also. The theory of post-industrialism advanced by Daniel Bell (1986) provides much of the conceptual background behind the Information Wave as the Information Society.). Bell's concept of postindustrial society has five dimensions:

1. There is a shift from a goods-producing economy to a service-producing one.
2. There is an increase in size and influence of the classes of professional workers.
3. The post-industrial society is organized around theoretical knowledge.
4. A critical aim is the management of technological growth.
5. There is an emphasis on the development of methods of intellectual technology.

Intelligent technology under the form of global computer networks dramatically expands the power of the brain into hyper-intelligence. With appropriate control programming, a network becomes a sensitive devise, not only as a physical devise, but also as an economic, social, and political one.

The spending on info-communication technology (ICT, the core of "intellectual technology) in the US reached $3.6 trillion in 2012 (*The New York Times*, July 9, 2012), which is about 22 % of GDP, which is 20% more what was spent on health care that year in the U.S.!

The 19th century eliminated wilderness through railroads. The 20th century developed science and technology that improved the well-being of many and pushed the planet to its limits resources-wise.

The 21st century perhaps will implement the Information Wave across all civilizations to improve knowledge-based, critical decisions about social life under the conditions of limited resources.

The mission of the Information Wave is:

To wisely control development and operations of the Agricultural Wave, Industrial Wave, Global Wave, and the other waves as well.

The goals of the Information Wave are:

1. To optimize development and operations of the Agricultural Wave, Industrial Wave, Global Wave, and the other ones in order to minimize the use of resources and ecology and to increase a citizen's choices and quality of life.
2. To sustain the development of human cognition in order to make conscious and wise decisions about: the sense of human possibility, life, education, health, politics, defense, business, entertainment and leisure time.

The strategy of the Information Wave is:

To develop and apply info-communication technology in control systems in a rational and human manner.

The role of the Information Wave in supporting other waves is shown in Figure 1.6.

These aims should be applied at all levels of civilization, including: national and local governments, schools & colleges, business and other organizations, homes, and individuals.

The Information Wave is composed of the following metaphoric elements (Figure 1.7):

- Info-factories, which generate information and seek new information; among them are the following: online enterprises, online schools and colleges, online communities, online governments, e-Republic, other.
- Info-malls, which provide the following services: e-mail, e-learning, e-banking, e-trading, e-job recruitment, e-information services, e-research, e-publishing, e-entertainment, e-calling, other.

- Infohighways, which transmit information content through info-communication services, such as: Local Area Network (LAN), Metropolitan Area Networks (MAN), Wide Area Networks (WAN), Global Area Networks (GAN), Value Area Networks (VAN), the Internet, TV, radio broadcasting, and others.
- Cyberspace is a digital information-based dark space: that is, a dispersed, infinite constellation of digital files, databases, home pages, bulletin boards, directories, menus, and others, where humans with a password interactively navigate in order to create, update, exchange, and retrieve information.
- Cybernauts (netcitizens), who are informed tele-computer users with a password to access billions of information tidbits and do everything on-line from shopping and learning to working and resting. Cybernauts can be "electronic immigrants" who can telecommute to work over great distances.

From Information Wave to Virtual Civilization 15

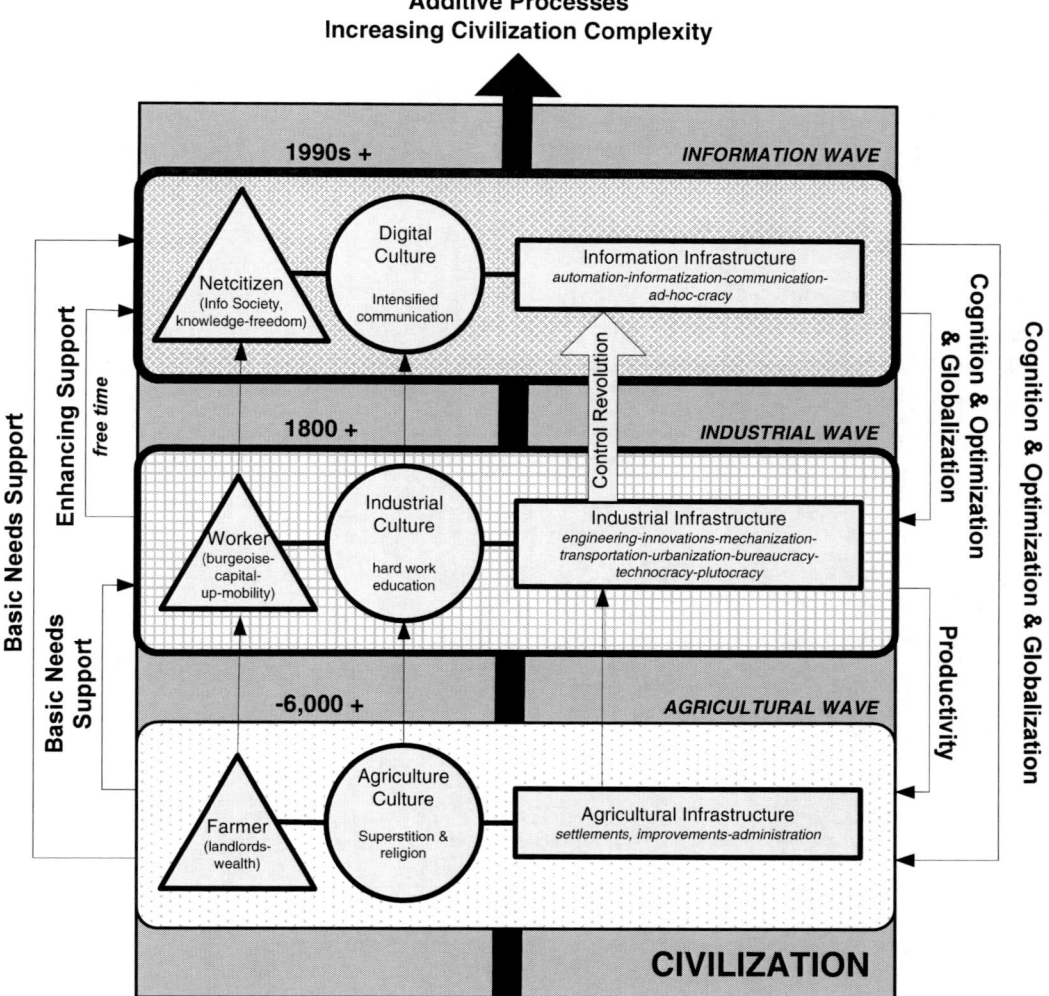

Figure 1.6. The Role of the Information Wave in Supporting other Civilization Waves.

The Information Wave is not just a matter of technology and economics. It involves morality, culture and ideas as well as institutions and political structures. It implies, in short, a true transformation of human affairs (Tofflers, 1994).

On the other hand, the unwise application of the Information Wave may be harmful for humans. Let's pose the following questions for civilization decision-makers:

- Is it wise to design automation, robotization, and informatization in such a way that their operators only watch the screens of many instruments but have little to say in the development control of a product? Sooner or later society will be divided into two groups of people: "thinking" designers and "thoughtless" users of such systems. It may lead to more productive solutions, but it may also degrade people and create a bifurcated society.

- Whether the world should unwisely apply automation, robotization, and informatization to reduce employment, when population growth and the demands of workers have interests often directly in contrast to strategies of efficiency?
- Whether the business and public administration should imprudently apply automation, robotization, and informatization to promote endless economic growth, while the reserves of strategic resources are depleting and sooner or later civilization as we know it will literally run out of gas?

There are plenty of such questions which face civilization now. Most of the time they are neglected, sometimes with catastrophic results. The potential of the Information Wave is in optimization of economic performance as well as to an even greater extent the wise control of civilization.

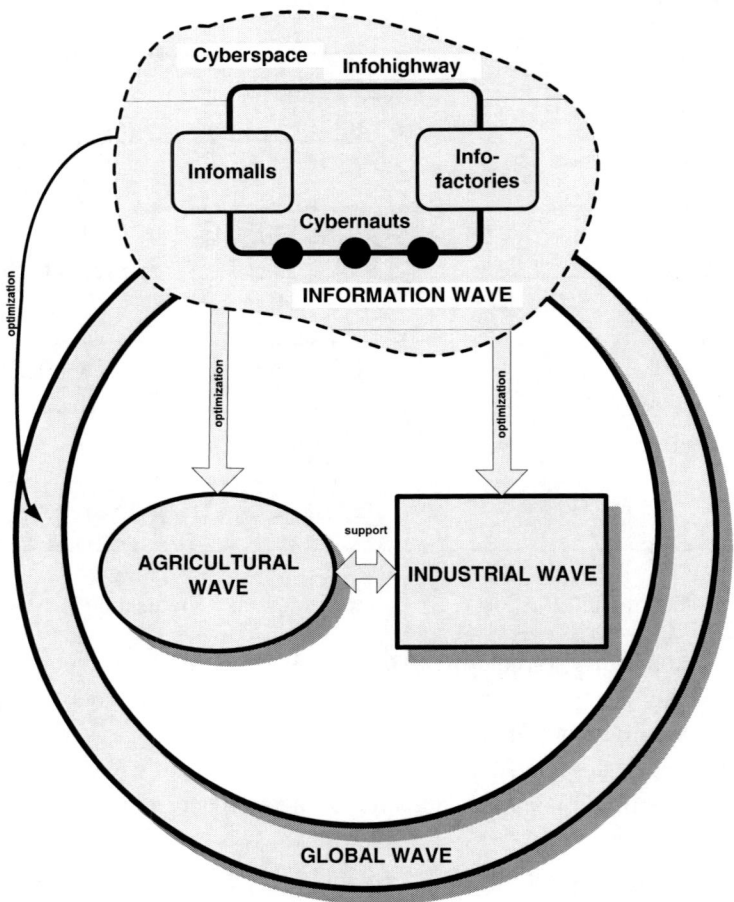

Figure 1.7. The Architecture of the Information Wave (2000) (Virtual and Communicating Things Waves Are Not Shown).

THE RISE OF THE VIRTUAL WAVE

When virtual was first introduced in information technology, it applied to memory simulated by the computer; that is, memory not actually built into the processor. Over time, though, the adjective has been applied to entities such as things, organizations, processes, and people that really exist and are simulated by means of information technology. For example, virtual conversations are conversations that take place over computer networks, and virtual communities are genuine social groups that assemble around the use of e-mail, webpages, and other networked resources. The adjectives virtual and digital and the prefixes e- and cyber- are all used in various ways to denote information, things, activities, and organizations that are realized or carried out chiefly in an electronic medium. Virtual tends to be used in reference to entities that mimic their "real" parallels. Thus a *digital library* would simply be a library that applies information technology, whether a brick-and-mortar library equipped with networked computers or a library that exists exclusively in electronic form, whereas a virtual library could only be the latter of these (The American Heritage® Dictionary of the English Language, Fourth Edition).[2]

Virtual worlds have exploded out of online game culture and now capture the attention of millions of ordinary people: students, husbands, wives, fathers, mothers, workers, and retirees. Devoting dozens of hours each week to massive multiplayer virtual reality environments – such as Civilization, World of Warcraft or Second Life – these millions are the start of an exodus to the refuge of the virtual, where they experience life under a new social, political, and economic order built around fun (Castronova 2007).

The development of the Global Economy in the 2010s is well established. The integrated information infrastructure has led to a boom in the development of social networks. In the past several years, some networks have thrived, some have vanished, and hundreds of new ones have appeared. It has become a huge area to follow, and nowadays one estimate is that about 500 large social networking sites offer services for about 1.242 billion users, as Table 1.1 illustrates the richness of this kind of info-communication-driven socialization.

These 1,635,000,000 users of global social networks today create the Global Virtual Society (GVS), which is mostly composed of young and middle aged people (a new emerging global information elite). They exchange information about facts, events, feelings, situations, activities, pictures, videos, and opinions faster and more frequently than they could in the real environment [117 million users visited Facebook every month in March 2010 (Time, May 31, 2010, p.37)].

These facts are very encouraging, since the world in the 2010s is not in good shape. Some civilizations such as Western, Eastern, and Islamic are in conflicts and wars. The global economy economically flattens the world at the cost of Western Civilization, which economically declines, because it is outsourcing its industry to less developed civilizations,

---

[2] The prefix e- is generally preferred when speaking of the commercial applications of the Web, as in e-commerce, e-cash, and e-business, whereas cyber- tends to be used when speaking of the computer or of networks from a broader cultural point of view, as in cybersex, cyber-church, and cyberspace. But like everything else in this field, such usages are evolving rapidly, and it would be rash to try to predict how these expressions will be used in the future (The American Heritage® Dictionary of the English Language, Fourth Edition).

where the cost of labor is low. The world needs new ideas and political will to improve its well-being. To do so, the hope is in the young generation which populated and even created the GVS (complex of social networks).

Table 1.1. The Ranking of the Largest Nations by its Citizenships/Memberships in 2012

Ranking	Nation	Population	Global Virtual Society
1	China	1.360 M	
2	India	1.234 M	
3	Facebook	1,100 M	1,100 M
4	United States	317 M	
5	MySpace	35 M	35 M
6	Indonesia	238 M	
7	Brazil	201 M	
8	Pakistan	184 M	
9	Russia	144 M	
10	Bangladesh	153 M	
11	Nigeria	174 M	
12	Japan	127 M	
13	Twitter	124 M	200 M
14	Mexico	118 M	
15	Vietnam	89 M	
15	Other Social Networks	Estimation	300 M
	TOTAL		1.635 B

In the spring 2010, just after being elected, Britain's Prime Minister David Cameron wanted a few tips from somebody who could tell him how it felt to be responsible for, and accountable to, many millions of people who expected things from him, even though in most cases he would never shake their hands. Prime-Minister Cameron turned not to a fellow of government but to Mark Zuckerberg, the founder and head of Facebook, the largest social network. These two men talked about ways for networks to help governments, for example how to generate ideas on cutting public spending. They talked as masters of two great nations (The Economist, p.59, 7-24, 2010).

Facebook is the fastest growing social network in the 2010s, which within a few years should reach 1.5 billion users. It will be a social network with the potential to become the first example of the Global Virtual Nation (GVN) in civilization. To become such a nation, Facebook must transform itself into a service not for profit and form a government, agencies and acquire citizens. This transformation should take some time in the near future, and it will require some strong societal and organizational will as well as initial capital.

The emerging social networks lead to the birth of collective "mindspheres" of intelligence, knowledge, and wisdom at global and national levels.

Figure 1.8 illustrates the architecture of these new collective mindspheres. Along with practice, these mindspheres can multiply at all levels of the nation, for example at the level of the village, town, township, county, city, and state. It will take time before such mindspheres can become organized. This certainly will not take place everywhere, but it will where there is social will and organizational might.

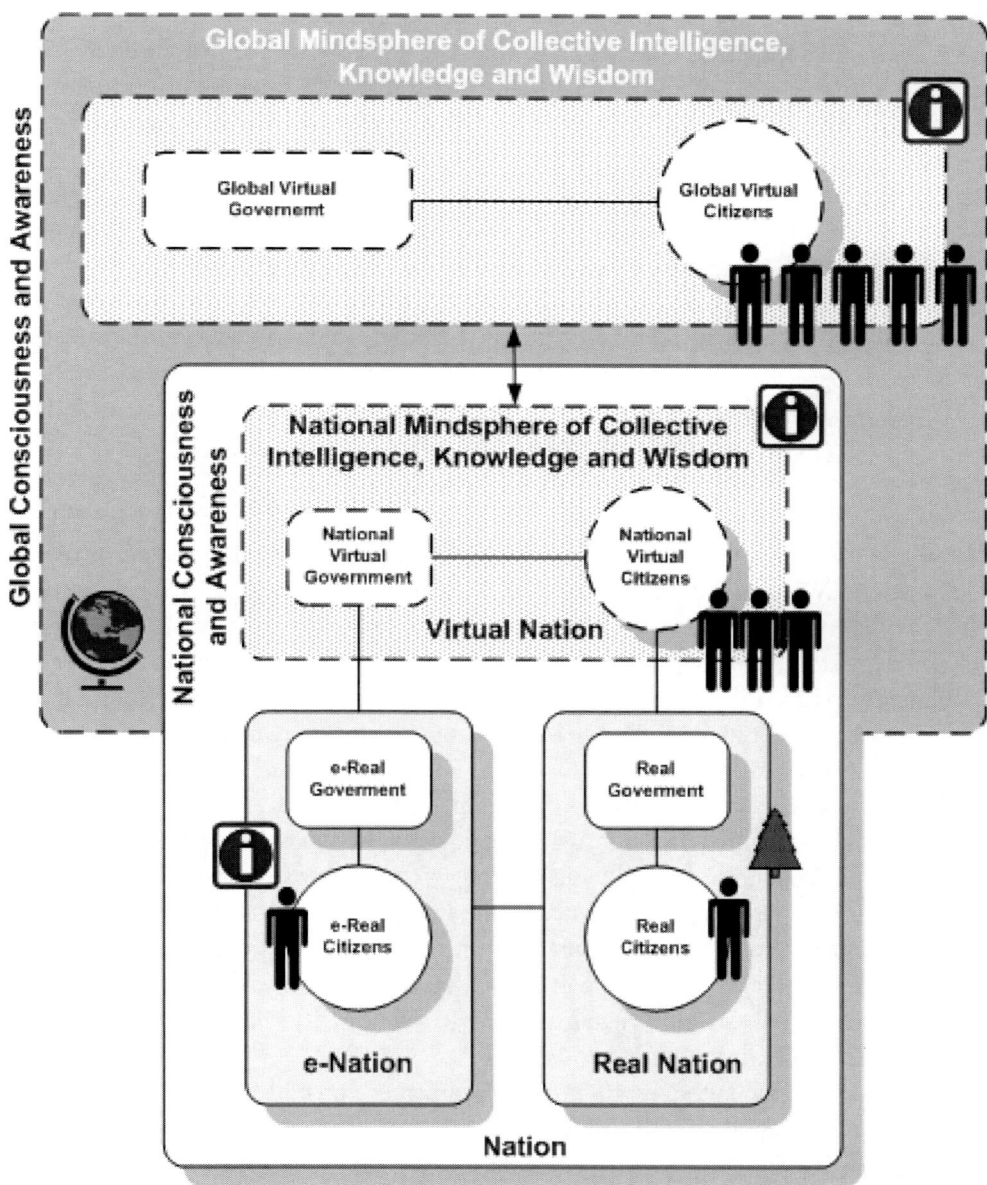

Figure 1.8. The Architecture of Emerging Collective Mindspheres at the Global and National Levels in the 21st Century.

These mindspheres working in universal cyberspace should facilitate the collection and exchanges of ideas and solutions which may liberate us from social and political hierarchies that stay in the way of mankind's advancement (Lévy 1997). Pierre Lévy says that perhaps "it is a utopia but is an achievable utopia." Furthermore, he thinks that "we cannot only exchange information but think together, share our memories and our plans to produce a cooperative brain." This collective brain, or rather mind, can multiply our social and cognitive potential. With such a powerful tool, mankind's consciousness can become broader, deeper, and more sophisticated, and perhaps be able to solve what are currently unsolvable problems. Will we be ready with such a collective mind to stop the depletion of strategic resources of our civilization, which will deplete completely within 50-200 years if we do not find good solutions?

Of course this "rosy" picture is full of unexpected motives and actions triggered by computer hackers, criminals, and anti-social agents. Since the new *virtual world* has the same or even more intensified crimes as the physical world, it is, therefore, not yet a paradise or utopia!

Rather it is a hope for a wiser and better civilization which would like to last as long as possible.

THE RISE OF VIRTUAL CIVILIZATION

How good and how much money must one possess to be elected president of the Global Virtual Nation? What would be the nature of the virtual election? Can it be made more available for more candidates? Can it be free from the pressure of groups? Can it be free of fraud? Today it is too soon to answer these questions. The coming operational practice of the GVN certainly will elaborate procedures of the political processes and systems. It will be fascinating since it will also be the birth of a new civilization, which can be called Virtual Civilization. It will be the next layer upon the existing civilizations. For example, in the 2010s Western Civilization is being transformed into Global Civilization and also is transforming into Virtual Civilization. An American or Portuguese citizen functions in these three civilizations concurrently! It is a big challenge to be successful in such an environment.

It will also be interesting to see whether the Global Virtual Nation, created by Western Civilization, will be pro-Western, against it or universal, which would be the most desirable position. Perhaps Virtual Civilization will be conducive for the development of Orwellianism; then again, it might just as well be against the Big Brother polity. Today it is too soon to state which way the new civilization will evolve.

In contrast to participative-representative democracy, practiced in Western Civilization today, the GVN will apply populist-direct democracy where to pass a bill, every citizen may vote electronically. Supposedly, every virtual citizen will belong to the information elite, which is well informed and aware of what is good or bad in a proposal being voted upon. The GVN will be dangerous for nations with authoritarian, dictatorial, and theocratic governments which neglect the public opinion. Today, China, Pakistan, Saudi Arabia and other counties block Facebook operations and censor the Internet. In 1970s, totalitarian Poland did not tolerate the INFOSTRADA project, which allowed bypassing governmental communication channels in delivering public information (Targowski 2009:193).

The impact of the GVN upon real global organizations (ex.: the U.N., IMF, TWO, and other stateless corporations) and national governments can be big and decisive. If virtual citizens of the GVN agree on an issue and strategy, they may enforce directions in the real world, since those virtual citizens are also real citizens in particular countries where real governments rule. Today, most people feel that they have little to say about what the government does; an overwhelming majority say that the government is run by a few big, selfish interests. Therefore, the GVN provides the opportunity to organize those unsatisfied people and pursue their (not the particular interests) issues and solutions.

There is a question whether the GVN will take over civilization and govern real national governments. A somewhat similar case took place when the unempowered society in totalitarian Poland beat the dictatorship in 1989. This happened when the underground press exceeded the volume and truthful content of the official press. It was the victory of a well informed and motivated solidarity movement which overcame a powerful, militarized government. Later the whole Soviet Empire collapsed, mostly due to info-communication oriented policy of *glasnost* and *pierostroyka* implemented by M. Gorbachev.

The generalized model of the dynamics of Virtual Civilization is provided in Figure 1.9.

Table 2.2. The Classifying Criteria of the Virtual Civilization

Criteria	Attributes
Space boundaries	World-wide unlimited, socially constructed work and leisure space in cyberspace. It is an extraterritorial space with a post-national culture and in some circumstances even post-nations.
Time span	Centuries/millennia - as long as info-communication technology is operational.
Religion (ideology)	Unlimited freedom, cyberspace, and progress supported by collective intelligence - to secure common good in an alternative virtual world, since the "real" one is going in the wrong direction in the 21st century.
Society	Virtual global, local and between communities, including the Virtual Global Society and Virtual Global Nation (possibly) living in spacial dispersion of social, political, and material processes.
Culture	Virtual techno-culture (Robins & Webster 1999) is the culture that has emerged, or is emerging, from the use of computer networks for communication, entertainment and business (Horn 1998). E-values: connected, expected feedback, rhythm, productivity, velocity, impatience, techno-centrism, cyber-ethics, informed, optimization, big-picture vs small-picture, global awareness, self-conciseness. E-behavior: net-centric, anytime, anywhere, "death" of distance, no-middleman, curiosity, discovery, digital & virtual divide, information wealth, poverty of attention (Targowski 2009:306). It is also the study of various social phenomena associated with the Internet and other new forms of network communication, such as online communities, online multi-player gaming, and text messaging (Jones 1997). In the 1990's information took a sharp turn away from the concrete and tangible to the abstract and intangible (Rheingold 1993).
Infrastructure	Computer networks and storage (online cyberspace as a repository for collective cultural memory, whose narrative is created by its virtual society)

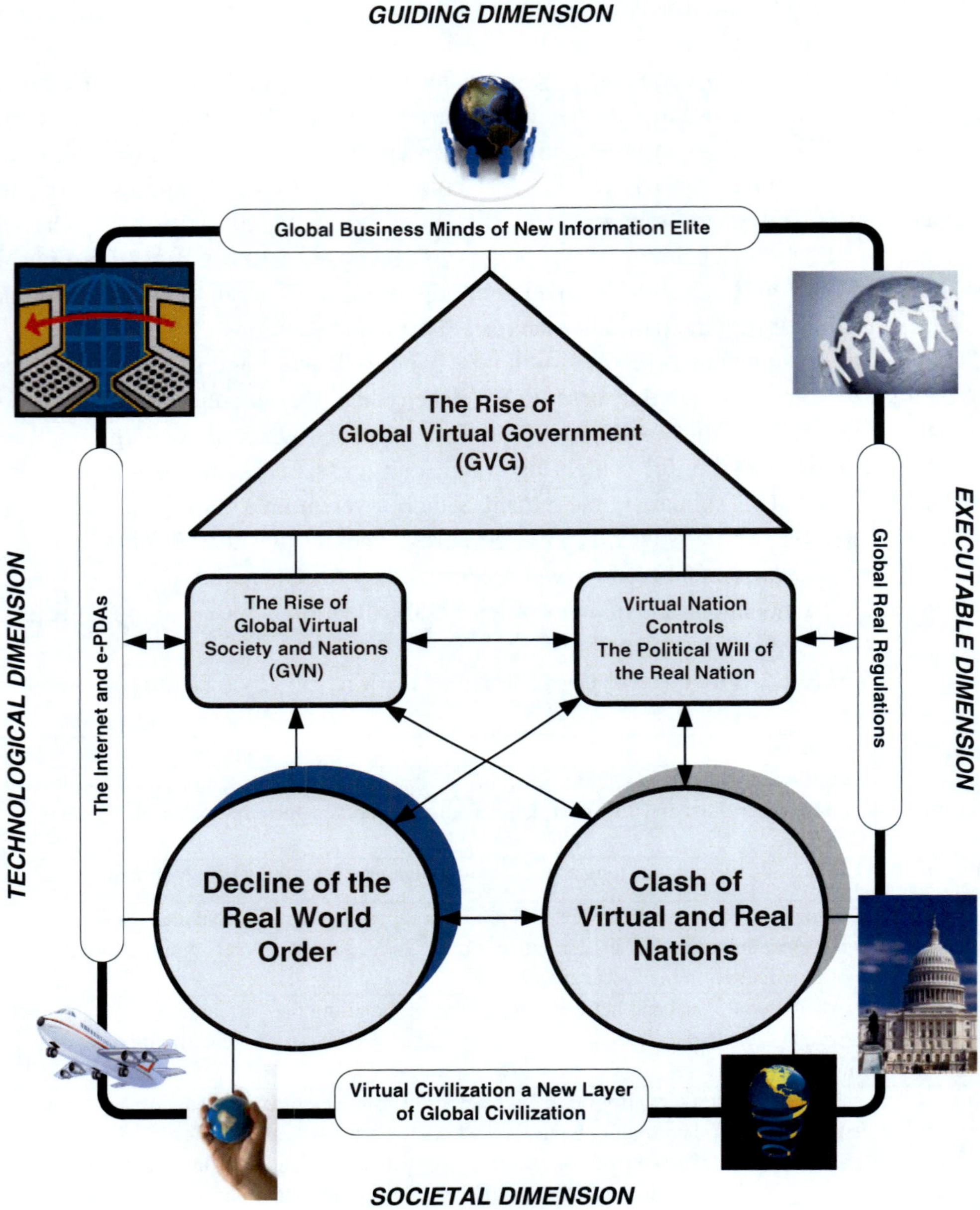

Figure 1.9. The Dynamics of the Virtual Civilization in the 21st Century.

One can expect that the GVN will create subunits under the form of virtual nations (VN). A virtual nation will organize a National Virtual Government (NVG) and National Virtual Citizens (NVC) around the important issues and solutions within the boundaries of a real nation. Lawrence Grossman (1995) already perceived the emergence of the *electronic republic*, where electronic voting and opinion-registering technologies will go from the bottom to the top (lawmakers). But as the practice shows, the lawmakers listen to the lobbyists rather than to their constituencies. It is true that the citizens' views are known in media and the political circles, but the citizens are rather passive and unable to implement their solutions through the official political parties, which are concerned with maintaining their own "jobs." It is a fact that the real citizens are unorganized and dispersed. An example of a certain kind of self-organization of unsatisfied citizens in America is the Tea Party in the 2010s.

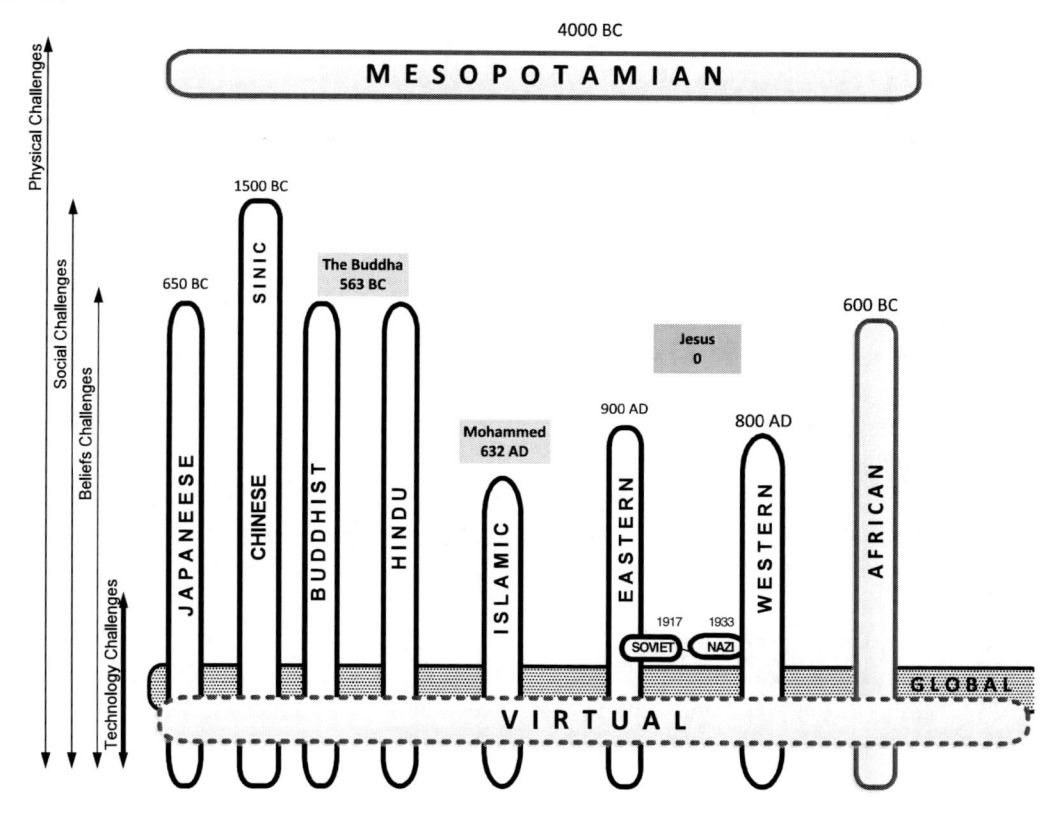

Figure 1.10. Virtual Civilization among other Civilizations in the 21st Century.

Why is the Virtual Wave considered to have become Virtual Civilization in the 21st century? Most outstanding, the latter satisfies all the criteria of a civilization as it is defined in Table 2.2 and has created its own independent, virtual society, parallel to the real one.

Virtual Civilization (of the infrastructural character) is to a certain degree a parallel entity to real Global Civilization in space and time. However, the former's goal is to control the latter for securing the common good. Virtual Civilization's main infrastructure is collective intelligence (Lévy 1997), which develops and shares a strong ability for solving problems among virtual members and is based on a word-wide retrieval of knowledge and wisdom kept in digital format.

Virtual Civilization penetrates horizontally all other autonomous civilizations as well as the Global Civilization, as it is depicted in Figure 1.10.

Conclusion

1. Virtual Civilization has transformed from the Virtual Wave into Virtual Civilization due to advancements in info-communication technology in the 21st century, exemplified by the ability of the Internet to secure operations of virtual organizations and social networks. Therefore, one can characterize Virtual Civilization as having infrastructural character.
2. The mission of Virtual Civilization is to control public policy of other real civilizations to secure the common good in the real societies. At least such a mission is exemplified in the practice of some virtual communities at the dawn of the 21st century.
3. Today it is too soon to judge the impact of Virtual Civilization upon the real ones. However, despite the positive aspects, like the quest for the common good, one can notice negative ones as well in the young generation, exemplified by a shortened span of attention and the desire for constant (electronic in fact) fun, playing computer games for long hours and engaging in "empty talk" in virtual mediums. For example students 18-24 years old learn less, since on average they send and answer about 100 text messages every day (Smith 2011). This is about 5 times more than a faculty is reading and answering e-messages every day. Some eager students send twice as many messages per day (200).
4. The quest for the common good by virtual society may limit or even replace representative democracy by direct democracy which although it eventually may create a few positive policies, it may also trigger permanent political chaos in real civilizations.
5. The many e-communications among people from different parts of the world is diminishing local interrelations and is intensifying connectivity among international or/and distant, parochial cultures, which eventually will separate, isolate and alienate individuals in their real living places.
6. At this time it is very improbable that virtual society can be regulated by real society. This means that Virtual Civilization, on one hand, can be positive, but on the other hand it can be harmful for humanity which is living in a declining civilization due to overpopulation, superconsumerism, depletion of strategic resources and environment degradation.

References

Castronova, E. (2007). *Exodus to the virtual world*. New York: Palgrave MacMillan.
Doheny-Farina, S. (1996). *The wired neighborhood*. New Haven, CT: Yale University Press.
Elmer-Dewitt, P. (1993). Here come the cyberpunks! *Time*, pp. 58-65.

Fernback, J. (1998). The individual within the collective: virtual ideology and the realization of collective principles. In Jones, St. G. (Ed.). (1998). *Virtual culture, identity & communication in cybersociety*. London: SAGE Publications.

Grossman, L. (1995). *Electronic republic*. Nw York: Viking.

Horn, S. 1998: *Cyberville: clicks, culture, and the creation of an online town*. New York: Warner Books.

Jones, S., (ed.). (1997). *Virtual culture: identity & communication in cybersociety*. London: Sage Publications.

Lévy, P. (1997). *Collective intelligence, mankind's emerging world in cyberspace*. New York & London: PLENUM TRADE.

McLuhan, M. (1962). *The Gutenberg galaxy*. Toronto: University of Toronto Press.

Melko, M. (1969). *The nature of civilization*. Boston: Porter Sargent Publisher.

Rheingold, H. (1993). "A slice of life in my virtual community." In Harasim, L. M. (ed.) *Global networks: computers and international communication*. Cambridge, MA: MIT Press, pp. 57-80.

Robin, K. and F. Webster. (1999). *Times of the technoculture*. London and New York: Routledge.

Simpson, G. (1991). *Montreux MetaResort brochure*. Reno, NV: Wellness Development Ltd.

Smith, A. (2011). *Americans and text messaging*. PewResearch Center. http://pewinternet.org/Reports/2011/Cell-Phone-Texting-2011.aspx

Targowski, A. (2009). *Information technology and societal development*. Hershey & New York: IGI Global.

Targowski, A. (2009b). Towards a composite definition and classification of civilization. *Comparative Civilizations Review*. No. 60, Spring, 2009.

Toffler, A. & Toffler, H. (1994). *Creating a new civilization*. Atlanta, GA: Turner Publishing.

Toynbe, A. (1995). *A study of history*. New York: Barnes & Noble.

In: Virtual Civilization in the 21st Century
Editor: Andrew Targowski

ISBN: 978-1-63463-261-4
© 2015 Nova Science Publishers, Inc.

Chapter 2

SOCIETY OF VIRTUAL CIVILIZATION

*Muhammad A. Razi**
Western Michigan University, US

ABSTRACT

The *purpose* of this chapter is to explore the makeup of Virtual Society and the impact of social media on various entities and on the users of social media. Virtual society is based on social media, and social media is any site that allows people a virtual place on the Internet to make connections and form networks of virtually connected people. The influence of social media on individual, and family life, industry, education, sports, globalization, governmental and political systems is enormous.

The seemingly innocuous technologies driving virtual societies have created a gold mine of consumer secrets that is fueling a booming business of consumer analytics.

A Solar Model of virtual society is proposed, social networking orientations are explored, and common elements of each orientation are identified. In addition, potential and future directions of social media are discussed.

The Solar Model and orientations, or social networking sites are intended to provide insight into the architecture of virtual society for practitioners and users.

INTRODUCTION

Virtual Society is based on Social Networking (SN) which is any site that allows people a place on the Internet to make connections, create relationships, communicate with participants, build followings and form networks of virtually connected people. Engaging in social networking activities has become a regular part of life for a majority of Americans and for a sizable portion of the world's population. Social Media (SM) is the media content (blog,

---

[*] muhammad.razi@wmich.edu.

video, e-book, slideshow, podcast, white paper) that one uploads on the internet for others to see, respond and comment (Burke 2013). Social media is a good way of preventing one's competence from becoming stale (Murillo 2008).

Behind all happy, not so happy, and reluctant users is the jockeying for position and revenue among the big players in social media: Facebook, Linkedin, Twitter and others. The influence of social media on individual and family life, industry, education, sports, globalization, governmental and political systems is enormous. New social media sites are popping up every now and then while young and older generations are trying to find an appropriate fit for their love of internet communication, exploration and virtual socialization. The seemingly innocuous technologies driving virtual societies have created a gold mine of consumer secrets that is fueling a booming business of spying on consumers while the impact of social media on education, industry, government, healthcare, communication, skill development, innovation, etc. is not well known. Big name sites as well as third party data collectors plant tracking files to track users every move on the Internet. These tracking data, in some cases, are sold to many companies.

Is it the formation of a multitude of social networking sites (SNSs) that will lead to the creation of virtual societies the next 'social glue', holding societies together in the future (Woolgar 2002)? Questions proposed by Woolgar in his book include:

1) 'Are fundamental shifts taking place in how people behave, organize themselves, and interact as a result of the new technologies?
2) Are electronic technologies bringing about significant changes in the nature and experience of interpersonal relations, in communications, social control, participation, inclusion and exclusion, social cohesion, trust, and identity?' What is the significance of the explosion of social media networks and a rapid increase of social networking members worldwide?

Since the impact of Internet based SNSs are present in all aspects of human activities, finding answers to the above mentioned questions are critical for formulating proactive and reactive policies on social media/social networks by all private and public industry sectors. The Internet, and specially SNSs have given voice to groups of people with concealable stigmatized identities or people who are isolated for any reason (Lea et al. 2000).

However, the question remains 'How social is a social networking site?' The pattern of social behavior on SNSs underlines the strengths and weaknesses of computer-mediated communications (CMC). On one hand, CMC opened the boundaries of communications and is considered more democratic and liberating. On the other hand, CMC is viewed as extreme, impersonal, anti-social, and tends to expose ways in which CMC is inadequate for replacing face-to-face interaction (Lea et al. 2000). The objective of this chapter is to explore the architecture of virtual society. This chapter is organized into five sections. The next section provides a history leading to the creation of virtual society followed by the solar model of virtual society. An analysis of the orientations of SNSs is presented in section three. Section four presents a discussion of the impact of virtual society on the current human social structure. Finally, the concluding section highlights the key points of this chapter.

FROM ONLINE COMMUNITIES TO VIRTUAL SOCIETY

Societies have been bound by mostly geographical territories, cultural influences, racial makeups, and religious beliefs. The emergence of the Internet and World Wide Web have basically eliminated the boundaries of traditional societies and opened up the opportunity for the creation of networks of virtual societies leading to virtual civilization. One of the earliest known online communities was the WELL (Whole Earth 'Lectronic Link) started by Stewart Brand and Larry Brilliant in 1985. WELL started as a dial-up bulletin board and email exchange system (Rheingold 2000). Talkomatic was the first online chat system created by Doug Brown and David R. Woolley in 1973 on the PLATO System at the University of Illinois. The PLATO system was originally designed for Computer-Based Education. However, according to David Woolley (1994) 'PLATO's most enduring legacy is the online community spawned by its communication features'. Before the release of the 'CB Simulator' in 1980, CompuServe allowed members to share files and access news and events (Goble 2012). The 'CB Simulator' was one of the first online real-time chat programs in the world. (Tweney 2009). The online social communities were still in their infancy until the rise of commercial Internet service providers like CompuServe, AOL, Prodigy, EarthLink and others in late 80s and early 90s (Simon 2009). Following is a chronological list of some of the early SNSs.

- 1995: Social networking site Classmates.com started as a way to connect and keep up with high-school classmates (Cerulo 2012).
- March 2002: About 3 million people joined the social networking site, Friendster, during its first three months. However, initial euphoria quickly disappeared since members did not know what to do or did not have the opportunity to do much while they were on the Friendster site. (Cerulo 2012)
- May 2003: LinkedIn, a professional oriented social networking site, was launched. (Cerulo 2012)
- September 2003: Myspace arrived with the ability for members to create profile page. Myspace provided many customization tools and was the most popular social networking site from 2005 to 2008. (Cerulo 2012)
- February 2004: Facebook, the most popular social networking site to date, was launched by Mark Zuckerberg. By April 2014, the number of Facebook accounts exceeded 1.3 billion.

Social media is now an inextricable part of social life of people around the world. This is however, a true testament of the digital divide. People with financial means, appropriate education and access to available technology are able to participate in this phenomenon. Table 2.1 provides selected statistics of several popular SNSs.

ARCHITECTURE OF VIRTUAL SOCIETIES (SOLAR MODEL)

The appetite for reaching and communicating with like-minded people, sports fans, consumers, patients, students, people with the same or similar interests, citizens of another country etc. has led to the creation of SNSs having many different orientations (domains).

In this section, an attempt is made to provide a model to depict the breadth and depth of social media. As shown in the Figure 2.1, at the core of the virtual society are social networking sites with their different orientations such as social, professional, educational, sports etc.

Table 2.1. Statistics for selected Prominent Social Networking Sites

Site	All Users	Popular Among	Market Valuation	When Launched
Facebook	1.31 Billion	All groups of people	$184 billion (Feb 2014)	2004 (February)
LinkedIn	227 million	45 – 54 year old	$24 billion	2003
Twitter	646 million	Young (18 – 31 years old)	$12.8 billion	2006 (March)
Pinterest	70 million	Women (25-35 years old)	$3.8 billion	2010 (March)
Instagram	150 million active users	Young (14 – 34 years old)	N/A (Facebook owns Instagram)	2010 (October)
YouTube	More than 1 billion active users	Young (18 – 34 years old)	N/A (Google owns YouTube)	2005 (February)
Google+	540 million active users	Older, working people	N/A (Google owns Google+)	2011 (September)
Tumblr (Smith 2014)	216 million monthly users	Young (13 – 35 years old)	N/A (Yahoo owns Tumblr)	2007 (February)

All orientations share some common elements; however, each orientation has its own distinguished elements as well. In terms of reach, social networking has been truly global in nature reaching people from all corners in all regions and all walks of life. Even though these sites have global reach, influence of local, regional, national and global attributes in the formation of a social networking site is very real. In addition, these social networking sites are influenced by language, religion, passion and other influential attributes. For example, the Chinese have a social networking site named Renren which closely resembles Facebook.

In a nutshell, the virtual social structure mostly follows a millennia old societal structure dictated by race, ethnicity, religion, language, and culture. These elements are considered influential factors in the solar model of virtual civilization (Figure 2.1). If we closely follow the communication, conversion, and following by members of social networks, it quickly becomes quite clear that most members communicate with other members of the same ethnic, religious, or cultural background. Of course, there are exceptions, and a truly virtual society where the exceptions become the rule is a long way off.

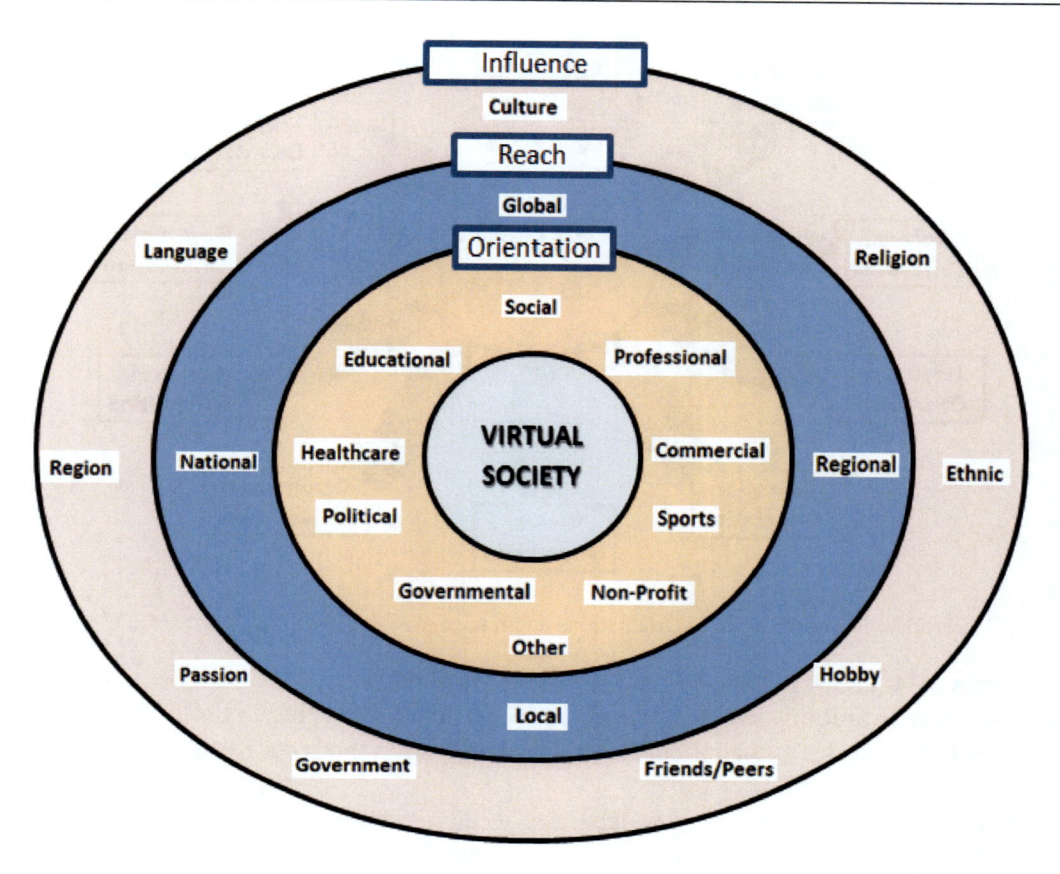

Figure 2.1. Solar Model representing the Architecture of a Virtual Society.

The next section presents a detailed discussion on the virtual community's orientations.

ORIENTATIONS AND ELEMENTS OF SOCIAL NETWORKS

Virtual Community Orientations

As discussed before, the orientation of each social networking site revolves around a particular theme or interest, for example, relationship building, keeping in touch with friends and family, building a community of experts or building a community for people with common interests like sports or music. Figure 2.2 provides a diagram of prominent Virtual Society Orientations and representative Networks.

A 2010 Harvard Business Review study reveals important statistics on social media use. The study found that social media use was most often reported in education (72%), communications (71%), services (66%), and retail/wholesale (61%) sectors. The least active were energy and utility companies (41%), manufacturing companies (32%), and government organizations (27%) (Harvard Business School Publishing 2010).

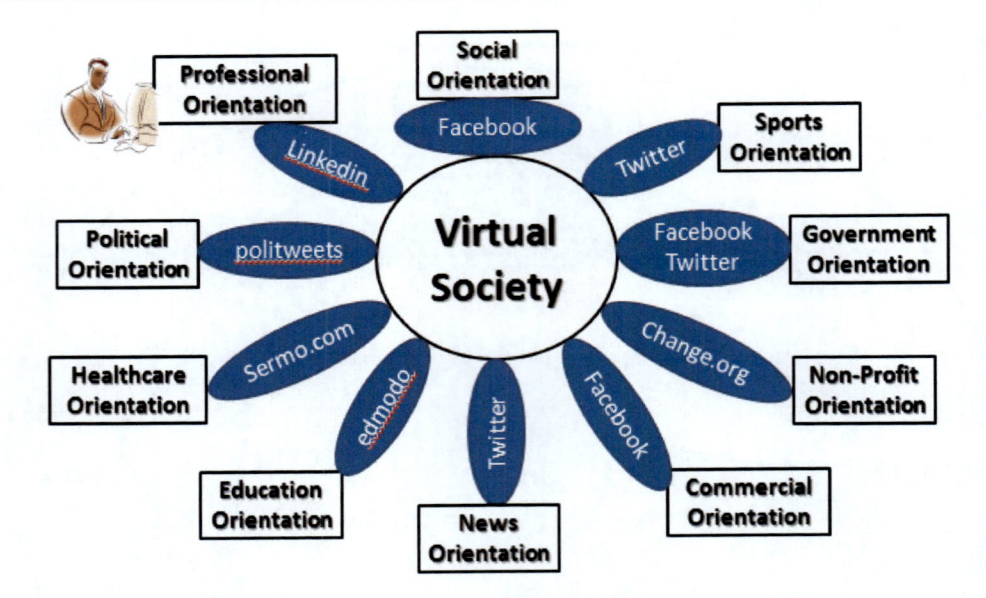

Figure 2.2. Prominent Virtual Society Orientations and representative Networks.

Irrespective of the orientation, many social networking groups share some common elements such as, information sharing, generating awareness, keeping in touch, fund raising etc. Figure 2.2 provides virtual orientations and examples of representative social networking sites.

Table 2.2 - 2.6 provide lists of widely used social networking orientations and elements for each orientation. Elements consist of use, activities, and the purpose of the social networking site. A brief explanation for each orientation is also provided. Abbreviations are provided for elements that are common in more than one orientation.

Table 2.2. Elements for Social Network Orientations SOC and PRO

Social Orientation (SOC)	Professional Orientation (PRO)
• Social Interaction • Family • Friends • Friends of Friends • Keep in Touch (KT) • Self-Presentation • Information Sharing (IS) • Photo/Video sharing • Showing popularity • Showing affection • Cyber Bullying • Posting articles/videos	• Connecting with other professionals, classmates, alumni, friends • Showing Expertise • Generating endorsements • Job searching • Hiring (HR) • Research (RES) • Posting articles/videos • Information Sharing (IS) • Keeping in Touch (KT)

Table 2.3. Elements for Social Network Orientations EDU and HCO

Educational Orientation (EDU)	Health care Orientation (HCO)
• Blogging • Collaborative learning • Collaborative mind mapping • Podcasting (POD) • Micro-Blogging/Micro-Sharing (BLOG) • Video sharing • Presentation sharing • Collaborative editing • Tutoring • Research (RES) • Posting Articles/Videos • Information Sharing (IS) • Information Rich Content (IRC) • Fund Raising (FR)	• Micro-Blogging/Micro-Sharing (MB/MS) • Patient engagement • Information Sharing (IS) • New Patient • Marketing/Patient Recruitment • Providing training • Photo/Video sharing • Research (RES) • Posting articles/videos • Providing preparatory information before a procedure • Keeping in Touch (KT) with Patient • Information Rich Content (IRC)

Table 2.4. Elements for Social Network Orientations COM and POL

Commercial Orientation (COM)	Political Orientation (POL)
• Fan/Member Page (FP) • Deliver Brand-focused message • Deliver Product-focused message • Product • Information Rich Content (IRC) • New Customers • Customer Profiling • Offering Incentives • Interactive, fun games for coupons, discounts • Marketing and promotion (MP) • Hiring (HR) • Posting articles/videos • Information Sharing (IS) • Podcasting (POD)	• Fan/Member Page (FP) • Campaigning (CAM) • Fundraising (FR) • Recruiting (REC) • Spreading message (posting articles/videos) • Information Sharing (IS) • Lobbying • Signatures Collection (SC)

Table 2.5. Elements for Social Network Orientations SPO and GOV

Sports Orientation (SPO)	Governmental Orientation (GOV)
<ul><li>Fan/Member Page (FP)</li><li>Increase Fan loyalty</li><li>Generate new Fans</li><li>Real-time engagement with Fans</li><li>Deliver brand-focused message</li><li>Marketing and Promotion</li><li>Information Sharing (IS)</li></ul>	<ul><li>Customer Service</li><li>Law & Order</li><li>Surveillance</li><li>Disseminating information</li><li>Reduce wasteful spending</li><li>Receiving feedback/complains</li><li>Education/Awareness (ED/AW)</li><li>Informing people about an epidemic</li><li>Emergency alert, severe weather</li><li>Social activities, registration, meetings</li><li>Public service announcements</li><li>Construction updates and road closings</li><li>Hiring (HR)</li><li>Information Rich Content (IRC)</li><li>Information Sharing (IS)</li></ul>

Table 2.6. Elements for Social Network Orientations NPO and NO

Non-Profit Orientation (NPO)	News Orientation (NO) (http://mashable.com/2009/03/11/newspaper-industry/)
<ul><li>Education/Awareness (ED/AW)</li><li>Posting schedule of activities</li><li>Mobilizing fans/members to support a cause</li><li>Connecting with people in need in remote areas</li><li>Service coordination</li><li>Recruitment/Volunteer (REC)</li><li>Fund raising (FR)</li><li>Campaigning (CAM)</li><li>Information Sharing (IS)</li><li>Information Rich Content (IRC)</li></ul>	<ul><li>News Headline Feeds/updates</li><li>Fan/Member Page (FP)</li><li>Social Media event to attract new readers</li><li>Engage with current readers</li><li>Promoting user generated content</li><li>Experimenting with the Social Networking platform</li><li>Community interactions hub</li><li>Reader engagement with local, personal news stories</li></ul>

Social Orientation (SOC)

SOC is about building a platform of social relations among friends, relatives, and people who share interests, activities, backgrounds or experiences.

A survey by pewinternet.org (2013) on trust, tolerance, social support, community, and political engagement has found that 'SNSs are increasingly used to keep up with close social ties and the average user of a social networking site has more close ties and is half as likely to be socially isolated as the average American'.

Professional Orientation (PRO)

Professional oriented SNSs focuses on industry professionals and is a good platform for professionals connecting with other professionals, advertising their expertise, gathering information, and meeting their needs. Many companies also search professional social networks for potential employees.

Educational Orientation (EDU)

Many SNSs have education oriented (EDU) groups and universities are one of the most frequent users of SNSs. Universities and colleges use social networking for reaching out to potential students, encourage networking and collaboration with other students. Educational institutions, however, are slow to start their own SNSs. The Milwaukee School of Engineering (MSOE) has started to engage with students through social media.

The objective is to build a lasting relationship starting from prospective students to accepted students, enrolled students and alumni. (Carr, D.F, 2013).

Healthcare Orientation (HCO)

Hospitals and Healthcare organizations have started using social media for communications, information sharing (except sharing of protected health information [PHI]), advising, sharing insights about diseases and medications, providing health tips and alerts, making appointments, educating patients, marketing and promotion. Physicians are able to collect information and views about the healthcare provider and patient experience during their visit.

Commercial Orientation (COM)

A 2010 Harvard Business Review article indicated that the commercial enterprises were still searching for the best practices and measurements for their use of social media. Even though the use of social media by commercial enterprises for promotion, data collection and analysis has grown since 2010, the efficacy of social media for commercial organizations is still unclear. Most companies are still struggling to justify their investment in social media. Results of a 2012 survey showed that 86 percent of marketers agreed social media was important and 46 percent were planning to increase their social media budget. However, only 12 percent of marketers felt capable of measuring social media ROI (Dubois, D. 2014).

Political Orientation (POL)

Social networking sites have become an important platform for political parties. According to a 2013 pewinternet.org study, SNSs are used to disseminate political news, information, searching for likeminded issue-oriented people, and for voter outreach.

As younger, more technology-savvy and social media user generation reach voting age, it is natural that activities related to politics also move on to the social media. Another 2012 pewinternet.org study found that younger users were more likely to post their thoughts on issues and political material. This group also encourages others to belong to a political group on a social networking site and take political action.

Sports Orientation (SPO)

Sports fans, in general, are emotionally attached to the teams they support. They are dedicated and not hesitant to voice their opinion. Social networking sites have been a game changer for sports organizations. Sports organizations now have the ability to start real-time engagements with fans eager for interaction, and specific social media strategies are very effective in increasing fan loyalty and delivering a positive return on their investment (LePage 2013).

Governmental Orientation (GOV)

One of many challenges of online user-generated content is the availability of a massive amount of information and misinformation. Governments around the world have started using social media to reach out to citizens to provide accurate information, and to promote and improve services and communications with citizens. Governments are also using social media for surveillance as well as for identification, monitoring and responding to issues concerning public service and safety. Therefore, the governmental orientation of social media revolves around providing information, service, and safety for its citizens (Kavanaugh et al. 2012).

Non-Profit Orientation (NPO)

More and more people are using the Internet and SNSs, and therefore, it is no surprise that more people are donating online. Nonprofit organizations have found Facebook and Twitter a very effective platform for fund raising. A post on Facebook about a cause reaches users faster than any other method, and about 39 percent of users who see the message actually donate for the cause. If Twitter is used for fundraising, the donations increase by tenfold (Huffingtonpost.com 2012). Non-profit elements of social media include education, awareness, fund raising, and volunteering among others.

News Orientation (NO)

Twitter has become a regular part of the daily news outreach by news organizations. News orientated social networking is basically one-way social media activity such as providing tweeter feeds of news headlines and uploading news headlines on SNSs. News organizations don't have much engagement with readers yet (Holcomb, Gross, and Mitchell 2011).

Some elements of social networking orientations are common for more than one orientation. For example, fund raising is common for political, non-profit, and for some education oriented sites. Similarly, commercial, political, and sports oriented sited have fan pages as a common element. Figures 2.3 and 2.4 provide examples of such clusters of orientations with common elements.

Understanding the elements for each orientation and the common elements among orientations are important information for potential users and for organizations. This information is helpful for marketing and promotion as well as for recruitment and other purposes.

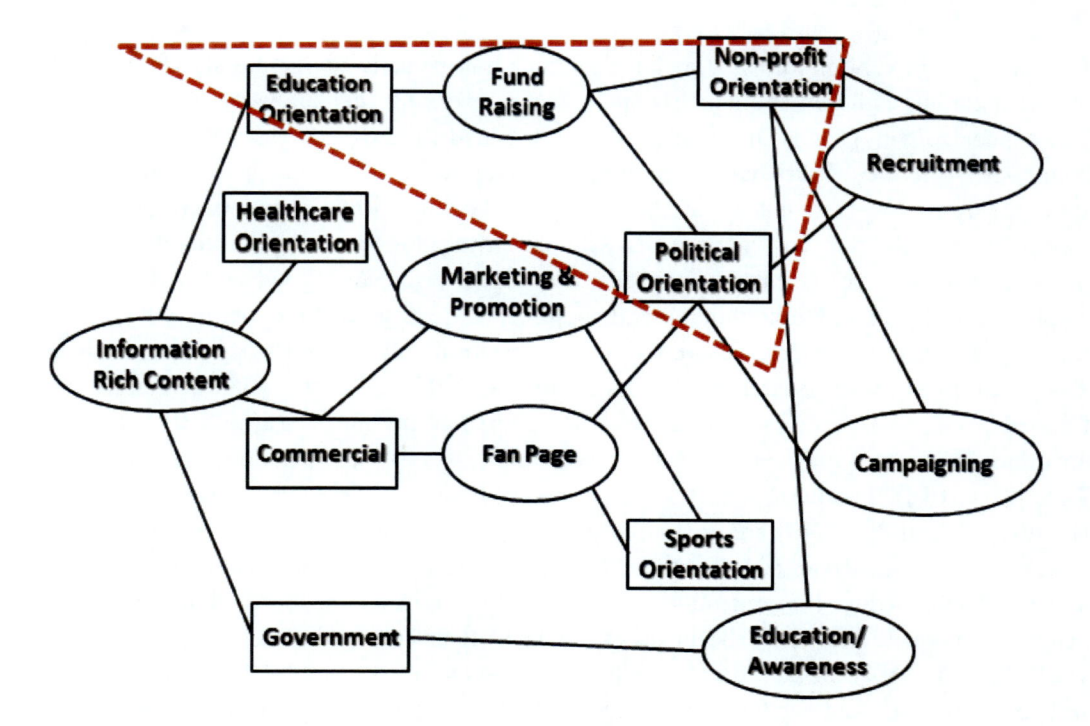

Figure 2.3. Cluster of orientations with common elements.

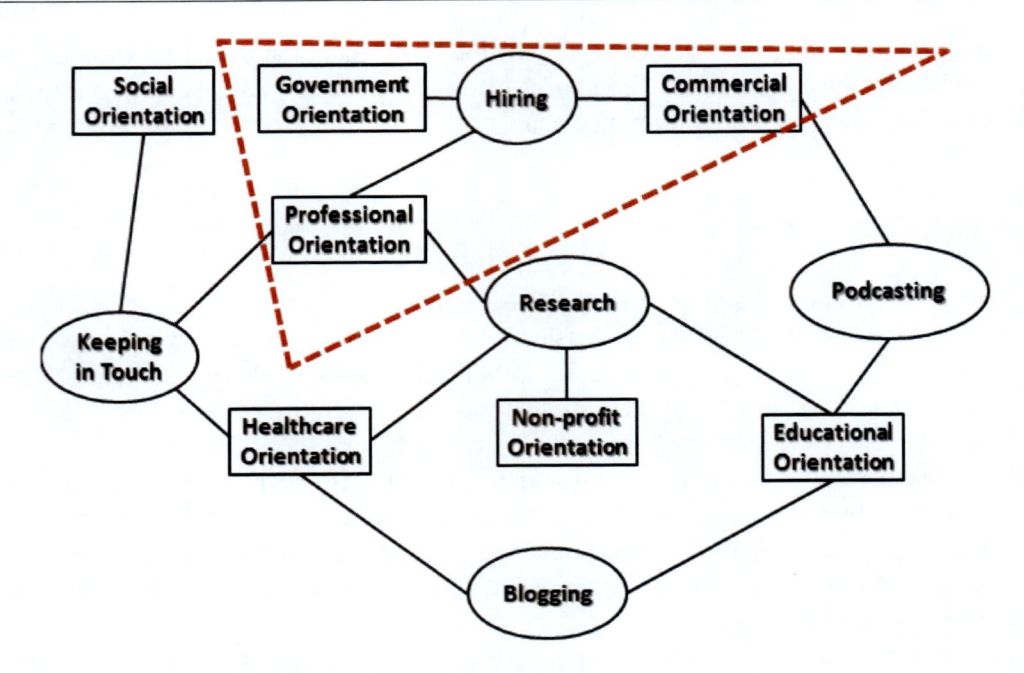

Figure 2.4. Cluster of orientations with common elements.

THE IMPACT AND FUTURE OF VIRTUAL SOCIETY

Engaging in various forms of social media is a routine activity that has shown to benefit people including children and adolescents. Social networking sites allow users the ability to stay connected with friends and family, make new friends, share pictures, exchange ideas and many other activities. Users have been pressing social media to enhance social and technical skills as well. However, not all of these sites are healthy virtual environments for users, especially, for children and adolescents. Children and adolescents are susceptible to peer pressure, and their self-regulating capacity and capacity to judge good and evil on social media is limited. In addition, children and adolescents are targeted for cyberbullying, clique-forming, and sexting. Internet addiction, distraction from studies and sleep deprivation are also cited in several research findings (Thompson 2013; O'Keefe, Clarke-Pearson, and Council on Communications and Media 2011; Kuppuswamy and Narayan 2010). It is not uncommon for teenage girls to send and receive well over 100 texts per day (Lenhart 2012; Thompson 2013). The number of texts for boys is about half. Franzen in his article for the Guardian argued that SNSs are creating a uniquely shallow and trivial culture, making kids unable to socialize face to face. (Franzen 2013). Scientist and writer Susan Greenfield warned about a future hedonistic generation who would live only by the thrill of the computer-generated moment and would be in distinct danger of detaching themselves from the real-world (Barton 2014). In fact, dire consequences of social media painted by many may very well be premature and far-fetched. There are extreme examples of teens who send 200+

messages each day (Thompson 2013) and spend too much time on virtual world; however, these behaviors are exceptions, not normal.

Amanda Lenhart, in her 2012 research, concluded that most avid texters were also most likely to spend time with friends and family in person. There is no conclusive evidence yet to suggest that virtual socialization is in the process of replacing face-to-face socialization. In fact, multiple authors argue that virtual socialization augments face-to-face socialization (Lenhart 2012; Thompson 2013). There is evidence to suggest that with the increase of texting, the use of phone conversations has gone down in recent years (Lenhart 2012). This is a natural phenomenon of one form of communication replacing other forms for some, but not for all communications. The bottom line is, virtual society through SNSs will continue to grow with more and more people going online. This phenomenon will have a significant positive impact on communication, collaboration, skill development, networking, information sharing, research and development, and many other areas in education, government, commerce, healthcare, sports, and politics. Of course, there are negative consequences of virtual socialization; however, negative consequences will probably be limited to an insignificant portion of social network participants.

Conclusion

The architecture and makeup of virtual society are discussed in this chapter. Recognizing the complexity, the Solar Model is proposed to provide the scope, depth and elements of the virtual society. Like any new tool, gazette or invention, virtual society has its share of good and evil. As always, how the technology and virtual space on the Internet is used will determine if the virtual society and communication are good for a person, community and society. It is a fact that people do more text-based computer-mediated communications than face-to-face or voice communication; however, above all else, this reflects the adoption of new and more efficient communication tools. Scientific evidence in support of the formation of a hedonistic generation that is detached from reality due to virtual society is yet to be found. Virtual society is here to stay and will benefit the human race if the engagements follow the line of morality.

References

Barton, J. (2014) Life in the social media bubble. http://www.frontiersin.org/blog/Life_in_the_ social_media_bubble/766 (Accessed 6/5/2014)

Burke, F 2013; http://www.huffingtonpost.com/fauzia-burke/social-media-vs-social-ne_b_4017305.html (Accessed 5/25/2014)

blog.hootsuite.com - http://blog.hootsuite.com/sports-social-media-white paper/

Carr, D.F, 2013. Universities Create Their Own Social Networks For Students. http://www.informationweek.com/universities-create-their-own-social-networks-for-students/d/d-id/1110997? (Accessed 6/5/2014)

Cerulo, 2012: http://www.details.com/culture-trends/critical-eye/201203 /social-media-timeline-evolution#/slide=4 (Accessed 5/20/2014)

Dubois, D. (2014). Measuring social networking success: more than just likes. http://www.forbes.com/sites/insead/2014/04/16/measuring-social-networking-success-more-than-just-likes/ (Accessed 5/20/2014)

Franzen, J., *The Guardian*, Friday 13 September 2013

Goble, 2012: http://www.digitaltrends.com/features/the-history-of-social-networking/#!SyCfK (Accessed 5/15/2014)

Google+ (http://www.nydailynews.com/news/national/google-540m-monthly-users-lags-behind-facebook-article-1.1500403 (Accessed 5/3/2014)

Tweney, 2009: http://www.wired.com/2009/09/0924compuserve-launches/ (Accessed 5/10/2014)

Harvard Business Review Analytic Services (2010). The new conversation: taking social media from talk to action. *Harvard Business School Publishing*.

Holcomb, J., Gross, K. and Mitchell, A. http://www.journalism.org/2011/11/14/how-mainstream-media-outlets-use-twitter/ (Accessed 5/5/2014)

Huffingtonpost.com (2012). How Nonprofits Used Social Media To Increase Giving In 2012 (INFOGRAPHIC). http://www.huffingtonpost.com/2012/12/18/nonprofits-social-media-2012_n_2325319.html

(Accessed 5/5/2014)

Kavanaugh, A, Fox, E. A., Sheetz, S., Yang, S., Tzy, L., Whalen, T., Shoemaker, D., Natsev, P., and Xie, L. (2012). Social media use by government: from the routine to the critical, *Government Information Quarterly*, Volume 29, Issue 4, Pages 480–491

Kuppuswamy, S. and Narayan P. B. S. (2010). The impact of social networking websites on the education of youth. *International Journal of Virtual Communities and Social Networking*, Volume 2, Issue 1, 13 pages.

Lea, M., Spears, R., Watt, S. E. & Rogers, P. (2000). *The InSIDE story: social psychological processes affecting online groups*. KNAW, Amsterdam.

Lenhart, A. (2012). Teens, Smartphones & Texting. http://www. pewinternet.org/2012/03/19/teens-smartphones-texting/ (Accessed 4/23/2014)

LePage, E. (2013). 3 Ways Sports Organizations Use Social Media to Increase Fan Loyalty. http://blog.hootsuite.com/sports-social-media-whitepaper/ (Accessed 5/5/2014)

Lewis, W (2009). 10 Ways newspapers are using social media to save the industry. http://mashable.com/2009/03/11/newspaper-industry/ (Accessed 7/2/2014)

Murillo, E. 2008; http://www.informationr.net/ir/13-4/paper386.html

O'Keeffe, G. S., Clarke-Pearson, K. and Council on Communications and Media (2011). Clinical Report—The impact of social media on children, adolescents, and families. *Pediatrics*, Published online March 28, 2011

pewinternet.org (2012) - http://www.pewinternet.org/2012/10/19/social-media-and-political-engagement (Accessed 4/23/2014) pewinternet.org (2013) - http://www.pewinternet.org/fact-sheets/social-networking-fact-sheet/ (Accessed 5/5/2014)

Rheingold, H. (2000). *The virtual community: homesteading on the electronic frontier.* Cambridge, MA: MIT Press.

Rheingold, 2000, http://www.maclife.com/article/feature/complete_history_social_networking_cbbs_twitter (Accessed 4/23/2014)

Simon, 2009: http://www.maclife.com/article/feature/complete_history_social_networking_cbbs_twitter (Accessed 5/5/2014)

Smith, C. (2014). How many people use 500+ of the top social media, apps and tools? http://expandedramblings.com/index.php/resource-how-many-people-use-the-top-social-media/9/#.U3DLpKPD_IU (Accessed 7/2/2014)

Thompson, C. (2013). Teenagers and social networking – it might actually be good for them. *The Guardian*, Friday 4 October 2013.

Woolgar, S. (2002) *Virtual society? Technology, cyberbole, reality.* Oxford University Press, Oxford. (ISBN 0-19-924875-3)

Woolley, D. R. (1994). PLATO: The emergence of online community, http://thinkofit.com/plato/dwplato.htm (Accessed 4/23/2014)

YouTube - http://www.youtube.com/yt/press/statistics.html (Accessed 7/2/2014)

Part II. Civilizing Virtual Culture

Chapter 3

RELIGION OF VIRTUAL CIVILIZATION

Andrew Targowski[*]
Western Michigan University, US
President Emeritus of the International Society
For the Comparative Study of Civilizations (2007-2013)

ABSTRACT

The *purpose* of this investigation is to define a secular religion of Virtual Civilization (virtuality). The *methodology* is based on an interdisciplinary big-picture view of the elements of development, their interdependency, and operations with respect to the religion of virtuality. Among the *findings* is that the religion of virtuality advocates for: unlimited freedom, cyberspace, and progress supported by collective intelligence for the purpose of securing the common good in an alternative virtual world, since the "real" world is going in a wrong direction in the 21st century. *Practical implications:* The purpose of virtuality's religion is to steer and motivate its users to act and behave within the boundaries of their secular religion. *Social implication:* The quest for the common good by virtuality's religion is good; however, the voiced values are not acceptable in reality. *Originality:* This investigation, by providing an interdisciplinary and civilizational approach at the big-picture level defined a religion of Virtual Civilization, which is evolving in our times and can be a golden solution to human well-being.

INTRODUCTION

The purpose of this investigation is to discover the religion of the Virtual Civilization, since according to Toynbee (1995) each civilization is characterized by its specific, key

---

[*] andrew.targowski@wmich.edu.

religion. It can be a sacred or secular religion. The latter is an appropriate kind of religion for a new civilization, driven by ICT tools.

According to the Oxford dictionary a religion is "the belief in and worship of a superhuman controlling power, especially God or gods." As an intentional oxymoron, the word combination "secular religion" can be used to describe ideas, theories or philosophies which involve no spiritual component yet possess qualities similar to those of a religion. Such qualities include a system of indoctrination, the prescription of an absolute code of conduct, designated enemies, unquestioning devotion to a higher authority and an ideologically tailored creation story and a millenarian narrative.

The secular religion operates in a secular society by filling a role which would be satisfied by a church or another religious authority. Social philosopher Raymond Aaron (1957) notably used the term to refer to Communism. Philosopher of science Michael Ruse (2003) made use of the term in discussing the theory of evolution and Darwinism. And last but not least, Thomas Frank (2011) suggested that the free market has become a secular religion in the United States. Ideologies such as atheism, agnosticism, skepticism, Marxism, secular humanism, and existentialism have also been recognized as secular religions since the Enlightenment (McDowell and Stewart 1991).

A New Secular "Religion" of Virtual Civilization

Since Westerners dominate Virtual Civilization, the justified question is what exactly is its religion? Christianity? Not at all. Granted, religion influences nearly everything in our daily lives, from buildings, the food we eat, and the books we read to the rituals of marriage and death, and the customs of court room and government. It shapes our beliefs, moral codes, and sense of national identities. Both individuals and nations describe themselves in religious terms -- Christian or Jew, Hindu or Muslim, Buddhist or Shinto, and so forth.

On the other hand, secularization has mounted since the seventeenth century, and today one's status as a business person does not require further *religious* identification, since business itself has become a "religion." Not only is greed good, as Gordon Gekko so persuasively insists in Oliver Stone's famous "Wall Street" episode, but, beyond that, it is virtuous, and in fact it is a religion of its own that is free and clear of its earlier involvement with Protestantism as described by Max Weber. It now throws a wider net than the northern European Protestant sect could ever have imagined.

In the United States, a country which is very strongly religious-oriented, there are many secular holidays celebrated like a "religious" event. In 1870, an Illinois representative introduced to the House of Representatives a bill to declare several days as federal holidays. The bill's language was approved by the House and the Senate, and signed into law by President Ulysses S. Grant in late June 1870. It included January 1, July 4, Thanksgiving Day and Dec. 25 as holidays. Congress acknowledged that Jan. 1 is "commonly called New Year's Day" and Dec. 25 is "commonly called Christmas Day." Thanksgiving, presumably, was identified by its name because its date changes from year to year.

Furthermore, there are also so called federal holidays, which are applied to federal employees and the District of Columbia. States and cities are free to adopt federal holidays or not, just as they are free to propose and approve their own holidays. The same is true for private employers; nothing forces them to stick to federal holidays. This bill, and other similar ones, did not establish a government religion or say that one faith deserved recognition over another; it simply recognized that certain days in the year are commonly celebrated. Federal employees, on the whole, would greatly benefit from having these days built in as holidays (Rienzi 2013). However, due to their celebration kind of rules, one can call them holidays of "secular religion."

Hence, the energetic creation of a new virtual layer of human experience upon the existing real one is associated with some strong new values and arguments that it is a new "better way to live" and those who "log in" to this new virtual world have a "better future." Most believers of this new mantra behave like "virtuality church" goers.

Virtual technology and its applications have been taking place during the time of Global Civilization's rise and have been steered by a secular religion which became business-oriented with values like super-consumerism and "greed is good." Virtuality, in a general sense, will supposedly make Global Civilization stronger yet at the same time weaker by antiglobalization movements, which organize themselves as virtual organizations.

BELIEFS OF VIRTUAL RELIGION

The belief in gods and goddesses was once important, but nowadays most e-communicating mortals—mostly young generations--take on virtuality to a certain extent. Virtuality as a societal trend began during the Clinton Administration (democratic, 1993-2001), when his opponent Speaker of the House republican Newt Gingrich tried to take the political spotlight as an intellectual who valued the opinions of futurists and spiritualists, self-improvement experts and cyberspace gurus -- all wanting to improve American society through the new forms of information technology. These new gurus even once argued that every American should know not only how to write in English but also how to program computers. Farther technological improvements proved that this advice was entirely wrong.

At the same time that e-nature was talking about the fourth instinct, and Mr. Gingrich was offering his "contract" for change in America, Alvin Toffler (1980) was talking about information dominance as the Third Wave. His wife Heidi Toffler, and his co-author, were arguing with Mrs. Huffington about Second- and Third-Wave diversity values. Eventually, a new conservative-futurist vocabulary was created with new terms such as: "byte cities," "brain lords" and "cyber-politics."

The day after the Republicans' historic takeover of the House of Representatives in the 1994 election, Newt Gingrich was off and running, giving a series of Fidel Castro-style speeches about "the Third Wave information revolution." It had the inimitable halo of language from his new-age gurus, Alvin and Heidi Toffler.

A few weeks later, when Newt was elected House Speaker by the incoming Republican conference, there was a small elderly couple standing by his side as he gave a one-hour acceptance speech. It soon became clear who they were once he issued a reading list to the Republican legislators. At the top of the list was a book by the Tofflers (*Slade* 2011-12-11).

At a conference today, for instance, his friends spoke about virtual economy, virtual government and virtual America (Dowd 1995). Their big idea is that the world is about to change faster than it ever had before, creating a technological explosion that would frighten and baffle the masses -- much like the electricity. The government must be prepared for it as well as the American society. Once Newt Gingrich himself delivered a talk titled "From Virtuality to Reality." His said that:

> "In a sense, virtuality at the mental level is something I think you'd find in most leadership over historical periods, but in addition, the thing I want to talk about today, and that I find fascinating, is that we are not at a new place. It is just becoming harder and harder and harder to avoid the place we are."

Apparently, the former #3rd politician on duty (after President and Vice-president) looked at virtuality as a new political solution. Of course politics at the illusionary level is nicer and easier to "implement." Gingrich and Toffler were working together on a new ideology of civilization. Alvin Toffler (1990) within 10 years published a book titled *Power Shift*, where he argued that a world division will arise – not between East and West or North and South, but between the "fast" and the "slow." The "fast" people will create wealth more rapidly simply by being more innovative, more individual, and better informed. This shift of power based on wealth supposedly will be at the global level, taking place at supermarkets, hospitals, banks, television, telephones, businesses, politics and personal life.

Eventually, Alvin and Heidi Toffler published a book on *Creating a New Civilization* (1994). Newt Gingrich wrote the foreword to his mentors' book. The authors argue that "the emerging new civilization writes a new code of behavior for people and carries us beyond the concentration of energy, money and power. The emergent new civilization has its own ways of dealing with time, space, logic and causality. And, its own principles for the future of the politics." Unfortunately, the authors mostly speak about the decline of industrial civilization and the rise of information civilization, where being informed may lead to being richer and knowledge mean more than capital. Once they hinted about semi-direct democracy, which is a shift from depending on representatives for representing ourselves. This kind of democracy is possible, because today, the mass society of industrial civilization is being transformed into a society of individuals of information civilization, who are communicating fast and broadly through e-means. The authors published their book on a new civilization 20 years ago, certainly thinking mostly about the real world.

Perhaps it would be a shock for them, who published the famous book *Future Shock* (1970) that within just 20 years since publishing about a new civilization, people are escaping from the real world into the virtual one. This escape is so fast, decisive, and broad that it leads to a new Virtual Civilization. This civilization is e-information and e-communication driven, and it aims at the radical improvements of real civilization, which is practiced by those who walk on the Earth's surface.

Since, as Arnold Toynbee (1995) argues, each civilization is characterized by a religion, let's characterize the religion of Virtual Civilization as follows: It is based upon a *virtuality doctrine* composed of the following elements in the 21st century:

Virtuality Faith emphasizes unlimited freedom, cyberspace, and progress supported by collective intelligence in order to secure the common good in an alternative virtual world, since the "real" one is going in a wrong direction in the 21st century. *Collective intelligence* (Lévy 1997) has limitless ability; "cyberspace is the limit." Virtuality faith develops and shares among its members a strong ability for solving problems, based on word-wide retrieval knowledge and wisdom kept in digital format. It has the permanent ability to be in e-touch, expanding world-wide membership, bottom-line opinions, recognizing individual views within boundaries of unlimited freedom of positions and views, downsizing societal solutions to satisfy almost every individual (toward the largest scale through virtual voting), seeing globalization as a platform for growing cyberspace and bigger market share for radical views, and the shared assumption that virtuality is "virtue."

Virtuality Knowledge should be free and should replace traditional education and real classrooms. The present curriculum is wrong because was created for the Industrial Revolution, which is *time passé*. The virtual curriculum should be based on online education anytime anywhere and should contain only knowledge which is limited to a few essentials and mostly emphasizes skills for how to live in the virtual society.

Virtuality Liturgy involves endless e-meetings/conferences via web-based media, all of which feature information convenient for the Virtual Doctrine in order to keep citizens as active members and faithful believers in unlimited freedom and Fun Society's simplistic lifestyle rooted in endless applications of computer games.

Virtuality Doctrine is what keeps virtuality as a religion. It is practiced by a billion plus devotees and some gurus, among them billionaires-owners of social networks who act as *Virtuality Bishops and Cardinals*. They are the virtual society's top elite who define vision, goals, strategies, principles and rules of current global opinion. As such it later becomes the *creed* for most of e-smart executives and managers of global organizations. For example, in the 2010s this doctrine was based on the following rules:
Rule 1: The elimination of governmental regulations is necessarily beneficial, since it encourages freedom of speech.
Rule 2: Intellectual property is an old concept which should be eliminated.
Rule 3: Most face-to-face meetings, particularly international conferences, should be replaced by virtual conferences to lower costs and broaden participation.
Rule 4: Printed books, journals, gazettes, magazines, and so forth should be replaced by e-publications to increase readership and decrease costs.
Rule 5: Face-to-face communication is too personal.

These five rules are highly debatable. Freedom is not free as we know through centuries of experience. The fact that we are civilized mostly means that our speech must be "civilized." We cannot say whatever we wish, since it can be against our cultural tradition and/or against our security, including the security of our nation, just to limit this issue to the most important criteria.

If the intellectual contributions (Rule 2) won't be protected then their production eventually will stop and there will be nothing to share. This issue was very strongly debated at the end of the 20th century when some businesses were freely distributing music. A solution was found which keeps the intellectual contribution as a private property.

Rule 3 in some cases can be applied but the most valid information is usually found in face-to-face communication. Body language and communication on impulse secure the highest level of information richness.

The Rule 4 is promoted by Big Business to secure higher income. For example Amazon.com waged the war against publishers of paper-based books, since it would like to be a sole distributor of e-books and e-book readers. Like-wise Google would like to possess all books in a digital form to sell access to them. After long negotiations Google agreed to pay some minimal royalties to authors. Needless to say, a printed book is a piece of our culture. It is kept on shelves to repeat that access on impulse once we visually located the book. Coffee table books cannot be of e-nature. Some magazines such Newsweek switched to digital format and after 1 year now went back to a printed version. A digital format of the Wilson Review is losing readership. All in all, we are overflown by large volumes of e-information and cannot absorb this constant and huge input anymore.

The Rule 5 is practiced by students who are in communication with "friends" from far away but do not know first names of colleagues seating in the same row at the elbow-to-elbow distance. This rule kills humanity as we used to know it.

Despite such negative meanings of the rules of virtuality, they are intensively practiced world-wide by younger generations, which have become addicted to it.

CLEARGY AND ELEMENTS OF VIRTUAL RELIGION

Each religion either sacred or secular has saints and apostols. Also the religion of virtuality has the following ones (Figure 3.1):

- *Virtuality Saints*: Tem Bernes – Lee (inventor of World Wide Web), Jerry Yang and David Filo (founders of Yahoo), Sergey Brin and Larry Page (founders of Google), Mark Zuckerberg (founder of Facebook), Reid Hoffman, Konstantin Guericke (inventors of LinkedIn), Jack Dorsey, Evan Williams, Noah Glass, and Biz Stone (founders of Twitter), and others.
- *Virtuality Apostols* – Marc Andreessen (Mosaic inventor), Eri Brynjolfesson and Andrew McAffee (advocates of the Second Machine Age, 2014), Albert-László Barbarási (advocate of "linked" people concept, 2003), Steve Woolgar (advocate of virtual society, 2003), Karen Mossberger (advocate of virtual inequality concept, 2003), Steven Jones (advocate of the Cybersociety 2.0 and virtual culture concepts, 1997, 1998), Richard Watson (advocate of future minds concept), Howard Reinhold

(advocate of online communities, 2000), Edward Castronova (advocate of exodus to the virtual word, 2007), and others.

Virtuality Doctrine is what codifies virtuality's values as a secular religion. The CEOs of Big Digital Business act as *Digital Business Bishops and Cardinals* and make decisions about updating the doctrine of virtuality as a religion. In fact, social networks function as marketing networks which make huge profits for their owners and executives out of personal data of naïve socially minded network members. The most influential of these virtuality leaders convene at *conclave*s to decide about the current curse of world digital business affairs. In turn *Digital Business Bishops* and *Cardinals* come to annual computer shows and share their virtuality doctrine's updates. Since cyberspace allows for direct democracy, some activists of online communities can contribute to these conclaves that may be kept in the digital mode.

Commission for Virtuality Faith Standards is composed of the following:

- Established practices of procedures applied in cyberspace which are automatically adapted by virtuality members, for example the symbol language used on Twitter.
- Several self-regulating committees, described by Tambini, Leonardi and Marsden (2008).
- U.S. Governmental committees, Congress' Task Forces, committees of the European Union, the Internet's committees, and so forth.
- Opinions expressed by Virtuality Saints and Apostols.

Practice indicates that many regulatory policies, particularly those ones defined by governmental authorities, are not accepted by the virtual society. The latter would like to have unlimited freedom in living as it is convenient for the virtuality users.

The main driving force of virtuality development is *virtuality education*, which means schools and colleges which push for digitalization and Internetization of the learning experience. Since they think that this way they are "progressive" and satisfying young generation's preferred e-cultural-driven behavior. Another factor is the lower costs of education if it is organized as an online-classroom. In such ways virtuality education teaches people how to be more a virtual user and less real person.

Virtual organizations are by products of virtuality; they are operating without real buildings but by real people, like Amazon.com or e-Bay, and others.

Virtuality Religion supports the basic needs of the digitized masses and makes them more aware of their mass power. If the virtual society wants to be lasting and successful, it must refine virtuality religion in order to serve virtuality users as well real people. Just as Christ's version of faith benefited from Paul's modifications, somebody somewhere in the virtual world must find a way to ameliorate the near-sighted ideological extravagance of the bottom liners today.

The *Digital Business Cardinals and Bishops* justify themselves by insisting that their strategy is to continue business growth till the level of the American Way of Life can be enjoyed in every corner of the world, particularly in China and India. However, two to three planets would be needed additional to the Earth to provide the needed volume of strategic resources for such an outcome, even assuming that the rest of the world would be satisfied with the high but gradually declining standard of life that Americans experience today. (Targowski 2009a:17).

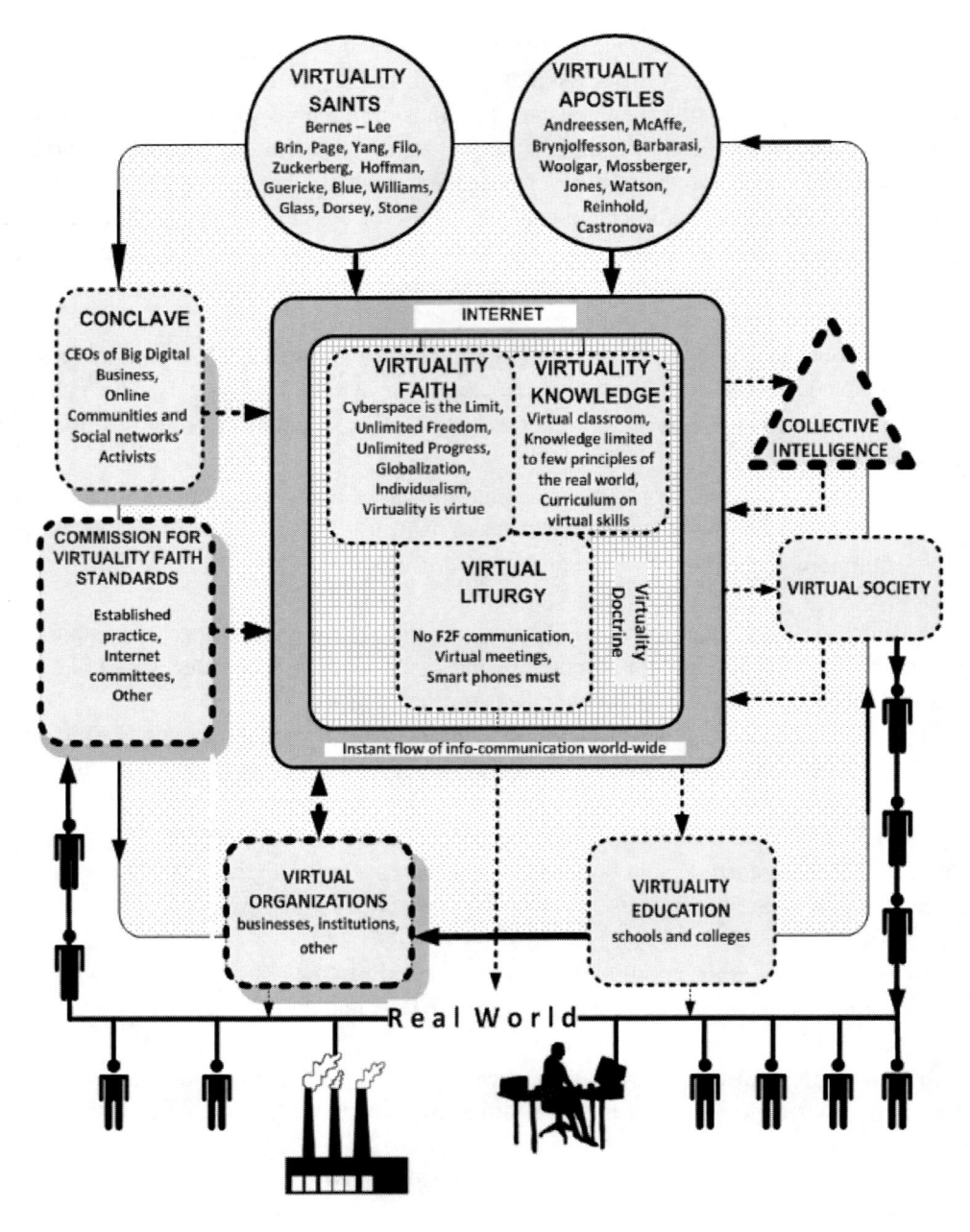

Figure 3.1. The Architecture of Religion of Virtual Civilization and the Main Relations among its Entities.

Conclusion

The religion of virtuality is one which "preaches" the value of unlimited freedom, cyberspace, and progress supported by collective intelligence in order to secure the common good in an alternative virtual world since the "real" one is going in a wrong direction in the 21st century.

1. The power of virtuality religion is generated by *collective intelligence* which has infinite ability - since "cyberspace is the limit" - to develop and share among virtuality members a strong capacity for solving problems, based on word-wide retrievalable knowledge and wisdom kept in digital format.
2. The liturgy of virtuality religion applies no face-to-face communication, virtual meetings, and smart phones as the must.
3. Virtuality religion is strongly supported by stock holders of social networks which in fact are of marketing rather than social character.
4. Virtuality religion is widely practiced by about 1.5 billion users in 2014, who feel that it strengthens their individual power in terms of opinion and impact upon the real world.
5. Virtuality religion contains some values, such as unlimited freedom, which are in disagreement with the religion of "normal reality" which accepts a notion that civilization limits freedom for the common good since the resources of our planet are limited. It is to be seen whether this disagreement will lead to a clash between those religions and what the repercussions for both of them will be.

In a broad and future sense, virtuality religion in its present formulation should be constantly enhanced and corrected to not only serve virtuality users but the real world inhabitants as well.

References

Aaron, Raymond (1957). *The Opium of the Intellectuals*. London: Secker & Warburg, pp. 265-294.

Barbarási, A-L. (2003). *Linked, how everything is connected to everything else and what it means for business, science, and everyday life*. London: A PLUME.

Brynjolfsson, E. & A. McAffee. (2014). *The second machine age*. New York: W.W. Norton & Company.

Castranova. Ed. (2007). *Exodus to the virtual world*. New York: Palgave Macmillan.

Dowd, M. (1995). The 104th Congress: the buzz; capital's virtual reality: Gingrich rides a 3rd wave. *New York Times*, January 11.

Frank, Th. (2011). *Pity the billionaire: the hard-times swindle and the unlikely comeback of the right*. New York: Picador.

Jones, St.G. (Edt). (1997). *Virtual culture, identity & communication in cybersociety*. London: SAGE Publications.

Jones, St.G. (1998). *Cybersociety 2.0 revisiting computer mediated communication and community*. London: SAGE Publications.

Lévy, P. (1997). *Collective intelligence, mankind's emerging world in cyberspace*. New York & London: PLENUM TRADE.

McDowell, J. and D. Stewart. (1991). *Understanding Secular Religion*. Manitou Spring, CO.: Summit Ministries.

Mossberger.K. et al. (2003). *Virtual inequality*. Washington, DC: Georgetown University Press.

Reisch, R. (2010). *After-shock*. New York: Alfred A, Knopf.

Reinhold, H. (2000). *The virtual community*. Cambridge, MA: The MIT Press.

Rienzi, M. (2013). Secular reasons to mark religious days. *New York Times*, February 17.

Ruse, M. "Is Evolution a Secular Religion?" *Science*, 7 March 2003.

Tambini, D., D. Leonardi & Ch. Marsden (2008). *Codifying cyberspace: communications self-regulation in the age of internet convergence*. New York: Routledge.

Targowski, A. (2004). From Global to Universal Civilization. *Dialogue and Universalism*, XIV(3-4), 121-142.

Targowski, A. (2009). *Information Technology and Societal Development*. Hershey & New York: IGI.

Toffler, A. (1980). *The third wave*. New York: Bantam Books.

Toffler, A. (1990). *Power shift*. New York: Bantam Books.

Toffler, A. & H. Toffler. (1994). *Creating a new civilization*. Atlanta: Turner Publishing, Inc.

Thomas. R. (2000). "The Rise Of Market Populism: America's New Secular Religion", *The Nation*, October 30.

Toynbee, A. (1995). *A Study of History*. New York: Barnes & Noble.

Wilkinson, P. (1999). *Illustrated Dictionary of Religions*. New York: A DK Publishing Book.

Woolgar, St. (2002). *Virtual society?* New York: Oxford University Press.

In: Virtual Civilization in the 21st Century
Editor: Andrew Targowski

ISBN: 978-1-63463-261-4
© 2015 Nova Science Publishers, Inc.

Chapter 4

CULTURE OF VIRTUAL CIVILIZATION

Kuanchin Chen[*]
Department of Business Information Systems
Western Michigan University, US

ABSTRACT

The main *purpose* of this work is to briefly outline the current debates regarding the dimensionality of national culture, and explore how that and other driving forces affect the development of digital culture. The *methodology* is rooted in a literature comparison across multiple disciplines, including management, information systems, communication and others. Our *findings* show that digital culture is similar to national culture in that the dimensionality view may better help delineate cultural variations (i.e., sub-cultures) within a larger form of culture. Unlike national culture, digital culture is frequently driven by or confined within digital means, which by themselves help formulate the unique contextual expectations of individuals who interact with the means. Among the *practical implications* are: human interactions on the Internet that usually drive a large part of evolution of digital culture can be innovated and enhanced to trigger another wave of digital and social evolution. Part of the *social implication* of this study includes how individuals build social cognition through leaning from or observing others. The *originality* of this work includes the explorations of possible frames of digital culture, their effects on individuals and societies, and the relationship of how theories from multiple disciplines are integrated.

---

[*] kc.chen@wmich.edu.

INTRODUCTION

Culture

The Oxford dictionary defines culture as "The arts and other manifestations of human intellectual achievement regarded collectively.", and the Merriam-Webster dictionary defines it as "the beliefs, customs, arts, etc., of a particular society, group, place, or time." Culture is also defined as "Values, symbols, and tradition-driven patterned behavior of people in society" (Targowski, 2009). Culture represents collective thoughts, beliefs and behaviors of a certain group, from which certain behaviors of individual members of that group are expected. Culture has long been a subject of interest across disciplines. With modern technological advances, gadgets and tools that were once only the "toys of the geeks" are now easily accessible to the typical consumers. We have thus grown more reliant on these technological tools that require little technical knowledge to operate. The ubiquity and the connectivity of these tools are becoming a reality in our day-to-day lives – a term called "the Internet of things" first coined by Kevin Ashton (1999). Although this definition has been refined by others, the term still refers to an environment where objects (gadgets, tools and others) are integrated with each other as part of our lives. Despite the fact that we are still far from reaching the perfect "Internet of things", we are beginning to see possibilities of ubiquity through today's technologies, such as Bluetooth, WiFi and the Internet. A smart phone is now multiple gadgets in one that can easily connect to other devices, computers and systems.

On a global scale, Friedman (2005, 2007) has called for action from businesses, governments and the like to stay competitive in response to the forces that had "flattened the world" (i.e., forces that had led to global competition). Of the ten forces, the ninth ("informing") and the tenth ("the steroids") are of most relevant to our discussion here in this article. The informing force originally referred to Google and other search engines that made information accessible to large numbers of populations in a rapid manner. This can now refer to all sources of information providers accessible by end-users. The "steroids" force refers to personal digital devices that have been part of our daily lives. As technology continues to improve, we are beginning to see a transformation of devices originally designed to be carried around as wearable devices (such as Google Glass and Sony SmartWatch). Therefore, Friedman's informing and steroids forces should not be treated as a static configuration, but rather as things that are fluid and evolving. All these changes have an impact on our lives ranging from the individual to national levels.

As a result of this digital impact, traditional cultures and societal norms have been shifting, converging and adapting. New ideas and new ways of life have been diffused more rapidly than ever because of the ease with which people can access the Internet. People have now become more aware of cultural differences through the means of global dissemination, rather than through traditional local stereotypes. Therefore, it is helpful to first delve into the current research debates on national culture and then explore culture elements of the virtual society.

Current Debates on National Culture

Hofstede (1980, 2001) was one of the pioneers who empirically identified national culture and its corresponding dimensions. In Hofstede's definition, culture is "the collective programming of the mind that distinguishes the members of one group of people from those of another." He further explains that "collective programming of the mind" can be in the form of education and socialization – experiences that occur early on in one's life. Hofstede (2001) defines the following five dimensions of national culture (p. 57 – 58):

- Individualism versus collectivism: the degree to which people derive their identity from either self (individualism) or social reference groups (collectivism).
- Power distance: the degree to which differences in power, status and privilege are accepted in society.
- Masculinity versus femininity: the degree to which the society favors achievement, heroism, and assertiveness (i.e., denoted as masculinity). The opposite is femininity where caring, cooperation and quality of life are preferred.
- Uncertainty avoidance: the degree to which uncertainty, novel phenomena and ambiguity are perceived as threats.
- Confucian dynamism: the degree to which the virtues of tradition and the present are valued against those of the future. It is later labelled as Short Term versus Long Term Orientation.

Hofstede's version of culture dimensions has attracted a lot of attention in many disciplines. Empirical validations of the clear separation and construct validity have been reported in recent studies. For example, using MBA students to assess the dimensionality of Hofstede's framework, Blodgett, Bakir and Rose's (2008) experiments suggest that Hofstede's framework may suffer from lack of reliability and validity. There are, however, studies using Hofstede's framework as the theoretical foundation to assess differences in behaviors. An example is Smith's (2011) work on delineating the difference in communication styles under different dimensions of national culture. The most salient cultural dimension leading to a difference of communication styles is individualism/collectivism.

Later House et al. (2004) embarked on a comprehensive study of national culture called the GLOBE project that involved 17,300 managers in 951 organizations from over 62 countries. Nine cultural dimensions were identified including Performance Orientation, Uncertainty Avoidance, Humane Orientation, Institutional Collectivism, In-group Collectivism, Assertiveness, Gender Egalitarianism, Future Orientation, and Power Distance. Although the GLOBE project aimed to validate Hofstede's dimensions as part of the goal, one key difference is that it took an approach which did not regard cultural values and practices as the same thing. In other words, it operated under the assumption that under a given norm of national culture, an individual may still behave differently due to their own value system. As a result, two sets of questions were developed (Javidan et al., 2006): one that measures the cultural norm (such as "In this society, power is …") and another that measures individual values (such as "In this society, power should be ..."). Their findings show that correlations between individual values and national cultures are mixed with positive correlations for some, negative correlations for others and no statistical correlation for the rest.

The studies reviewed thus far point to a couple of very interesting ideas regarding culture and behavior. First, national culture is a source of influence on individual behavior, but it is far from the only source of influence. Other sources include an individual's value system, which is derived from experience, education, social norms, and group norms. Second, individual values and national culture are intertwined and cross-pollinated which lead the value system to "co-evolve" into new forms. A similar pattern is observed with digital culture in that sub-cultures with different forms of the values system are possible under the big umbrella term of digital culture. In the sections below, we will first look at this umbrella term of digital culture. After that, we will delve into the factors that affect one's own value system.

Digital Culture

Individual values may be affected by their national cultures, but for a large part they may venture away from the national culture along their own path. The difference could in one way be attributed to an individual's projection of how a society should have been like, which is a view rooted in one's own experience in search of a solution to meet one's own needs. Such needs may not be fulfilled in the physical world. When the digital world becomes accessible and allows one to assume an identity which does not necessarily accord with one's true identity in the physical world, this opens the door for both many good and bad possibilities of meeting one's needs in cyberspace. For example, using a gender neutral ID allows one to hide their true identity in online conversations. Therefore, digital culture, or cyberculture, may cross the boundaries of national cultures to become a truly interesting phenomenon.

Levy (2001) defines cyberculture as "the set of technologies (material and intellectual), practices, attitudes, modes of thought, and values that are developed along with the growth of cyberspace." Despite the fact that many consider cyberspace as a form of technological infrastructure (Levy also defines it as "the new medium of communications"), Levy nonetheless cautions that it is society that creates technologies, and technologies "condition" (not determine) the societal norms. Technologies condition the societal norms by providing access to certain possibilities "that certain cultural or social options couldn't seriously be contemplated without its presence." (p. 7). As there are a growing number of technologies that make up the "technologies" of cyberspace, it is possible that the cyberculture is not a monolithic form, but rather intertwined forms of sub-cybercultures that together form the larger version of the cyberculture. For example, the cyberculture of those using Instagram or Selfie emphasizes expressiveness of pictorial forms of oneself and surroundings or other objects, while twitter focuses on short and intermittent communication messages – a form of self-expression in text messages. These subcultures may include fundamentally different populations, or a similar population immersed in multiple virtual environments.

Research also confirms variations of subcultures within a national culture. For example, Lenartowicz and Roth's work (2001) offers evidence of subculture variations across motivational domains in business. Of the five motivational techniques (achievement, enjoyment, restrictive conformity, security, and self-direction), four (with the exception of enjoyment) were statistically different across the four subcultures studied. With respect to the rank-order of the motivational techniques, all subcultures were found to have the exact rank order – a situation that indicates that there might be some common elements that are shared collectively across subcultures. In other words, this could be due to the larger form of culture (i.e., national culture).

The sections below are designed to identify key driving forces of digital culture (or subculture), the effects should these driving forces actualize and the net effect of digital culture on society or national culture. As subcultures vary in their course of action compared with the national culture, it is useful to view the driving forces from two angles – the macro angle and the micro angle. It is also important to point out that the two angles should not be treated as mutually exclusive approaches, but rather two forces that overlap to jointly affect an individual's decision in the virtual society.

DRIVING FORCES OF DIGITAL CULTURE – THE MACRO VIEW

Technology advances have enabled opportunities that were once difficult, and sometimes not even possible, in the physical world, but these advances were not adopted at same time or at the same rate. Without the right condition(s), an invention will not receive its intended adoption. These conditions, however, have become available through the history of evolution. As Igbaria (1999) puts it, "The virtual society transcends towns, states, and countries, and represents an evolutionary, as opposed to a revolutionary, movement." The evolutionary aspect of it clearly shows incremental progression of the required conditions for a technological advance to be successful.

Igbaria's framework includes four main driving forces for a virtual society from a macro level:

- Global economics:
- Policies and politics:
- Enlightened and diversified population:
- Information technology:

The debate on Net Neutrality (a term coined by a Columbia Law Professor Tim Wu, 2003) is a nice example of Igbaria's multiple driving forces in action. Net Neutrality is the principal that Internet service providers and governments should treat all Internet services, content and data equally without discriminating by the purpose of use, the type of data, the person who uses it, and the mode of usage. The ongoing debate centers around global competition, government policies, laws, consumer rights as well as technology, which basically cuts across all driving forces of Igbaria's framework. In a recent blog post by the FCC's chair Tom Wheeler (April 29, 2014), he indicated that treating consumers differently by creating fast and slow lanes, and degradation of existing services to force consumers to pay a higher price for a better service are not in the spirit of preserving an Open Internet – an idea he made a priority of the FCC. He continues with the blog by citing President Obama's comment "Preserving an Open Internet is vital not just to the free flow of information, but also to promoting innovation and economic productivity."

DRIVING FORCES OF DIGITAL CULTURE – THE MICRO VIEW

Technology has been the centerpiece of digital evolution, but a technological invention does not always guarantee adoption. Technology adoption at a higher or national level does not necessarily mean adoption at the individual level unless it is something forced onto an individual. In this section, we focus on an individual's willful or voluntary choice to adopt and continue using a technology. This assumption is consistent with the many forms of digital culture, for the choices of using an Internet service are largely individual decisions.

Technology Acceptance

To drive use, a technology has to be proven useful. However, usefulness is in the eyes of the end users. A product with designed usefulness does not automatically translate into perceived usefulness by the end users. For example, 3M developed a special kind of glue that can be used to temporarily attach one object to another. It can be removed easily by detaching two objects. The product was not considered useful for some time until an engineer spread the glue on a piece of paper and stuck the paper on his office wall to remind others of important things. As a result, stick-it notes were born. Frequently features designed in a product may not be perceived to be useful by consumers. In the software industry, it has long been recognized that products built based on the specs unilaterally determined by the developers are going to have a hard sell to end users. This is a key reason that user testing, requirements elicitation and certain software development methodologies (such as agile methodology) all require heavy user participation.

From the research standpoint, the practical elaborations expounded in the previous paragraphs are fully supported in the literature.

The Technology Acceptance Model (TAM) (Figure 1) is perhaps one of the most important theories in information systems frequently used to model use intention. In this model, perceived usefulness (PU) and perceived ease of use (PEOU) jointly affect one's attitude towards using a technology. PEOU is also an antecedent variable for PU, and PU has a direct effect on behavioral intention.

This model has been empirically verified in various applications ranging from smart phones to ERP systems. A majority of TAM-based models (Figure 4.1) show that PU affects attitudes and intentions more than PEOU. Therefore, it makes sense to treat PU as one of the first drivers to explain the digital culture. Since technology is the channel that connects users in the digital world, usefulness of a technology is an influential driver for a technology to be adopted for a certain task.

After all, users do not come to use a technology if it is not useful. With PU alone, it is difficult to support sustainable use.

Countless technologies failed because users had trouble operating the technologies. If one takes a look at the history of computer operating systems, we see a lot of examples of user interface improvements because of this exact reason.

For example, operating systems have evolved from the command-line user interface to graphical user interface (GUI) and from GUI to tablet-like interfaces (e.g., Microsoft's Metro UI on Windows 8). Although we still see all these types of user interfaces in use today, the ones that feel more consistent to the ways we do things will likely draw more non-technical users into the world of information technology.

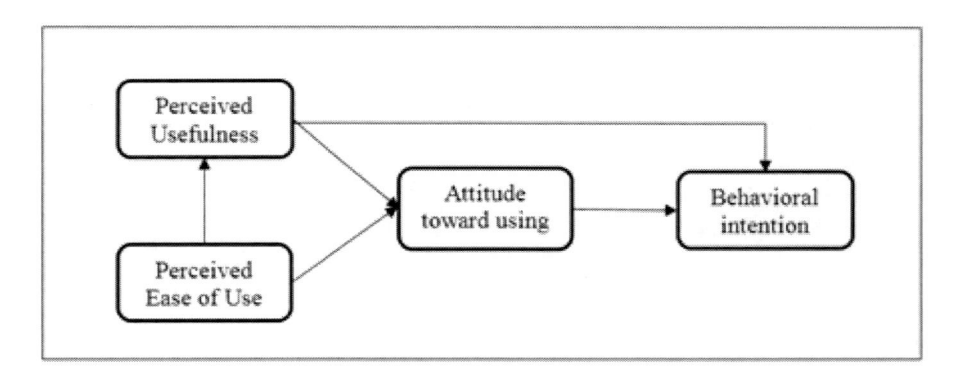

Figure 4.1. Technology Acceptance Model (Davis 1989).

Despite the wide applications of TAM in many fields and technologies, researchers also delve into factors other than PU and PEOU that have effects on attitudes and intentions. After all, TAM may be limited in certain applications of technology. For example, social influence plays a larger role for someone using social networking web sites than the combined effect of PU and PEOU alone. One may not use a social network site only because the site is useful and easy to use. Most people use social networking sites because their friends are already using them, or the sites give them a better way to connect with their friends. On the other hand, one's perceived capability in technology (i.e., self-efficacy or perceived behavioral control) has an effect on the perceived level of usefulness and ease of use. Non-technical users with less proficiency on a certain technology (i.e., lower self-efficacy) will likely perceive the usefulness of that technology differently than the technical users. Literature abounds in studies that expand the antecedents of PU or PEOU, or the antecedents of attitude or intention. TAM3 (Venkatesh & Bala, 2008) is a notable example that represents a multitheory model with theories such as TAM, Roger's diffusion model (Rogers, 1983), Ajzen's Theory of Planned Behavior (Ajzen, 1991), computer self-efficacy (Compeau and Higgins, 1995), and others.

Media Richness

As modern social media primarily rely on sponsorship and advertisements as their core business model, charging end users is a rare practice (unless for premium services). Users have come to expect free services with loaded features that they can use with their friends. One key element that enables relationship building for both business-related and individual reasons is communication. Social networking tools build the best communication by either making it easier to communicate or offering better sharing capabilities that are more likely to be adopted.

In the realm of computer-mediated communication, the media richness theory (Daft & Lengel, 1984) suggests that all media vary in their capabilities to support a vast amount of cues during the course of a communication session. The "richer" media are those that are equipped with more communication cues (e.g., visual, auditory, etc.), which are expected to help deliver a clearer message to the intended recipients, especially when equivocality of messages become a problem. On the other hand, the "leaner" media supports less supplemental information for the communication message. If modern communication tools are laid out in a media richness continuum, text and email messages are on the low end of media richness as the only cue available is the text. Elements (such as emoticons) have to be artificially inserted into an email to enhance the text with supplemental information. Face-to-face communication is on the high end of media richness that concurrently offer visual, gesture, auditory and other forms of cues during a session of communication. Daft & Lengel (1989) further suggest that media richness is a function of media capabilities in four areas:

1. The ability to handle multiple information cues simultaneously.
2. The ability to facilitate rapid feedback.
3. The ability to establish a personal focus.
4. The ability to utilize natural language.

Not all communication requires rich media all the time. If the goal of a communication is to deliver information, most likely text media would suffice. Chen, Yen, Hung and Huang (2008) provide further evidence through their experiment of media richness in equivocal messages. Email was found to be most effective and of higher quality compared to instant messaging for resolving conflicts and differences.

For leisure use of technology, social networking sites continue to build media richness into their offering. It is rare to see any social networking site today that has little capability in user interaction. Multi-way communication, presence information, and short messages all characterize the movement into richer media, closer to face-to-face communication. However, the momentum in that direction does not go unconstrained. When communication is used as a form of self-expression, tools that allow for disassociation of communication messages from one's true identity encourages the willingness to communicate. This is one reason some Facebook users take a very prudent approach in their activities and/or messages on Facebook, the same way one behaves in face-to-face communication when their identity is known to the audience. Figure 4.2 shows Facebook's Name Policy. The same true identity is not strictly required in Twitter. As a result, Twitter enables a very different kind of communication compared to the one available on Facebook. This makes one wonder if a "dislike" button was implemented in both Facebook and Twitter, would Facebook users be less inclined to use it due to their identity being known in their circle of friends. Additionally, some Twitter users still opted to provide their true identity for credibility, promotion and authenticity reasons. Unlike in Facebook, all communications from this latter type of users on Twitter who choose to provide their true identity will likely be of its own kind. Therefore, the exact richness of the media needed for a communication session depends on the task on hand, the purpose of communication, as well as the types of messages one wishes to deliver.

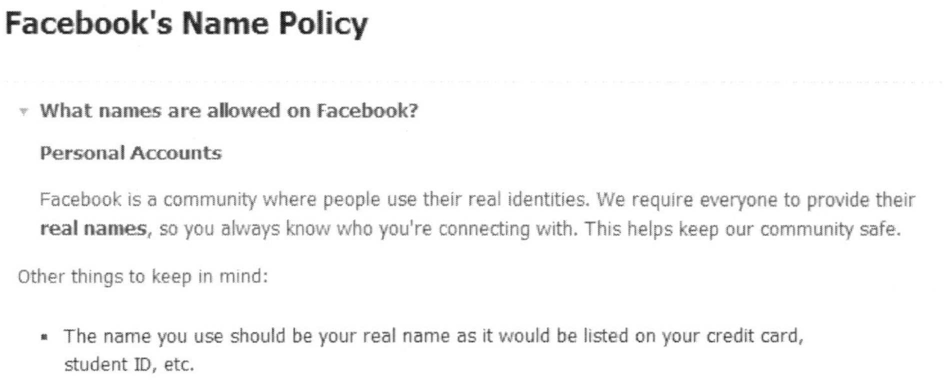

Facebook's Name Policy

▼ What names are allowed on Facebook?

Personal Accounts

Facebook is a community where people use their real identities. We require everyone to provide their **real names**, so you always know who you're connecting with. This helps keep our community safe.

Other things to keep in mind:

- The name you use should be your real name as it would be listed on your credit card, student ID, etc.

Figure 4.2. Facebook's Naming Policy.

Other Driving Forces

Thus far, we have addressed the driving forces of digital culture from two basic perspectives: tools (technology acceptance, perceived usefulness and perceived ease of use) and needs (communication needs, self-expressiveness, etc.). Other forms of driving forces are also possible. For example, TAM3 cited in the above sections goes beyond tools into one's capabilities to handle tools, perceived outcomes of tool usage, reactions of peers and past experiences. Furthermore, there are also other reasons that have the potential to entice someone to a social networking site in addition to communication and social needs. Without being comfortable with tools, demonstrated usefulness and meeting one's needs, adoption of a certain technology can be slow or even stagnant. Therefore, the tools and needs reviewed in the previous sections are the critical prerequisites for the blossoming of the digital culture. If the desired tools and needs are fulfilled for an individual, it is at best an isolated fulfillment of one's desire. The impact is quite limited to culture. When this same fulfillment happens to a group of people, it results in a collective pattern of behavior (as noted in the Oxford and Meriam-Webster's definitions) which leads to a refinement of an existing digital culture.

THE RISE OF DIGITAL CULTURE

Culture adapts, evolves and morphs as members of a culture continue to explore new ways of adaptation. For examples, instant messaging, SMS, tweets and texting are a collection of tools that enables communication with short messages. As members of a digital culture adapt to this new way of communication, the changes in the structure of communication (from long discussions to short messages) require a certain level of adaptation, which may deviate from the traditional social and culture expectations. If only a few people take this route, they are early adopters, pioneers or even "outliers". When more buy into the same new way of adaptation, it gradually becomes a societal norm and eventually forms a sub-culture.

Much of the transformation from a small-scale adoption to a new societal norm takes learning and observation of how others perform the tasks and how the results are compared to the existing approach. Technology (especially the Internet) is a catalyst that helps make learning and diffusion of new approaches more rapid than other traditional forms (such as newspaper). Social cognition is a sub-discipline of psychology that focuses on how people store, process and apply information about other people. Social Cognitive Theory (SCT) posits that acquisition of knowledge and social norms are primarily done through observing others within the context of their social encounters (Bandura, 2001). As a result, the triadic reciprocal relationship among learning, behavior or cognition, and environment is formed (Figure 4.3). These elements interact with each other to form the basis of reference for behavioral decisions.

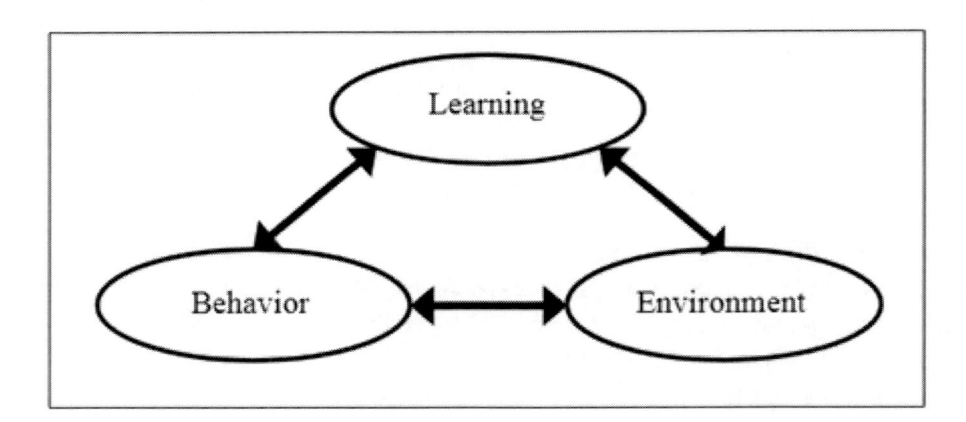

Figure 4.3. Triadic Reciprocal Relationship in Social Cognitive Theory.

SCT does not limit the source from which an individual emulates to be a real person. Media sources and experiences of others are possible models for imitation. Therefore, diffusion of a new norm, fad or style can be greatly enhanced with modern forms of technology. This is even more so when technology becomes more pervasive or even more ubiquitous in our daily lives. Not only do the new norms spread faster and wider than before with modern technology, but commonalities across sub-cultures also gradually grow as a result. Operating parallel to this is the development of digital culture that grows out of the common platform provided by modern social networks. Total homogeneity in a national or digital culture may not happen any time soon (or even ever), but some common elements (e.g., self-expressiveness) of digital culture certainly have spread across different national cultures.

MODERN SOCIAL NETWORKS

The older forms of social networks (such as early forms of listserv and gopher) primarily attracted technology savvied users in the early days. The digital culture which formed through people with technology know-how was very different from that of which we see today. As discussed in previous pages, the improvement of user interface from command-line interface to GUI, or from GUI to cloud-based user interface, had greatly removed the largest entry barrier to technology (more specifically social networks). Users with little training can now comfortably use modern social networking web sites due to the extreme simplification of user interface to click and type activities within a browser. A wider range of users are now on the social network sites than ever before.

As with groups formed naturally (e.g., common interest) or artificially (e.g., military) within a society, social networks attract all types of social groups. Most interestingly the tools themselves also influence social expectations, norms and behaviors. For example, the professional focus of LinkedIn.com carries the expectations of professionalism in social interactions and self-expressions on their web site, while Facebook is open to a wide range of communication styles for personal accounts.

Table 4.1. Comparison of Social Networking Sites

	Audience	Potential for Privacy Risks	Media Richness	Identity
Facebook	Personal and business	Personal information, relationships, affiliations, and other common privacy risks associated with social networking sites	Presence information, chat, asynchronous messages/feeds	Required
Linkedin	Personal and business	Personal information and affiliations, other common privacy risks associated with social networking sites	Limited media richness similar to those seen on dynamic web sites.	Required
Twitter	General public	Common privacy risks associated with social networking sites	Asynchronous and near synchronous interactions	Not required
Instagram	General public	Common privacy risks associated with social networking sites	Rich media when connected to other social networking sites	Not required

Table 4.1 shows a brief comparison of popular social networking web sites. The Potential for Privacy Risks column is the most important here. Generally the more personal and sensitive the information the web site requires, or the more such information the web site entices the user to provide, the higher potential for privacy risks. The requirement of a certain form of private information (such as name) on Facebook is the start of a possible privacy risk. The photo locations on Facebook, where one can easily associate with the uploaded photos, give out information about where someone has been, and more importantly where they live. The messages, postings and sharing are sources that reveal one's affiliation and relationship with others. Although this does not necessarily mean that there are already established privacy risks, the potential alone is enough to cause concerns. For example, when a friend's account has been hacked, his friend list is also likely known to the hackers. In the traditional email environment, this means that the email addresses, and possibly other contact information of those listed in the address book, are compromised, which might cause phishing, junk or spam emails. In today's social network web site, a compromised account also means that the private information, activities, affiliations and relationships are also compromised leading to a potential of more serious privacy issues, such as identity theft. Despite that privacy awareness still needs to be promoted to the general Internet population, the larger issue is not just lack of knowledge, but also willful rendering of private information when posting and sharing things on social networking sites. Additionally, the Identity column in Table 1 shows whether some form of identity is required when registering for an account on a social network site. As we explored before, communication style on the web site can be very different with or without a true identity being recorded or revealed.

EFFECTS OF PERVASIVE DIGITAL CULTURE

Digital Divide

The Digital Divide refers to an inequality between groups in accessing information and communication technologies (Chinn & Firlie, 2004). When the digital divide is applied to countries to assess inequalities in their access to information technology, it is usually referred to as the Global Digital Divide. Wikipedia (2014) shows approximately 7.2 billion people were on the Internet in 2013. The top ten countries with the highest internet penetration rate are mostly European countries (e.g., Iceland, Norway, Sweden, Netherlands, Denmark, Luxembourg, Finland) with an overall Internet penetration rate as high as 90% or above. U.S. is ranked 28 with a penetration rate of 81.0%. Several African countries (such as Niger, Ethiopia, Guinea, and Eritrea) have a very low penetration rate well below 2%. Globally there is such a wide range of internet penetration that it has created a digital divide.

However, Internet penetration usually offers a high level view of a possible divide. Several other factors are also relevant to how far the divide could be (even among the countries that have a similar penetration rate). For example, it would greatly hamper access to certain information on the Internet if Internet access is slow or intermittent. Akamai's State of the Internet report (2013) shows that the top countries or regions that had the fastest broadband connection were South Korea, Japan, Netherlands, Hong Kong, Switzerland, Czech Republic, Sweden, Latvia, Ireland and the U.S., ranked in the order listed. By cross examination of the data between Wikipedia and Akamai's reports, certain countries (such as Netherlands and Sweden) stand out with a high internet penetration and a high overall connection speed. A high level of internet penetration also means that citizens are likely to be kept current with the many forms of digital culture. As such, the diffusion of the digital culture is faster in countries with a high Internet penetration rate. On the surface level, high broadband connections indicate that more multimedia contents may be transmitted easily among users. A deeper implication is that multiple cues become available in a communication session (which is generally better according to the media richness theory) in a cheaper way. An example in the business context is the opportunity to adopt better or more modern video conferencing technology, which eventually translates to economic benefits (such as cost-cutting and competitiveness).

The digital divide, as the definition cited above shows, refers to inequality among groups. These groups are not necessarily countries, even though a good amount of research has been focused on the digital divide at the country level. A digital divide can happens within the same country as well. Recent publications began to distinguish the difference between two generations: digital natives versus digital immigrants. Digital natives, coined by Marc Prensky (2001), are those "who are native speakers of the digital language of computers, video games and the Internet". According to Prensky and related studies, digital natives were born roughly between 1980 and 1994 and they process information differently compared to generations before them. Digital immigrants were not born into the e-generation, but are those who welcome and adopt the digital language. A more precise distinction between digital natives and immigrants should be based on how they use the ICT, rather than when they were born. An example includes those who were born before the said time of digital natives, but closely work with ICT either professionally or at leisure. Several professions (e.g., software developers, people work in engineering and technology fields, and designers) characterize this latter form of digital natives. Therefore, digital natives are those who are comfortable working with ICT. Because of the frequent exposure to ICT (or more specifically, the Internet), these digital natives usually have a better opportunity to initiate the first waves of changes in the digital culture. Prenksy describes digital immigrants as those who learn to be proficient in ICT, and retain their "accent" (their foot in the past). Such differences between the natives and immigrants are enough to trigger the dynamics of different digital cultures. Therefore, we see digital culture as an evolving norm, rather than something that is fixed in form or shape.

Dependency and Behavioral Addiction

As the digitally inclined population grow and ICT continues to improve its ease of use, more and more are drawn to the virtual world. In the literature of Internet dependency and addiction, we have also seen transformations due to the improvements made possible by the driving forces discussed in the previous sections. Early technology "addicts" were those who were very computer savvy. These "geeks" had come to embrace technology as part of their lives, which might not be considered a group that represents the norm of the general population. After the entry barrier was removed through improvements in user interface and other areas of software systems, "computer addicts" (or a gentler term "computer dependents") are now those who have grown dependent on ICT as part of their lives. This is the reason the Internet Addiction Survey (created by Dr. Kimberly Young who also coined the term "Internet Addiction") includes questions such as "stay online longer than intended", "feeling depressed or nervous when not online", "frequent email-checking", "performance suffers due to Internet use", and "attempts to cut down but failed". As one can see, longer duration of use is not the only criteria one should use to consider someone as an "addict" or dependent. It is a necessary, but not a sufficient condition for Internet Addiction (or Dependency). Withdrawal (similar to what happens to the withdrawal syndromes of substance-based addiction) and degradation of performance are also key elements of the problem.

Young (1998) considered Internet addiction as a form of non-substance based pathological addiction, but some early works in the psychology discipline (e.g., Glasser, 1976 and Perkins, 1988) suggest that people can show addictive behavior with little or no impact on their performance at school or work. Therefore, Glasser was one of the first who coined the term "Positive Addiction". Examples of positive addiction include jogging and meditation. When people perform a healthy activity frequent enough for a long period of time, it could become a habitual form of addiction that does not necessarily interfere with one's performance. This is the reason Chen (1999), and Chen, Tarn and Han (2004) started exploring behavioral differences among the positive and negative Internet dependency groups. Those with some dependencies (no matter positive or negative) were found to have a higher interest in online shopping and online education than those with little or no signs of dependency.

If using ICT long and frequent enough does not make one an addict, and groups of people with Internet dependency (positive or negative) share similar behavioral patterns, one would expect to see digital sub-cultures to be formed due to the behavioral or preferential difference among the digital population. Based on the Internet Addiction literature, we see that different dependency groups are themselves separate sub-cultures when they are engaged in similar computer applications. More importantly different digital sub-cultures may also share some common traits in their behaviors as well.

CONCLUSION

Culture is a complex concept. If one tries to make generalizations about a culture, he or she will soon find themselves wading through a sea of variations under a known culture. Added to the complexity is the fact that while the dynamics of a national culture may slowly change, this pace is faster in the virtual world. With this in mind, this study tries not to over-generalize, but rather offers a summation approach that draws implications from the existing literature. We started with the debates of the dimensionality of national culture as it is the traditional connotation of what culture means to the general public. With the basic understanding of cultural dimensions, one would no longer treat culture only as a monolithic concept. In what follows, we further explore the concept of digital culture, the driving forces from both macro and micro perspectives, the main road blocks that prevent spreading of digital culture, and the effects of digital culture on society and individuals.

Throughout the entire investigation, we have also briefly discussed existing theories that relate to digital culture. Due to limitations of space, readers may want to consult the cited references for the origins of these theories and their implications. Many of these theories have been empirically verified across multiple contexts. For example, the Technology Acceptance Model (TAM) has been used across disciplines to explain use and adoption intention. In a similar fashion, the Media Richness Theory has also received a wide range of recognition in disciplines outside of its birth place – Management and Information Processing. Theory of Planned Behavior (TPB) is now empirically used to explain behavioral intention beyond a psychological context.

In sum, digital culture is similar to national culture in that the dimensionality view (as opposed to monolithic view) may better help delineate its variations or sub-cultures. Both types of culture evolve, adapt and change in response to external environments, although digital culture evolves easier and faster as it carries less historical baggage that sometimes slows down the speed of evolution. Unlike national culture, digital culture may be constrained by the tools, the features made available through tools, and even the contextual expectations (i.e., professionalism) designed in tools. It will be interesting to see future research that compares and contrasts the structural differences of national versus digital culture, and the directions where they are heading.

REFERENCES

Ajzen, I. (1991). "The theory of planned behavior". *Organizational Behavior and Human Decision Processes*, 50 (2): 179–211.

Akamai (2013). *State of the Internet* – Q4 2013 Report, 6(4), retrieved from http://www.akamai.com/dl/akamai/akamai-soti-q413.pdf?WT.mc_id=soti_Q413

Ashton, K. (1999). *That 'Internet of things' thing – In the real world, things matter more than ideas.* Retrieved February 2, 2014 from http://www.rfidjournal.com/articles/view?4986

Bandura, Albert (2001). Social cognitive theory: an agentic perspective, *Annual Review of Psychology*, 52 (1), 1–26.

Blodgett, J. G., Bakir, A., & Rose, G. M. (2008). A test of the validity of Hofstede's cultural framework. *Journal of Consumer Marketing*, 25(6), 339–349. doi:10.1108/07363760810902477

Chen, K., Yen, D.C., Hung, S.-Y., & Huang, A.H. (2008). An exploratory study on the selection of communication media: The relationship between flow and outcome, *Decision Support Systems*, 45(5), 822-832.

Chen, K. (1999). Factors that motivate internet users to use business-to-customer electronic commerce (Doctoral dissertation). *Available from ProQuest Dissertations and Theses database.*

Chen, K., Tarn, J. M., & Han, B. T. (2004). Internet dependency: Its impact on online behavioral patterns in e-commerce. *Human Systems Management, 23*, 49–58.

Chinn, M. D. & Fairlie, R.W. (2004). The determinants of the global digital divide: a cross-country analysis of computer and internet penetration. *Economic Growth Center.* Retrieved from http://www.econ.yale.edu/growth_pdf/cdp881.pdf. Accessed May 12, 2014

Compeau, D. R., & Higgins, C. A. (1995). Computer self-efficacy: development of a measure and initial test. *MIS Quarterly*, 19, 189–211.

Daft, R.L.; Lengel, R.H. (1984). Information richness: a new approach to managerial behavior and organizational design. *Research in organizational behavior.* Homewood, IL: JAI Press, 6: 191–233.

Lengel, Robert; Richard L. Daft (August 1989). The selection of communication media as an executive skill. *The Academy of Management Executive*, (1987-1989): 225–232.

Davis, F. D. (1989), "Perceived usefulness, perceived ease of use, and user acceptance of information technology", MIS Quarterly, 13(3): 319–340

Hofstede, G. J. (2001). Adoption of communication technologies and national culture. *Systèmes d'Information et Management, 6*(3), 55–74.

Friedman, T.L. (2005). *The world is flat: A brief history of the twenty-first century*, New York: Picador.

Friedman, T.L. (2007). *The world is flat 3.0: A brief history of the twenty-first century*, 3rd ed., New York: Picador.

Glasser, W (1976). *Positive addiction*, New York: Harper & Row.

Hofstede, G. (1980). *Culture's consequences: international differences in work-related values.* Beverly Hills, CA: Sage Publications.

Hofstede, G. (2001). *Culture's consequences- comparing values, behaviors, institutions and organizations across nations.* 2 edition, Beverly Hills, CA: Sage Publications.

House, R.J., Hanges, P.J., Javidan, M., Dorfman, P. and Gupta, V. (2004) *Culture, leadership, and organizations: the globe study of 62 societies.* Thousand Oaks, CA: Sage Publications:

Igbaria, M. (1999). The driving forces in the virtual society. *Communication of the ACM, 42*(12), 64–70.

Javidan, M., House, R. J., Dorfman, P. W., Hanges, P. J., & Sully de Luque, M. (2006). Conceptualizing and measuring cultures and their consequences: a comparative review of globe's and Hofstede's approaches. *Journal of International Business Studies, 37*(6), 897–914.

Lenartowicz, T., & Roth, K. (2001). Does subculture within a country matter? a cross-cultural study of motivational domains and business performance in Brazil. *Journal of International Business Studies, 32*(2), 305–325.

Levy, P. (2001). *Cyberculture*. Minneapolis, MN: University of Minnesota Press:

Perkins, H. (1988). P.A. and running - a report on a replication study. *Journal of Reality Therapy*, *7*(2), 27–30.

Prenksy, M. (2001). Digital natives, digital immigrants. *On the Horizon*, (9)5: 1–6.

Rogers, Everett M. (1983). *Diffusion of innovations*. New York: Free Press.

Smith, P. B. (2011). Communication styles as dimensions of national culture. *Journal of Cross-Cultural Psychology*, *42*(2), 216–233.

Targowski, A. (2009). *Information technology and societal development*. Hershey, PA and New York: Information Science Reference.

Venkatesh, V. & Bala, H. (2008). TAM 3: advancing the technology acceptance model with a focus on interventions. *Decision Sciences*, 39(2), 273-315.

Wekipedia (2014). *List of Countries by number of Internet users*, retrieved 4-25-2014, from http://en.wikipedia.org/wiki/List_of_countries_by_number_of_Internet_users

Wheeler, T. (April 29, 2014). Finding the best path forward to protect the open Internet, retrieved 4-25-2014 from http://www.fcc.gov/blog/finding-best-path-forward-protect-open-internet

Wu, T. (2003). Network neutrality, broadband discrimination. *Journal of Telecommunications and High Technology Law*, (2):141-180.

Young, K.S. (1998). *Caught in the net*. New York: John Wiley & Sons, Inc.

In: Virtual Civilization in the 21st Century
Editor: Andrew Targowski

ISBN: 978-1-63463-261-4
© 2015 Nova Science Publishers, Inc.

Chapter 5

THE VIRTUAL DIVIDE AS ONE OF CIVILIZATION'S DIVIDES

Andrew Targowski[*]
Western Michigan University
President Emeritus of the International Society
For the Comparative Study of Civilizations (2007-2013)

ABSTRACT

The *purpose* of this investigation is to define the central contents and issues of the Virtual Divide of real civilization. The *methodology* is based on an interdisciplinary big-picture view of the Virtual Divide in the context of other civilizational divides such as: digital, information, and knowledge. Among the *findings* are: the Digital and Virtual Divides of civilization lead to the dichotomy of Society into developed and undeveloped citizens. It may lead to a strong civic unrest or even societal revolution. *Practical implications:* The gap created by the Virtual Divide should be minimized by better development of common good-oriented policies. *Social implication:* The quest for the common good by virtual activists may limit or even replace representative democracy by direct democracy and its ability for chaos creation. *Originality:* This investigation, by providing the interdisciplinary and civilizational approach at the big-picture level defined several crucial repercussions of the Virtual Divide of real civilization, which is evolving in our times and can be either a dangerous solution or a boon for human well-being in the democratic environment.

---

[*] andrew.targowski@wmich.edu

INTRODUCTION

Inequality as a Forming or Weakening Force of Civilization

In pre-civilization times, people lived in nomadic tribes with a leadership not based on land and/or animals ownership. When 6000 years ago civilization was increasing social stratification was also increasing which began to distinguish social and economic roles and ownerships of early elites. This stratification immediately created the minority of "haves" and majority of "have nots". The "haves" possessed some "surplus" from better farming and/or larger land and even from others who paid them some rent, for example for irrigation services. These additional revenues allowed the elites to support their empowered life style, which through the last 6000 years has still remained the main goal of the elites.

Surplus of all sorts of income has been creating wealth in an additive manner which in turn led to the need for military, administration, and law to protect the elites by top-down means keeping the social order. One of the first laws was property rights. Property, however, made humans combative and ready to die just to get a piece of the new wealth, eventually possessing that which makes people see each other as enemies.

Social inequality was the force which created civilization, where the society is composed of the minority which rules and the majority which is ruled. To increase the scope and deepness of ruling, the elites develop education, technology, and architecture which signify their ruling legacy. For example the Egyptians pyramids could not be built by an egalitarian society since it was a large-scale project and required thousands of laborers working 20 years, just to benefit one ruler who could pay them or use concurred slaves.

Among the "haves nots" since the early times of civilization were children and women. Since poverty was broad, and in order to limit the number of those who eat, circumcision was practiced on girls and boys. Despite the passing of six millennia, children and women are still discriminated in the undeveloped world. One of form of current discrimination of children and women is world-wide human trafficking. Human trafficking is the trade of humans, most commonly for the purpose of sexual slavery, forced labor or commercial sexual exploitation for the trafficker or others (Amnesty International 2009), or for the extraction of organs or tissues (United Nations 2009) including surrogacy and ova removal (Council 2004). Human trafficking can occur within a country or trans-nationally. Human trafficking is a crime against the person because of the violation of the victim's rights of movement through coercion and because of their commercial exploitation. Human trafficking is the trade in people, and does not necessarily involve the movement of the person to another location. Human trafficking represented an estimated $32 billion of the total $650 billion per annum of illegal international trade in 2010 (Haken 2011).

Philosophers were the first people who understood that civilization needs reason and morality to minimize social inequality. They were and still are playing the role of monitoring civilization and warning the world about civilization's progress which in their eyes is done at the expense of morality. As Jean Jacque Rousseau (1754-1755) stated "There is an inverse relationship between cultural and moral development: Culture does generate much learning, luxury, and sophistication—but learning, luxury, and sophistication all cause moral degradation[1]."

He also argued that the foundation of the Enlightenment Project is Reason, which is the foundation of civilization.

As the philosophes were indicating the achievement and importance of reason in the world, Rousseau wanted to demonstrate that "all the subsequent progress has been in appearance so many steps toward the perfection of the individual, and in fact toward the decay of the species." It is true that power of reason led to the Industrial Revolution, which through technology and goods, the factory system made mankind become soft, lazy, and put him in economic and social conflict with himself.

However, reason led humans also to desire removing social inequality through a chain of revolutions in the last 400 years, such as: English (1640-60), American (1776), French (1789), Mexican (1910), Bolshevik (1917), Civil Rights Movement (1955-1968), and Polish (1989). These revolutions steadily minimized all sorts of social inequality, arguing that eventually liberal democracy and Capitalism will make all people happy.

Even F. Fukuyama announced *The End of History and the Last Man* in his popular book in 1992 – stating that "What we may be witnessing is not just the end of the Cold War, or the passing of a particular period of post-war history, but the end of history as such: that is, the end point of mankind's ideological evolution and the universalization of Western liberal democracy as the final form of human government."

Unfortunately he was wrong; rather, he should have waited a few years after the fall of Communism to see how the New World Order would look.

The world is not now more peaceful at the dawn of the 21st century. In fact, it is even more dangerous since the *Clash of Civilizations* (Huntington 1996) is run by terrorism which is almost impossible to eliminate. This clash is not about material resources but is about setting standards of morality by different contemporary civilizations, mostly Islam Civilization versus Western and Eastern Civilizations.

It looks as though morality is becoming the main issue of contemporary civilizations. Islamic morality is of religious kind, while Western morality is of secular kind; is the West's morality triggered by turbo-Capitalism today? The latter morality, which is rapidly declining leads to large levels of inequality within Western Society, first in the scope of money, then later in political power, education, consumption and so forth.

This inequality in the Western society is justified and promoted without any doubts by the elite since competition among people is supposedly embedded in the capitalistic order. Furthermore, this leads hypothetically to more innovations and civilization progress.

The elite and their chaplains have argued that inequality is a noticeable and expected consequence of civilization.

---

[1] A recent book that summarizes vast interdisciplinary research work in anthropology and archaeology arrives at the conclusion that Rousseau's idealized reconstruction of the origin of inequality is surprisingly correct on historical grounds. See Flannery & Marcus (2012). The Creation of Inequality: How Our Prehistoric Ancestors Set the Stage for Monarchy, Slavery, and Empire by Kent Flannery and Joyce Marcus (Harvard University Press, 2012).

The elite does not accept the notion that such inequalities are damning because all inequalities "such as being richer, more honored, more powerful" are "privileges enjoyed by some at the expense of others," as J.J. Rousseau argued 260 years ago and triggered the French Revolution for the sake of abolishing social inequality.

In contemporary civilization, this lack of compassion becomes more than a sin of omission.

Rousseau argues that, having succeeded in the competitions of civilized life, the winners now have a vested interest in preserving the system. Civilization's advocates—especially those who are living at the top of the heap and therefore insulated from the worst of the harms—go out of their way to praise civilization's advances in technology, art, and science. But these advances themselves and the praise heaped upon them serve only to mask the harms civilization does (Hicks 2011).

WEALTH DIVIDE AND VIRTUALITY

Wealth divide can be evaluated by income inequality metrics, including Gini coefficients, as these indicators have been accepted by the United Nations (UN), the World Bank, and the Organization for Economic Co-operation and Development (OECD). The Gini coefficient is a number between 0 and 1, where 0 corresponds with perfect equality (where everyone has the same income) and 1 corresponds with perfect inequality (where one person has all the income and everyone else has zero income). Income distribution can vary greatly from wealth distribution in a country. "The top 10 per cent owned 71 per cent of world wealth, and the Gini coefficient for the global distribution of wealth is estimated to be 0.804, indicating greater inequality than that observed in the global distribution of consumption or income" (Davis 2008).

According to James Davis et al. (2008) roughly 30 per cent of world's wealth is found in each of the following regions: North America, Europe, and the rich Asian-Pacific countries. These areas account for virtually all of the world's top 1 per cent of wealth holders. On an official exchange rate basis India accounts for about a quarter of the adults in the bottom three global wealth deciles while China provides about a third of those in the fourth to eighth deciles. If current growth trends continue, India, China and the transition countries will move up in the global distribution, and the lower deciles will be increasingly dominated by countries in Africa, Latin American and poor parts of the Asian-Pacific region. Thus wealth may continue to be lowest in areas where it is needed the most.

A study entitled "Divided we Stand: Why Inequality Keeps Rising" by the Organization for Economic Co-operation and Development (OECD) reported:

> "Income inequality in OECD countries is at its highest level for the past half century. The average income of the richest 10% of the population is about nine times that of the poorest 10% across the OECD, up from seven times 25 years ago." In the United States inequality has increased further from already high levels. Other traditionally more

egalitarian countries, such as Germany, Denmark and Sweden, have seen the gap between rich and poor expand from 5 to 1 in the 1980s, to 6 to 1 today" (Gurría 2011).

A study by the World Institute for Development Economics Research at United Nations University reports that the richest 1% of adults alone owned 40% of global assets in the year 2000. The three richest people in the world possess more financial assets than the lowest 48 nations combined.[2] The combined wealth of the "10 million dollar millionaires" grew to nearly $41 trillion in 2008.[3] A January 2014 report by Oxfam claims that the 85 wealthiest individuals in the world have a combined wealth equal to that of the bottom 50% of the world's population, or about 3.5 billion people.[4] According to a Los Angeles Times analysis of the report, the wealthiest 1% owns 46% of the world's wealth; the 85 richest people, a small part of the wealthiest 1%, own about 0.7% of the world's wealth, which is the same as the bottom half of the population (Puzzanghera 2014). According to PolitiFact and others, the top 400 richest Americans "have more wealth than half of all Americans combined" (Kretscher & Borowski 2011).

Research has shown an inverse link between income inequality and social cohesion. In more equal societies, people are much more likely to trust each other, measures of social capital (the benefits of goodwill, fellowship, mutual sympathy and social connectedness among groups who make up a social unit) suggest greater community involvement, and homicide rates are consistently lower. The Nobel laureate economist Joseph Stiglitz (2012) has argued that economic inequality has led to distrust of business and government.

In the United States most of the growth has been between the middle class and top earners, with the disparity becoming more extreme the further one goes up in the income distribution (Noah 2010). A 2011 study by the CBO[5] found that the top earning 1 percent of households increased their income by about 275% after federal taxes and income transfers over a period between 1979 and 2007, compared to a gain of just under 40% for the 60 percent in the middle of America's income distribution[6]. In 2012, the gap between the richest 1 percent and the remaining 99 percent was the widest it's been since the 1920s. Incomes of the wealthiest 1 percent rose nearly 20 percent, whereas the income of the remaining 99 percent rose 1 percent in comparison (Wiseman 2013).

This trend of growing inequality helped in the fall 2011 to ignite the "Occupy" protest movement in the U.S. and in Europe (mostly in Spain). According to many opinions it is the most important problem that we are facing now today. Pope Francis echoed this sentiment in his *Evangelii Gaudium*, stating that "as long as the problems of the poor are not radically resolved by rejecting the absolute autonomy of markets and financial speculation and by attacking the structural causes of inequality, no solution will be found for the world's problems or, for that matter, to any problems" (Nichols 2013).

---

[2] http://articles.moneycentral.msn.com/News/StudyRevealsOver/, Retrieved 2014-1-30.
[3] "Growth of millionaires in India fastest in world ". Thaindian News. June 25, 2008.
[4] Rigged rules mean economic growth increasingly "winner takes all" for rich elites all over world. Oxfam. 20 January 2014.
[5] CBO-Congress Budget Office.
[6] Congressional Budget Office: Trends in the Distribution of Household Income between 1979 and 2007. October 2011.

Economist Robert Frank, a journalist concerned about social separation in the US, noted that:

> Today's rich had formed their own virtual country .... They had built a self-contained world unto themselves, complete with their own health-care system (concierge doctors), travel network (Net jets, destination clubs), separate economy. .... The rich weren't just getting richer; they were becoming financial foreigners, creating their own country within a country, their own society within a society, and their economy within an economy (Frank 2007).

Wealth inequality has reached such a high level today in Western Civilization that the rich live in the virtual world (the 1% virtual society), detached from the reality of 90 or even 99% of people. This 1% virtual society cannot last a long time just as Wall Street cannot last a long time without Main Street. The remaining 99% of desperate people perhaps will trigger one day strong social unrest or revolution applying e-communication among the members of the 99% virtual society. Perhaps it will look like a science fiction war between both virtual societies. However, at stake will be the real world and well-being for those beyond the 1% virtual society. The main weapon in this war will be virtual technology, collective intelligence, collective threat, and the 1% minority's fear.

The typology of the wealth divide is illustrated in Figure 5.1 which differentiates four membership categories.

The membership categories of wealth divide can be characterized as follows:

- The poor and disconnected people with the real world this includes the sick, dreaming, or those isolated from the dynamics of the real society. These people have no hope for better life.
- The wealthy who are detached from real society's dynamics. This includes the rich elite living in virtual society. Among there are ones who promote turbo-Capitalism and applying Darwinian 1:0 strategy, here and today. Among these people are global financiers and executives of stateless global corporations who do not care about their society and country, mostly having in mind continuous growth of business and fat bonuses.
- The wealthy and realistic. This includes the rich elite, which is composed of capitalists with a human face, socially responsible, contributing to the common good. Among them were or are such ones as: Henry Ford, Warren Buffett, Bill Gates and others.
- The needy majority of people who straggle with the reality of daily life.

The good future of society depends on the wisdom of the C-elite, whether they can curtail the B-elite's desire to possess the whole wealth of the world. This can be done through right politics, education, and inter-elite power games. So far, Bill Gates and Warren Buffett asked, at the beginning of the 21st century, that their richest peers of the world share their wealth 50/50 with society. Furthermore, Warren Buffett in 2012-13 argued that the richest people should pay higher taxes, surprising many members of the financial elite. Needless to say that he is an exceptional person, whose annual income is about $2-3 billion, but his personal budget is about $150,000; the rest of his income is donated to foundations, mainly to the Melinda and Bill Gates Foundation, the largest in the world. This philanthropic appeal had some headlines in media but did not solve any social problems of society. If this kind of attempt fails, then the D-majority may solve it through civic unrest or even through a social revolution.

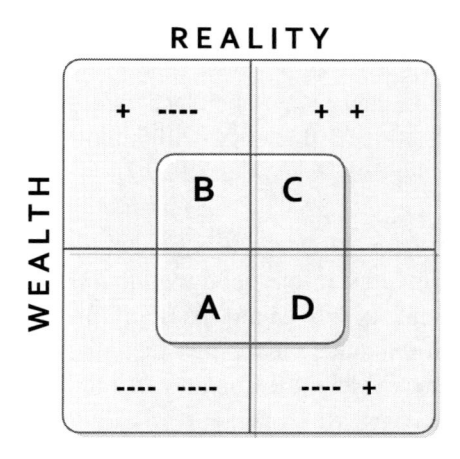

Figure 5.1. The Typology of Wealth Divide Membership Categories.

POLITICS DIVIDE AND VIRTUALITY

In a liberal democracy, all citizens—the rich, middle-class, and poor alike—supposedly have some capability to effect what their government does. Few people would expect that influence to be identical: those with higher incomes and better connections will always be more influential. But if influence becomes so unequal that the needs of most citizens are ignored most of the time, a country's claim to be a democracy is cast in doubt. Leveling the political playing field is as important as leveling the economic field; therefore, in the past, unions provided workers with a powerful voice in the political field.

But unions have largely faded from the scene due to capital's quest for low wages, leaving workers with very little organized political power. Correcting the political imbalance as it is today should be done through a renewed political empowerment of the working class. This quest ought to be a part of any attempt to improve society's response to serious economic downturns (Thoma 2012).

Following the collapse of Communism in 1991, Capitalism lost its competitor and triumphantly went on to dominate the world. In the political West it assumed the form of managerial capitalism, super-capitalism or turbo-capitalism, sometimes dubbed undemocratic capitalism. The uncontrolled managers have intercepted almost all profits due for shareholders, which they have had paid out in the form of multi-million or multi-billion bonuses and share options, which, though, was consistent with their contracts; these contracts were drafted by colleagues from the board of directors. The established criteria of business growth make such bonuses justified and this is among the reasons why so much production is being transferred to and outsourced to Asia, making it possible to reap huge profits thanks to sweatshop labor there.

Today's Capitalism is also called undemocratic capitalism (Reisch 2010) because it is lobbyists rather than representatives who regulate (in fact deregulate) the economy on behalf of corporations, which is to the detriment of the citizens – those who have elected the representatives and who have forgotten about their pre-election promises.

Managerial capitalism has entered the phase of global capitalism (approx. the year 2000), when, thanks to the Internet, distance was "abolished" and production was moved to countries with cheaper labor. The West invested about 2 trillion dollars in production infrastructure in those countries and made them great manufacturers.

As the result of this strategy Western Civilization's middle class is disappearing but the political class supports the status quo since it is funded by global corporations. They do not even have to provide their identity to the public while they provide funding. The American Congress is in constant gridlock; they cannot pass any important law which could improve the well-being of diminishing middle class. Nowadays, the approval rating of how Congress is handling its job is at a very low level - 14 (Gallup 2014).

The electorate of many countries no longer trusts its elected representatives. Particularly this negative opinion has taken place in the U.S., Russia and Eastern and Central European countries as well as in PIGS counties (Portugal, Italy, Greece, and Spain). Moreover, the election process in certain countries requires huge funding, For example, to be elected President in the United States, a candidate has to collect a fund close to $1 billion. This is the barrier for many potentially good candidates to parliaments and high ranking public offices.

Since the internauts found that their voice can impact political decisions, they plan to elect own candidates through virtual society. It will even cost little, since spreading a message through the Internet cost nothing in comparison to the cost of TV election commercials. If this is implemented, it will be a huge shift in practicing politics. Perhaps it will even overpass accomplishments of the English, American, and French Revolutions. It will be the Virtual Revolution in enforcing a new social order.

The typology of the political divide is illustrated in Figure 5.2 which differentiates four membership categories.

The membership categories of politics divide can be characterized as follows:

- The poor and disconnected people with the real world – This includes the sick, dreaming, or those who are politically isolated from the dynamics of the real society. These people have no hope for better political participation in the real life.
- The wealthy people who are detached from the real society's dynamics. This includes the rich elite living in virtual society. Among these are ones who promote turbo-Capitalism and applying Darwinian 1:0 strategy, here and today. Among these people are global financiers and executives of stateless global corporations who do not care about their society and country, mostly having in mind continuous growth of

business and fat bonuses. They are not involved directly in politics, but very often try to enforce their impact upon it through large donations to candidates for high elected offices, such as congressmen, governors, and president. Their donations may vary from high thousands to millions of dollars. Since they are disconnected from average citizens' reality, their political programs are very specifically aimed at the strategy of deregulating the real world and they hold the motto "the sky is the limit," while every educated citizen knows that such a world is not sustainable nowadays.

- The wealthy and realistic people who either support right politics or even want to be full time politicians. It includes the rich elite, which is composed of capitalists with a human face who are socially responsible and contribute to the common good. Examples of such persons include John Kennedy, president of the United States (1961-63). Also Mitt Romney can be considered another example, who was a presidential candidate in the 2012 election, even though very often during his campaign he shown surprising detachment from the life of average citizens. As a bishop of the Mormon Church he had some human touch for others.

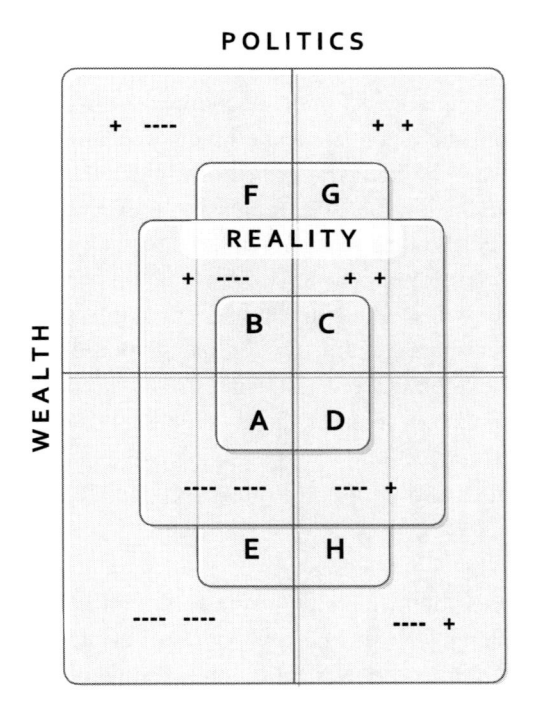

Figure 5.2. The Typology of Wealth Divide Membership Categories.

- The needy majority of people who struggle with the reality of daily life and enter politics to change the *modus operandi* or vote to do so. However, sooner than later they are disappointed by how politics is practiced. Since the end of World War II, all American presidents, with the exception of John Kennedy, were recruited from this kind of pool of indigent people. A case of president Barak Obama (2008-2016) shows that even a very well-motivated and aware political leader can do little if he/she is facing the impact of big business and capital.

The crucial point of this political membership categorization is that the real politics or common sense politics is not any more practiced, since the virtual rich elite is too economically powerful to allow for it. To keep positive social balance, the virtuality of the rich should be met by the virtuality of the indigent people. The weapon of the former is wealth; the weapon of the latter is or will be the info-communication technology (ICT), making their virtual society fast in using collective intelligence at the level of minimal spent financial resources.

The conflict between the F-Virtual Rich Elite and H-Indigent Community is the most important clash of values, goals, and strategies in Western Society in the dawn of the 21st century. This could even lead to a social revolution if the clash develops to an unmanageable level of governing of western nations.

DIGITAL DIVIDE AND VIRTUALITY

The concern of the "digital divide"[7] – or inequalities in info-communication technology based on income, education, race, gender, and ethnicity – captured headlines as the Internet made otherwise steady progress in advanced Western society (Mossberger et al. 2003). There is wide spread apprehension that the impressive growth of the Internet is intensifying existing inequalities between the information available to the rich and poor. A global digital divide is evident between developed and developing nations. In turn, a social divide as the result of the digital divide is also evident between the rich and poor within each of 200 nations in the 2014. Furthermore, within the online communities there is evidence for a democratic digital divide between those who do and those who do not use Internet resources -- those who do not apply the Internet have problems in engaging, mobilizing, and participating in public life (Norris 2001).

Access to the Internet allows for the use of the following info-communication applications:

- E-mail - the transmission of messages over communications networks. The messages can be notes entered from the keyboard or electronic files stored on disks. Most mainframes, minicomputers, and computer networks have an e-mail system. Some electronic-mail systems are confined to a single computer system or network, but others have gateways to other computer systems, enabling users to send electronic mail anywhere in the world. Companies that are fully computerized make extensive use of e-mail because it is fast, flexible, and reliable. Most e-mail systems

---

[7] The term "digital divide" was popularized by the U.S. National Telecommunication and Information Administration (NTIA) under the Clinton administration (1993-2001) to refer to the gap between those who do and do not have access to computers and the Internet.

include a rudimentary text editor for composing messages, but many allow you to edit your messages using any editor you want. You then send the message to the recipient by specifying the recipient's address. You can also send the same message to several users at once. This is called broadcasting.

Sent messages are stored in electronic mailboxes until the recipient fetches them. To see if you have any mail, you may have to check your electronic mailbox periodically, although many systems alert you when mail is received. After reading your mail, you can store it in a text file, forward it to other users, or delete it. Copies of memos can be printed out on a printer if you want a paper copy.

- The World Wide Web (WWW, or the Web) - A system of Internet servers that support specially formatted documents. The documents are formatted in a markup language called HTML (HyperText Markup Language) that supports links to other documents, as well as graphics, audio, and video files. This technology creates a network of "web pages" presenting information in multimedia formats, with links from page to page often created associatively, to allow multiple ways of navigating using user-friendly browsers through the information content of websites or set of websites called web vitrines. Many people use the terms Internet and World Wide Web (also known as the Web) interchangeably, but in fact the two terms are not synonymous. The Internet and the Web are two separate but related things.
- Chatrooms, online communities, virtual groups - A virtual room where a chat session takes place. Technically, a chat room is really a channel, but the term room is used to promote the chat metaphor. It is similar to e-mail; chat rooms are public sites where users can type messages to each other or to the community/group and receive answers in real time or delayed time.
- E-commerce - refers to the purchase and sale of goods and/or services via electronic channels, such as the Internet. Online retail is convenient due to its 24-hour availability, global reach and ease of customer service. Though purchasing items online is a major facet, e-commerce is more than that. This type of commerce can be useful at the enterprise level as well. E-commerce is not just on the Web — it was first introduced in the 1960s via electronic data interchange (EDI) through value-added networks (VANs). In the mid-1990s, e-commerce was transformed with the introduction of Amazon and eBay. Amazon started as a book shipping business, out of Jeff Bezos' garage in 1995. EBay, which enabled consumers to sell things online, introduced online auctions in 1995 and exploded with the 1997 Beanie Babies frenzy.
- Web services - a method of communications between two electronic devices over the World Wide Web. Web services are a software function provided at a network address over the web with the service always on as in the concept of utility computing. For example, the Wix is web service provider with over 37 million users worldwide. Wix makes it easier for an inexperience user to create a stunning website for free by giving the user all the essentials. A user can choose from 100s of

designer-made web-savvy templates. Using the powerful drag n' drop Editor, one can change anything like fonts, text, background, colors and more. Also, Wix provides top-grade, reliable & secure hosting. Wix' service can enhance a website by adding popular web Apps & Services like Facebook Comments, Instagram, Google Maps & SoundCloud. So whether one is a designer, programmer, musician, artist or small business owner, Wix has some web-oriented service for everyone.
- The semantic web - this is driving the evolution of the current Web by enabling users to find, share, and combine information more easily. Humans are capable of using the Web to carry out tasks such as finding the Estonian translation for "twelve months", reserving a library book, and searching for the lowest price for a DVD. However, machines cannot accomplish all of these tasks without human direction, because web pages are designed to be read by people, not machines. The semantic web is a vision of information that can be readily interpreted by machines, so machines can perform more of the tedious work involved in finding, combining, and acting upon information on the web. The Semantic Web, as originally envisioned, is a system that enables machines to "understand" and respond to complex human requests based on their meaning. Such an "understanding" requires that the relevant information sources be properly structured semantically. The Semantic Web is a collaborative movement led by a body of international standards, the World Wide Web Consortium (W3C). The standard promotes common data formats on the World Wide Web. By encouraging the inclusion of semantic content in web pages, the Semantic Web aims at converting the current web, dominated by unstructured and semi-structured documents, into a "web of data". According to the W3C, "The Semantic Web provides a common framework that allows data to be shared and reused across application, enterprise, and community boundaries."[8] The term was coined by Tim Berners-Lee (the inventor of WWW) for a web of data that can be processed by machines (Feigenbaum 2007).

ICT technologies, such as these above, have transformed both work practice and leisure activities into more of an "info-communication mode." They have intensely changed the way we relate to others, both distantly and locally. In fact, for some unexpected reason we prefer to be in e-touch more remotely than locally. This new mode of inter-relations among people has developed new crimes, new arts, new sources of complications and new types of misperceptions.

To possess the ability to access the Internet, a digital storage or a digital "library" of similar size to Information Ocean, full of e-documents, which could feed a few billion of books – all this means that a user can be better informed about the past, presence and future. This kind of learning can be fast and cheap since it is done electronically, where each such document on the Web has own address which can be accessed by a hyperlink that takes a user from one page to another just by clicking it manually. Furthermore, a web search engine like

---

[8] W3C Semantic Web Activity". World Wide Web Consortium (W3C). November 7, 2011. Retrieved 2011-10-23.

Google, Yahoo, or Bing can find for a user quickly stored documents complying with the search question.

Up until the use the Internet (until e-browsers became available—around 1995), people had rather easier access to locally stored information in the real world, but not to information which was kept far away. The Internet killed the problem of distance, and once information was digitalized and put into the Internet, a user could read and print it for use in the real world. Therefore, the Internet provides the virtual platform for discussing political issues and elections in online communities; however, later developments of the Internet can be applied in the real world. Virtually motivated votes are done in the real world at the voting booths and counted by the real world's machines and people. Customer orders done electronically require a real delivery at someone's address. Even if packages are one day delivered by drones (Amazon's plan), they need a real "pilot," sitting somewhere in a real room. Therefore, the use of the Internet is as good and beneficial as is access to it by the real people.

The premise of the quest for the elimination of the digital divide is to effectively integrate ICT tools into communities, institutions, organizations, and individuals' activities. The physical capabilities of computers and the Internet are not as important as are people's capabilities to participate in meaningful social practices, enhanced by the digitalization and Internetization.

On the other hand, internetophilia neither causes neither cures; therefore the social context is very important in which ICT tools appear. Mark Warschauer (2003:215) argues that:

> "Technology and the mind cannot be separated...Just as technology becomes part of the neural network of the mind, it also becomes part of the social network of humanity. ...information and communication technology function not only as the electricity of the 21st century but also as the printing press, library, television, and telephone, not to mention school, social club, mall debating society, and gambling dan."

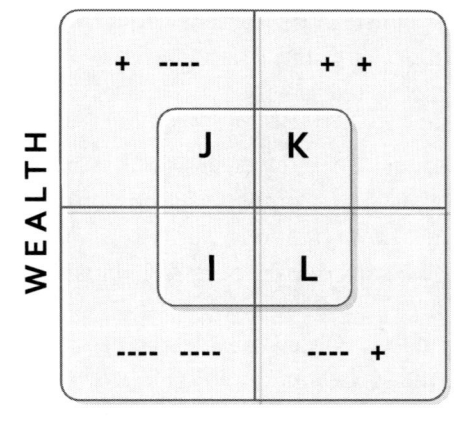

Figure 5.3. The Typology of Digital Divide Membership Categories.

In this context one must remind what Mark Poster (1997) said that *"the Internet is not much a tool as a new social space that reconstructs social relations."* Since, as Pierre Lévy (1997) noted due to the Internet, humanity has gained a new virtual ability of thinking and applying *"collective intelligence as mankind's emerging world in cyberspace."*

These new realities of the virtual landscape leads to issues of a global divide among counties, a democratic divide, the new virtual political system, the impact on civic engagement, and so forth (Norris 2001). The gap of these divides, simply speaking, depends upon types of the digital divide.

The typology of digital divide (access and skills) is illustrated in Figure 5.3 which differentiates four members-oriented categories of that kind of divide.

The membership categories of digital divide can be characterized as follows:

- I - The poor and disconnected people with reality who do not have access nor the skills to use the Internet and its applications to enhance their engagement in social life. These people are in a helpless situation without any tangible sign of possible change of their status.
- J – The rich elite with so called "old money," who usually are older people, neglecting the use of ICT tools, relying mostly on traditional communication and sources of information, and traditionally relating with a well-established circle of people. Their social engagement is mostly through the power of wealth which in most cases is heard and not successfully countered by less privileged people. This rich elite informationally and communicationally are disconnected with the real world's issues, living in a closed virtual society, not being interested in increasing its wealth but rather preserving it.
- K – The digital rich elite who are wealthy and info-communicationally well connected. They have a strong impact upon the real world and engage in social life to protect their status.
- L – The digital savvy people who want to use ICT tools to gain wealth and change the state of the social order which puts them in a disadvantaged state of *modus operendi*. These are the strongest proponents of a new info-communication technology which is considered as their social weapon with more potential for success than traditional wealth. These people argue for the development of Teledemocracy and the virtual society.

The digital divide issue adds a new layer to social justice which can be called digital justice. It is wrong to think that the I-members can be eliminated by providing access and skills on a wide-range. Practice shows that one can lead a horse to water but cannot make it drink, which means one can give someone the access & skills to do something on the Internet, but cannot force them to do it.

While the conflict between the J-virtual rich elite and L-digital savvy indigent people will increase in the 21st century, the K-wealthy and digital savvy elite will increase their social reach and potential for more social gains. The latter will play a role of Hollywood's celebrities who used to be examples for strong success in the pre-Internet era. Nowadays, there are plenty of examples of millionaires who have tremendously surpassed Hollywood's actors and producers' wealth. For example; Sergey Brin (co-founder of Google) aged 41 is worth an estimated $24.4 billion, the 24th richest person in the world (Wikipedia); Lary Page (co-founder of Google) aged 41 is worth an estimated $20.3 billion, the 25th richest person in the world (Wikipedia); Mark Zuckenberg (Facebook funder) aged 26 is worth an estimated $17.5 billion; Dustin Moskovitz (Facebook co-founder) aged 26 is worth an estimated $1.4 billion; Andrew Mason (founder of Groupon) aged 29 is worth an estimated $600 million and so forth.[9] Needless to say that the richest American, Bill Gates, (software business magnate) aged 59 is worth an estimated $72 billion, and according to the Bloomberg Billionaires List, he was the world's richest person in 2013.

The growth of human culture is centered upon the development of the tools of civilization. And the tools which man utilized in his rise from barbarism were effective just to the degree that they freed man's power for the accomplishment of higher tasks. Among such civilization developing tools were the following:

- The taming of fire.
- Iron-based handy tools and weapon.
- The domestication of animals.
- The enslavement of captives.
- Private property.
- Wheels.
- Dynamite.
- Magnetic compass.
- Printed books
- Ocean going ships.
- Engine.
- Electricity.
- Medications.
- Machine.
- Mechanization.
- Automation.
- Computer.
- Informatization
- Internet.
- Internetization (WWW)
- Digitalization.
- Virtualization.
- Internet of things.
- Other.

---

[9] http://www.incomediary.com/top-young-entrepreneurs, Retrieved 2014-1-31.

The depersonalization of the so-called natural phenomena of the cosmological nature has required millennia, and the knowledge about the world and universe has not yet been finalized. But the constant search for true causes gave birth to modern theoretical science about 500 years ago. Eventually it turned astrology into astronomy, alchemy into chemistry, and magic into medicine. In the 19th century engineering tools mechanized muscle power and in the 20th century the electronic tools automated mechanized systems; however, in the 21st century digital tools are going to inform human judgment and choices, and develop a well-established virtual layer of real civilization.

The digital rich elite is so rich and powerful, and able to develop and implement widely social-intensive change triggering *digital tools* that they must be watched for their possible irrational undertakings, coming from their youthful thinking about a new, "wonderful world," where no one will work and people only will be playing computer games, googling for interesting information and communicating world-wide in promoting one's own ego or frustration. Who will pay taxes and utility bills, and who will provide food, as these do not seem to be of their concern.

INFORMATION DIVIDE AND VIRTUALITY

Local or remote access to the Internet does not immediately make a given user information savvy, since one must be an educated person to be aware of the quality of accessed information. Today, the digitalization of e-documents which can be retrieved and read is infinite in number; this means most of us do not read at all this information; rather, we "scan" it. Hence, the question is how to write for those who do not read?

The printed word is under unprecedented assault by digitalization and network-driven dissemination. The battle is not just a duel among businesses and technologies – what is being decided is the future of how we think and how we perceive the world. The proliferation of image and text on the Internet has exacerbated solipsism [the belief that the only thing somebody can be sure of is that he or she exists, and that true knowledge of anything else is impossible (Boorstin 1987)], because it allows us to read in a broad but shallow manner. We do not read more - we scan more. The fast invading streams of displayed images on a screen minimize our control over the written word. As Rosen (2009) argues, *"we find ourselves in the position of living in a highly literate society that chooses not to exercise the privilege of literacy – indeed, it no longer views literacy as a privilege at all."*

Due to the ease of the Internet's use, we prefer to scan The Huffington Post's links to hundreds of articles from other publications every day. Even focused information can be delivered to our e-mail boxes by all sorts of "aggregators," unfortunately, together with advertisements for more intensive consumerism. The power of virtually simulated events transforms us from participants to viewers, from readers to scanners. More and more we are satisfied by these secondhand experiences.

Numerous studies have shown that we do not read deeply online as much as we scan material. In a study conducted by Jacob Nielsen (a former Sun Microsystems engineer) and Don Norman, a cognitive scientist, the eye movements of Web surfers were tracked as they skipped from one page to the next. They found that only 16 percent of subjects read the text on a page in the order in which it appeared. The rest jumped around, picking out individual words and processing them out of sequence. Their web "reading" is quite different than book paper-based text reading.

A survey of 1,300 students at the University of Illinois, Chicago, found that only five percent regularly read a blog or forum on politics, economics, law, or policy. Nearly 80 percent checked Facebook, the social networking site. However, this famous social network is full of our pictures, resumes, and activity reporting. It is modest in interpersonal communication and in producing new knowledge/wisdom based on communicated parties. But it does not make us better readers or more knowledgeable and wise (Rosen 2009).

According to Maryanne Wolf, director of the Center for Reading and Language Research at Tufts University,

> "It's not just what we read that shapes us, but the fact that we read at all. With the invention of reading, we rearranged the very organization of our brain, which in turn expanded the ways we were able to think, which altered the intellectual evolution of our species." She asks, "What would be lost to us if we replaced the skills honed by the reading brain with those now being formed in our new generation of 'digital natives?'" (Rosen 2009).

Electronic info-communication technology is honing our ability to do many more things at once and to do them faster. Multitasking may even be making us smarter but are we more intelligent and wiser? According to Courage & Cowan (2009), *"It is true that we access and absorb information more quickly than before, and as a result, we often seem more impatient."* Using Google we can find information faster than in an encyclopedia and due to easy information that is globally accessible, we can be better specialist and better generalist also. We may be overloaded by the volume of downloaded information but some filters may help in sorting the right one for us. Furthermore, we are as we were in the 1980s when we learned how to operate a PC computer steered by its hectic operating system, DOS. We have since learned how to operate iPhones and other related technologies (e.g., electronic tablets, smart phones, and notebook computers) in order to know how to get the right information. Young people usually know how to use these devices; in fact, they are more active participants and creators of culture. This is a new benefit of digitalization. However, knowing how to use new info-communication devices does not make us more knowledgeable and wiser. Being a better car driver does not make us a better tourist. We may drive better but not necessarily know where to go and what we should like for.

The intensive applications of ICT in society at the dawn of the 21st Century has led to a strong divergence of among media users. Figure 5.4 illustrates at least four main groups of citizens, classified by their knowledge and skills in handling information by old and new ICT.

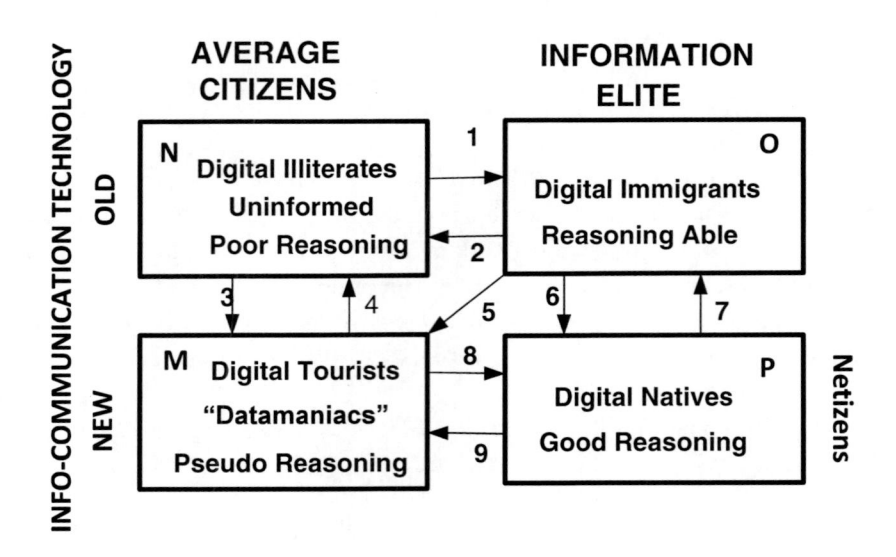

```
                            AVERAGE              INFORMATION
                            CITIZENS                ELITE
         ┌──────┐      ┌─────────────────┐  1  ┌─────────────────┐
         │      │  OLD │ N                │────▶│ O               │
         │ INFO-│      │ Digital Illiterates│    │ Digital Immigrants│
         │COMM. │      │ Uninformed       │     │ Reasoning Able  │
         │ TECH.│      │ Poor Reasoning   │◀────│                 │
         │      │      └─────────────────┘  2  └─────────────────┘
         │      │           3 │  ▲ 4      5 ╲    6 │  ▲ 7
         │      │             ▼  │            ╲    ▼  │
         │      │      ┌─────────────────┐  8  ┌─────────────────┐  Netizens
         │      │  NEW │ M                │────▶│ P               │
         │      │      │ Digital Tourists │     │ Digital Natives │
         │      │      │ "Datamaniacs"    │     │ Good Reasoning  │
         │      │      │ Pseudo Reasoning │◀────│                 │
         └──────┘      └─────────────────┘  9  └─────────────────┘
```

Figure 5.4. The Typology of Information Divide Membership Categories.

The membership categories of information divide can be characterized as follows:

- M - Digital Tourists are good "Netizens" (mostly young generation) who spend hours using the Internet, but their knowledge/skills of handling and understanding cognition units is shallow, as is their level of reading. They collect a lot of data and become "Datamaniacs" but their reasoning is pseudo-reasoning, sometimes good, but mostly it is questionable. If they improve their knowledge and skills of handling information, they may become "Digital Natives" (path 8).
- N - Digital Illiterates apply traditional (OLD) ICT. They are uninformed and reason purely; however, if they improve their knowledge/skills they may advance (path 1) to Digital Immigrants who work on the adaptation to new conditions of handling information. They may improve skills in using the Internet and its resources as Digital Travelers (path 2).
- O - Digital Immigrants have good knowledge/skills in handling information but mostly apply OLD ICT. They only occasionally apply NEW ICT, usually with the help of other people. They may improve digital skills to advancing to Digital Travelers (path 5) or to Digital Natives (path 6). They are able to reason well.
- P - Digital Natives (Prensky 2001) belong to the information elite and apply NEW ICT. They reason very well.

If the specialists do not practice their knowledge/skills, they may lose them (paths 2, 4, 7, and 9).

It is wrong to say that since Digital Natives reason best, we should educate only this kind of graduate. One cannot forget that they are not only good in digitalization but also belong to the Information Elite. This kind of elite has a very comprehensive education in humanities and given professions, and ICT knowledge/skills are the second layer of their education.

Furthermore, in order to belong to the Information Elite, they cannot be separated from the nature of a simulated virtual/digital environment, since they may lose their human biological drive.

Hence, it is a "done deal" with traditional ways of handling information, since F2F communication or P2F or F2P (P-paper) is still richer information then electronic communication.

Therefore, it is important to keep equilibrium in the society between OLD and NEW ways of handling information in order to minimize the dichotomy of people (Figure 5.5 illustrates this equilibrium). It should be done by intensive development of techno-psychology, techno-philosophy and public policy (regulations) how intensively and broadly ICT should be applied. The required regulations may dramatically challenge many well already established values in certain civilizations. Certainly they challenge the values of Western civilization.

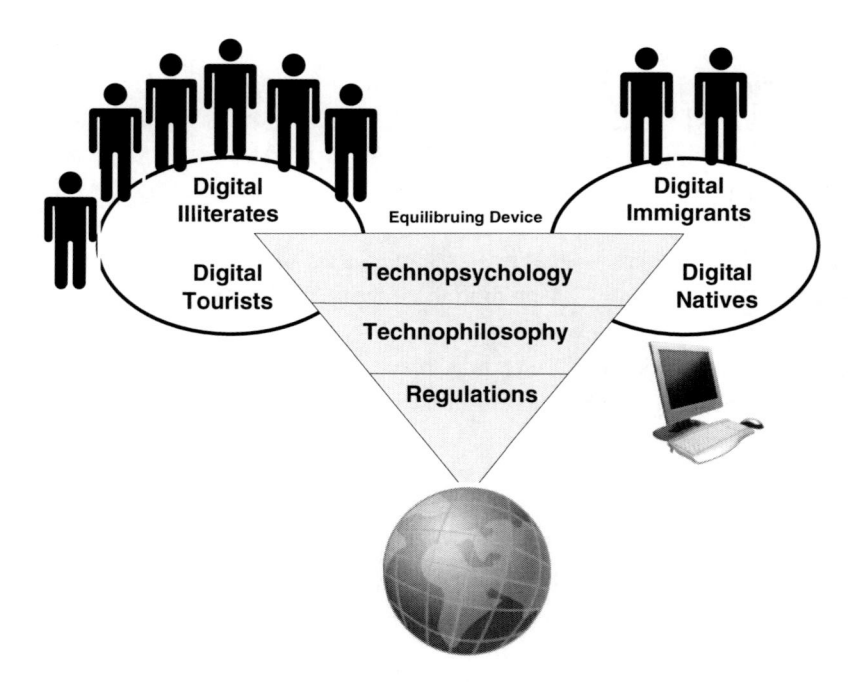

Figure 5.5. The Information Society in the Developmental Process of Digitalized Equilibrium.

KNOWLEDGE DIVIDE AND VIRTUALITY

The emergence of the concept "the knowledge society" is triggered by the omnipresent influence of info-communication technologies, and brings about a premise that knowledge is reshaping the global economy. Its significance goes well beyond the publicizing of the Internet. What is underway is a style of thinking that knowledge is the transforming force of our economy and society.

Knowledge has always been a factor of production, and a driver of economic and social development. Agricultural economy depended, for example, on knowledge about how to farm and how to build while industrial economy depended on knowing how to manufacture. However, the current capacity to process, store and transmit large quantities of information cheaply has increased at a staggering rate over the recent 40 years. Unfortunately technology-driven information processing does not mean that knowledge is also "fast processing".

The digitization of information and the Internet's distribution of digital information to a certain degree enhance humanity's level of knowing. It is a new source of e-business activities, which has become the major factor in the creation of new wealth. As much as 70 to 80 percent of economic growth is now said to be due to new and better information processing which results in better "knowing." ICT is the main facilitating factor in a rapid globalization of business activities.

Digitalization as a new technology leads to a broad scope of innovations, which fuels new businesses and job creation, and economic growth. It is quickly becoming the key factor in global competitiveness among global-minded inventors and business people. Innovation fundamentally means coming up with new ideas about how to do things better or faster.

Knowledge in a broad sense as being better informed about "things" has become the key resource. Better knowing has value, but so too does information about knowing. Creating value as the mantra of current business practices is about creating new knowledge and capturing its value.

The ability of individuals to generate and apply data on a global scale does not essentially result in knowledge formation. Contemporary media distributes almost infinite amounts of data and information and nevertheless, the data and information alone do not create knowledge. For knowledge creation to take place, reflection and definition are obligatory to form awareness, meaning, understanding, and rules/laws/principles. The Absence of one of these attributes in thinking will not lead to knowledge, which means that such information is in fact "non-knowledge;" perhaps it is still data or information but it could be false or inaccurate (Harvey 2010).

The anticipated Semantic Web 3.0 and Ubiquitous Web 4.0 perhaps will move both information and knowledge creation forward in their capacities to use intelligence to digitally create meaning independent of user-driven ICT. A precise definition of Web 3.0 is difficult to identify, but most descriptions agree that a fundamental characteristic of it is the ability to make connections and infer meaning – essentially, the Web is going to become more 'intelligent'. This has led to the coining of expressions such as the semantic Web, or the intelligent Web, in reference to Web 3.0.[10] Furthermore, Web 4.0 is about empowering

---

[10] Macmillan Dictionary, http://www.macmillandictionary.com/us/buzzword/entries/web3.html, Retrieved 2014-02-2. The defining aspect of Web 1.0 was search. In other words, think Yahoo! in the early 1990s. Web 2.0 is a form of social media, which involves collaborative projects like Wikipedia, social networking sites like Facebook, blogs and micro-blogs like Twitter and many other examples. So what's Web 3.0? According to the futurist and business strategist and Big Think blogger Daniel Burrus, this is all happening faster than the transition from Web 1.0 to Web 2.0 due to processing power, bandwidth and storage, "creating a curve of exponential change." So Burrus describes the third iteration of the Web as "the 3D Web." By that does he mean 3D glasses? No. "We already have that with video games where you go in to environments in 3D," Burrus says. "What you're going to see is "3D on phones and tablets coming up very shortly." Burrus says the

customers with the tools to engage their business in the right place, at the right time. It's about closely replicating the customer experience in the offline world on the Internet. The result is the ability to get sales and service force to the customer earlier in their need-state, improving web-based reaction time for customers, and entering into meaningful dialogue with the customer on their terms. Those companies who adopt Web 4.0 will be in a position to effectively cut off their competitors at the pass (Larson 2013).

As the examples of the advanced ICT technologies show, they will be more intelligent in satisfying a user with respect to how to apply information in making real world deals; however, this does not mean that this information will become knowledge or even wisdom.

To understand what is the difference between data and information and knowledge and wisdom let's see the Semantic Ladder as it is shown in Figure 5.6. This model of semantics defines the following units of cognition as follow:

- *Data*. Dow Jones index, of say 10,000 points on a Monday of a given month and year, will be the data.
- *Information*. The fact that on the following Tuesday Dow Jones was 8,000 points, that is, 20% less than the day before, will be information. This is a rather unpleasant kind of information, which characterizes the change of the index by minus 20%. This information demands that the investor conceptualizes a new solution.
- *Concept* may be about the choice of one of three option-concepts. Because the stocks fell in price and are cheap, a new package of shares can be bought (C1); in other words, having slumped so much, they cannot keep falling; another option (C2) will be the sale of one's stocks in order not to make bigger losses. Finally, the third solution (C3) will be neither selling nor buying stocks. Now, having three concepts/options of a solution, a judgment needs to be made as to which solution is the best.
- *Knowledge* is a set of principles, rules and research data which the investor will make use of in the assessment of each of these options. *Basic knowledge* indicates: buy shares when they are cheap and sell when they are expensive. *Theoretical knowledge* might indicate that a decline in the prices of stocks may result from the economy entering a recession. *Global knowledge* suggests that a war with state X is imminent and this fact will increase the needs for the sake of war. What *universal knowledge* implies is that when the economy enters a recession, profits from trading stocks dwindle but money can be made on trading bills of exchange (bonds).
- *Wisdom*. The investor has received an assessment of the situation in the four categories of knowledge and now has to make a choice between three options/solutions. Since he would lose by selling the stocks, he rejects the option C_1. As war is coming, and stocks might increase in value, he does not buy but, rather,

---

real game-changer will be the 3D web browser: "You can go into inter-spatial places. You can go into rooms, in to convention centers, in to showrooms." http://bigthink.com/big-think-tv/web-40-the-ultra-intelligent-electronic-agent-is-coming, Retrieved 2014-02-02.

decides to keep his shares and waits. So, he selected option C_3 and time will tell whether this was a good, and hence wise, choice.

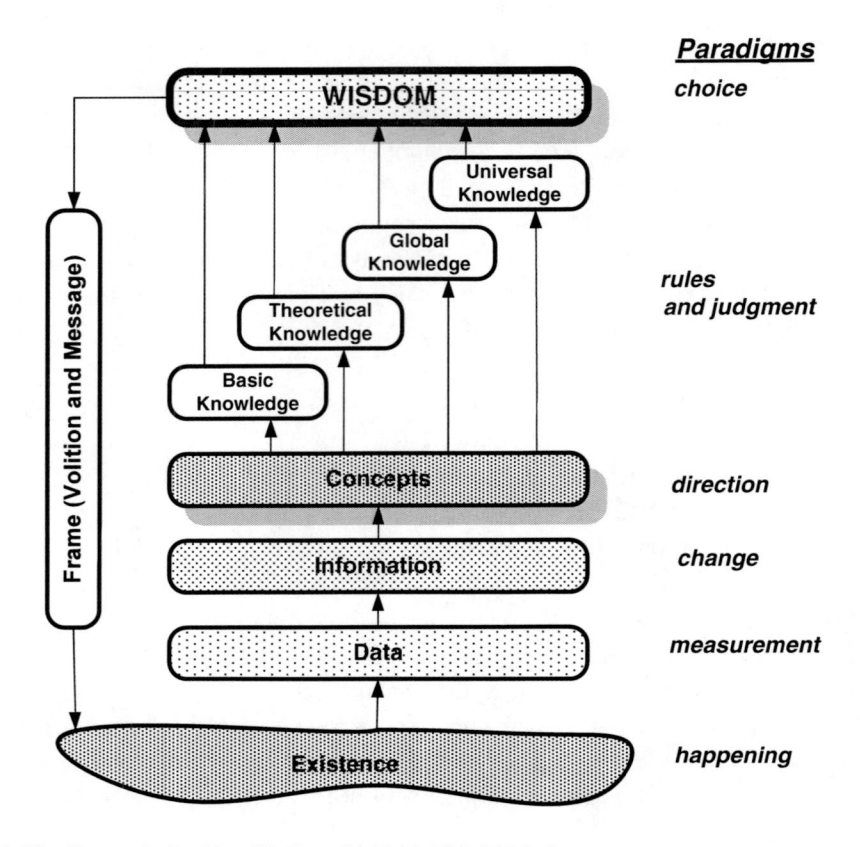

Figure 5.6. The Semantic Ladder (Targowski 1990:136, 2013:6).

The Semantic Model explains that wisdom is not knowledge, neither is it information nor data. It is judgment, and the choice of concepts of thinking and action. Moreover, in order that the concept be properly formulated, one needs to be well-informed; that is, one has to have verifiable data. In order to make a wise assessment, one needs to have good knowledge: basic, theoretical, global and universal. Not all have such kinds of knowledge, and therefore their judgments are not wise within the range of knowledge that a decision-making subject has.

This is not to say that if one has a wide the range of knowledge at their disposal, one is guarantee of a wise judgment. There are other factors, such as emotions, intuition, luck or a will to implement a wise action, etc. All these attributes reflect an art of living. The word 'art' used here refers to an intuitive and innovative approach to the known and right principles of judgment and an ability to create new principles and breaking rules when outdated for the case in question.

The Theory of Semantic Ladder is a contemporary approach of the 21st century. It clearly distinguishes knowledge and wisdom from the remaining units of cognition. In approaches from centuries ago, wisdom was a concept of the totality of the wisdom of mankind, which an individual man was incapable of attaining, and therefore was not wise. In a contemporary psychological approach, wisdom is an expert attitude, inaccessible to the rank and file. In this cognitive IT approach, wisdom can be possessed by any sane individual (Targowski 2013).

The Semantic Ladder clearly indicates that it is not easy to convert information into knowledge and wisdom. However, data mining "Big Data" may provide some rules about a given business or institution's development and/or operations.

For example Walmart found that on Mondays the best selling goods are baby pampers and beer. Hence, a store manager is more knowledgeable and can select one of possible strategies; 1) to satisfy a customer - baby pampers and beer should be kept in the same alley, 2) to satisfy business - these two items should be spread apart to different alleys to stimulate a customer to buy other items on impulse.

The typology of the knowledge divide memberships is illustrated in Figure 5.7 which differentiates four members-oriented categories of that kind of divide.

The membership categories of the knowledge divide can be characterized as follows:

- P - Digital Illiterates with basic knowledge who have little awareness of information quality retrieved through the Internet: This user, even if having digital skills, has limited understanding of the quality of information accessing. He has perhaps even reached a level of a "data-maniac" who is able to apply only pseudo-reasoning. Among this group are pupils from secondary schools, who know how to use the Internet but do not know the value of information and knowledge.
- R - Digital Tourists who have limited awareness of information quality who are, however, aware of globalization: This fact improves his/her awareness of the information possessed. Among this group are military personnel on duty in foreign countries.
- S - Digital Tourists who have limited awareness of information quality, but have better judgment of it since they know universal knowledge: Among this group are graduates of schools in certain countries where universal values are important in social life. This includes pupils of schools managed by religious executives and/or are owned by religious institutions. Of course secular ownership and management of schools may teach values of a given civilization too.
- T - Digital Tourists who have limited awareness of information quality but have better judgment of it since they know global and universal knowledge: Among this group are graduates of schools in certain countries where universal values are important in social life and travelling abroad is facilitated.
- U - Digital Immigrants who know the value of information and theoretical knowledge but they have limited digital skills. Among this group, one can distinguish old faculty and retiring and/or retired professionals.
- Z - Digital Immigrants who know the value of information and theoretical as well as global knowledge, but have limited digital skills: Among this group one can distinguish old faculty and retiring and/or retired professionals, also some well-educated tourists can be included too.

- V - Digital Natives (Netcitizens) who know a value of information, theoretical, and global knowledge. Among this group one can distinguish travelling professionals.
- W - Digital Natives (Netcitizens) who know a value of information, theoretical, global, and universal knowledge (possess a complete knowledge). Among this group one can distinguish: university faculty, intellectuals, top national and international politicians, travelling professionals and others.

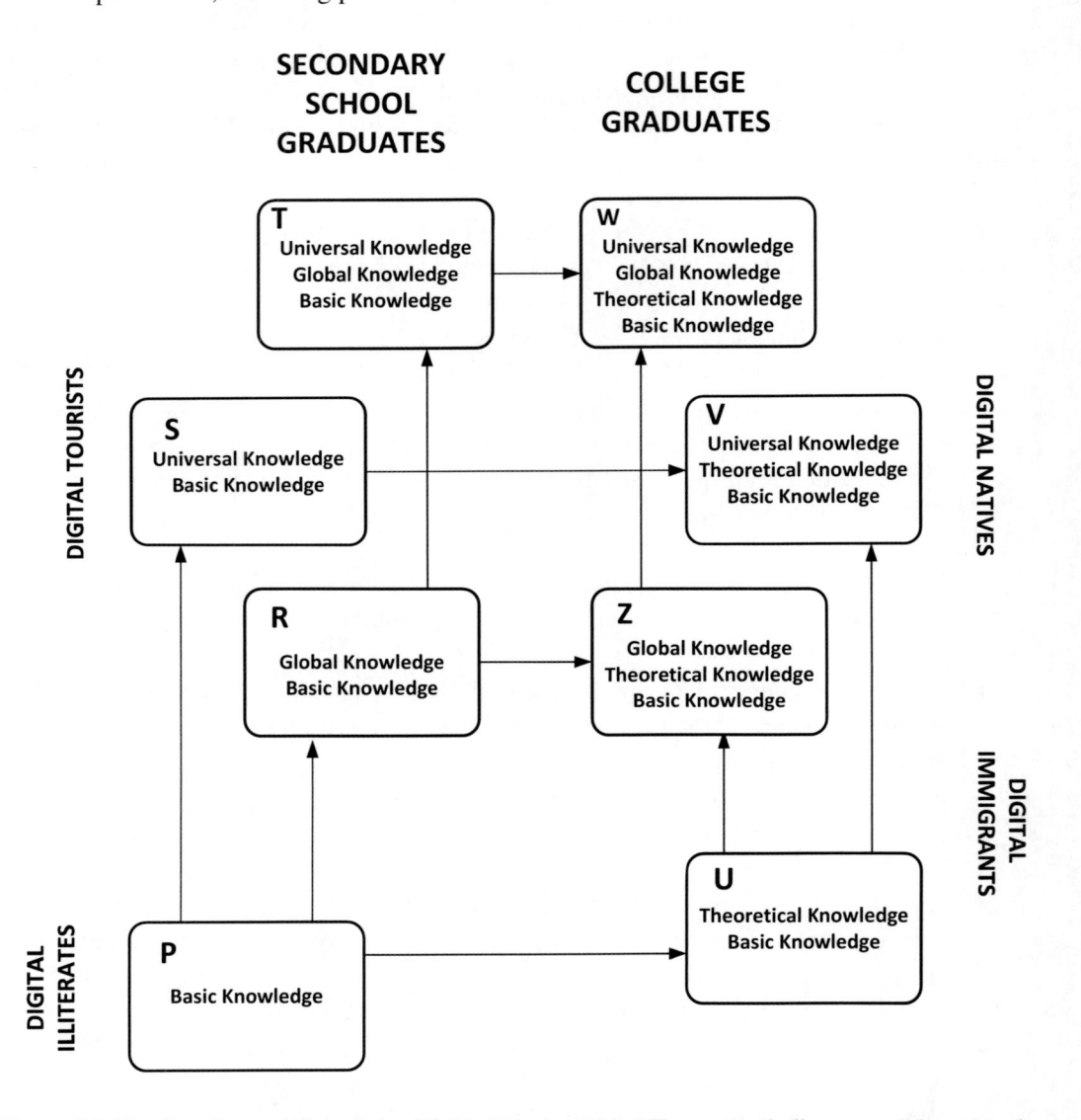

Figure 5.7. The Typology of Knowledge Divide Memberships. (The arrows indicate possible paths of advancement)

ICT tools significantly improve the awareness level of information and knowledge quality. Even secondary school graduates may in this way enhance their awareness of enhanced cognition in terms of globalization and universal knowledge. However, this awareness is limited since they do not possess theoretical knowledge; they only have so called "common sense." If it is good, then it has strong value; however, it is not enough to compete with people in possession of theoretical knowledge. Among the latter, those who have complete knowledge (at the level of an individual capacity) and are netcitizens – they gain the most from Internetization. Their professional careers can be very successful. Also, their civilization contribution can be meaningful. The arrows shown in Figure 5.7 illustrate the possible advancements in the status of this knowledge divide.

It is evident that important property is now intellectual property about "knowing", not physical property, and this property is coming from the minds of people, rather than from its traditional form of labor, which is essential to sustainable growth and eventual prosperity in the Global Civilization. Workforces at all levels in the 21st century's emerging knowledge society will need to be lifelong learners, who, besides having common sense knowledge, should possess theoretical knowledge, global knowledge and universal knowledge. In Western Civilization college graduates number about 15-30% depending on the country. It is impossible that 100% or even 50% of a given Western society will have college degrees. Therefore, the argument that jobs are plenty for college graduates in the digital economy is a misleading statement. From the nation point of view, the question is: what should secondary school graduates and those with less than a high school diploma do? These people comprise about 105 million out of 155 million of labor force in the U.S. in 2013.[11]

VIRTUAL DIVIDE

That there is a "digital divide" which demarcates those who have and can afford the latest ICT tools and those who have neither in our society is certain. On the other hand, the Virtual Divide redefines the issue as it explores the cascades of that divide, which involve access, skill, political participation, as well as the obvious economic status and personal/group purpose to change the status quo in the societal realm. While computer and Internet access are becoming more available as time passes since the invention of World-Wide-Web and easy to use browsers at the end of the 20th century, the issue of the digital dived is losing its message's powerful urgency at the dawn of the 21st century.

The Virtual Divide enhances the digital divide thoughtfully in its human dimensions and quest for the common good. The Virtual Divide also is the most dangerous, socially-speaking, out of all divides that have already been discussed. The Virtual Divide should remind us that it is unacceptable, and that either strong civic unrest or even social revolution in developed nations could be created by it.

The typology of Virtual Divide memberships is illustrated in Figure 5.8 which differentiates four members-oriented categories of that kind of divide.

The membership categories of Virtual Divide can be characterized as follows:

---

[11] http://www.dlt.ri.gov/lmi/laus/us/usadj.htm. Number of graduates with the bachelor degrees was about 50 million in 2013- --http://www.bls.gov/news.release/empsit.t04.htm. Retrieved 2014-02-02.

Online Communities, Virtual Groups, Social Networks

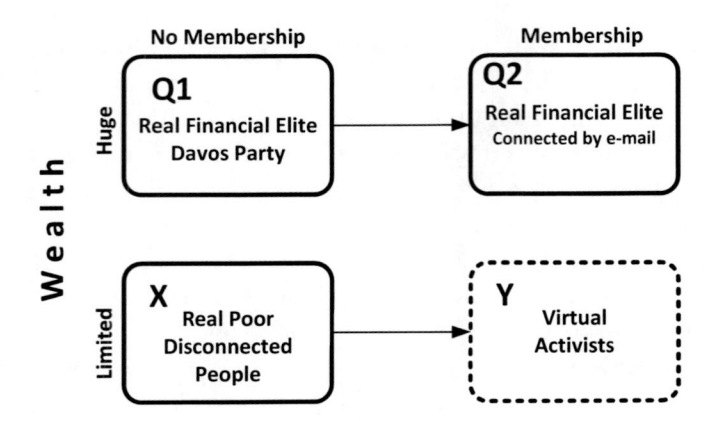

```
                    No Membership              Membership
                ┌──────────────────┐    ┌──────────────────┐
         Huge   │ Q1               │    │ Q2               │
                │ Real Financial   │───▶│ Real Financial   │
Wealth          │ Elite            │    │ Elite            │
                │ Davos Party      │    │ Connected by     │
                │                  │    │ e-mail           │
                └──────────────────┘    └──────────────────┘

                ┌──────────────────┐    ┌ ─ ─ ─ ─ ─ ─ ─ ─ ─ ┐
         Limited│ X                │    │ Y                │
                │ Real Poor        │───▶│ Virtual          │
                │ Disconnected     │    │ Activists        │
                │ People           │    │                  │
                └──────────────────┘    └ ─ ─ ─ ─ ─ ─ ─ ─ ─ ┘
```

Figure 5.8. The Typology of Virtual Divide Memberships. (The arrows indicate possible paths of advancement).

- X – Real poor, disconnected no-members who do not have money and digital, information, and knowledge skills who have no ability to actively participate in the virtual space.
- Q1 – Real Financial Elite-Davos Party who have good information and knowledge skills but prefer to use face-to-face communication, not only for security reasons but mostly for profiting from personal friendships and relations. These people stay away from social networks, online communities and virtual groups. They are, nonetheless, well informed what is going on in the virtual space, since they employ special agents to penetrate and spy in that space. Up till now these elites have looked for ways to increase their wealth, and the common good has perceived this as a sphere where money is "unnecessarily" lost.
- Q2 - Real Financial Elite who may communicate by e-mail among a narrow circle of business-oriented people. They are also well informed about the issues discussed in the virtual space, since they employ specialists to do so for them. Up till now these elites have looked for ways to increase their wealth faster and in a less regulated way, and the common good has perceived this as a sphere where money is "unnecessarily" lost.
- Y – Virtual activists who empathetically participate in online communities, virtual groups, and social networks for the purpose of supporting common good policies.

The Virtual Divide has only 2 paths of improving the status quo. The X no-members can move to Y members if they would have motivation and resources. The Q1 people can move to Q2 people which is rather an active path nowadays.

Furthermore, the Virtual Divide is very strong between the Q1-Q2 and X-Y groups; it is almost impossible to minimize the gap between them today. This gap is even widening as the former is increasing rapidly its income and the latter is increasing its grasp of the virtual groups' communication ability for defining common goals and strategies and motivating a vast number of followers. The "Occupy Wall Street," and similar other movements in the U.S. and Europe, particularly in Spain are good examples of this kind of engaged groups and their virtually active members.

The rising social conflict between these two groups may lose its steam if the former looks more responsibly for the common good and latter is more tolerant and patient. These attitudes are not yet even on the horizon, rather they strengthen their isolationist "fortress" mentality, perhaps leading to a confrontation in the real world.

CONCLUSION

1. The Digital and Virtual Divides of real civilization:
   - Improve reasoning of the Information Elite because they make a broad scope of information for problem solving and decision making instantly available.
   - Worsens the reasoning of Average Citizens because they do not have good knowledge/skills of handling information as the Information Elite do. They become "Datamaniacs" whose reasoning sometimes is good, but sometimes is bad.
2. The Digital and Virtual Divides of Civilization lead to the dichotomy of Society into developed and undeveloped citizens. To minimize this process one must develop Techno-psychology and Techno-philosophy and Regulations for how to apply society friendly ICT. Whether society is able to regulate the technological change is another question. This author is rather pessimistic.
3. The Virtual Divide is the most dangerous, socially-speaking, out of all divides that have already been discussed. This should remind us that this is unacceptable and that either strong civic unrest or even social revolution in developed nations is a situation that could be created by it. If the financial elite won't look better for the common good, the virtual activists may replace representative democracy with direct democracy which is able to create social chaos.
4. The Virtual Divide is very strong between the members of financial elite and the disconnected poor as well as with virtual activists; it is almost impossible to minimize the gap between them today. Even this gap is widening as the former is increasing rapidly its income and the latter is increasing its grasp of the virtual groups' communication ability for defining common goals and strategies and motivating a vast number of followers.
5. The divergence of paper and electronic media looks like a "done deal" in the dawn of the 21st century; in fact, it must be transformed into the convergence of these media if the dichotomy of society should be minimized, and if society would like to be well informed and civilized.

REFERENCES

Amnesty International (2009). "People smuggling." *Amnesty.org.au*. 2009-03-23. Retrieved 2011-04-20.

Boorstin, D. (1987). *The image: a guide to pseudo-events in America*. New York: Vintage Books.

Council (2004). "Human trafficking for ova removal or surrogacy." *Council forresponsiblegenetics.org*. 2004-03-31. Retrieved 2012-11-20.

Courage, M.L., & Cowan, N. (Eds.). (2009). *The development of memory in infancy and childhood*. Hove, U.K.: Psychology Press.

Davis, J.B. et al. (2008). *The world distribution of household wealth*. Helsinki, Finland: UNU-WIDER.

Lee Feigenbaum, L. (May 1, 2007). "The semantic web in action". *Scientific American*. Retrieved 2010-2-21.

Flannery, K. & J. Marcus (2012). *The creation of inequality: how our prehistoric ancestors set the stage for monarchy, slavery, and empire*. Cambridge, MA: Harvard University Press.

Frank, R. (2007). *Richistan: a journey through the American wealth boom and the lives of the new rich*. New York: Three Rivers Press.

Fukuyama, F. (1992). *The end of history and the last man*. New York: Free Press.

Gallup (2013). "Congressional Approval Sinks to Record Low." *Gallup Politics*. Retrieved 2014-1-30.

Gurría, A. (2011). *Divided we stand: why inequality keeps rising (report)*. Paris: OECD. Retrieved 2011-11-15.

Haken, J. (2011). "Transnational crime in the developing world." *Global Financial Integrity*. Retrieved 2011-06-25.

Harvey, P.L. (2010). Applying social systems thinking and community informatics thinking in education. In Rudestam, K.E., & Schoenholtz-Read, J. (Eds.), 91-128. *Handbook of online learning*. Thousand Oaks, CA: Sage Publications, Inc.

Hicks, St. (2011). *Explaining postmodernism: skepticism and socialism from Rousseau to Foucault*. Tempe, AZ: Scholarly Publishing.

Huntington, S. (1996). *The clash of civilizations and remaking of world order*. New York: Simon & Schuster.

Kertscher, T. & G. Borowski. (March 10, 2011). "The Truth-O-Meter Says: True - Michael Moore says 400 Americans have more wealth than half of all Americans combined". *PolitiFact*. Retrieved 2013-08-10.

Larson, L. (2013). Web 4.0. the era of online customer engagement. *B2C Customer Service Research*. http://www.business2community.com/online-marketing/web-4-0-the-era-of-online-customer-engagement-0113733#!uckNj, Retrieved 2014-02-02.

Lévy, P. (1997). *Collective intelligence, mankind's emerging world in cyberspace*. New York, London: Plenum Trade.

Mossberger, K. C.J. Tolbet & M. Stansburg (2003). *Virtual inequality, beyond the digital divide*. Washington, D.C.: Georgetown University Press.

Nichols, J. (December 2, 2013). Pope: "King Money" Culture is Hurting Young and Old." *Moyers & Company.* http://billmoyers.com/ 2013/12/02/the-pope-versus-unfettered-capitalism/ Retrieved 2013-12-08.

Noah, T. (2010). "The stinking rich and the great divergence." *Slate.com.* 2010-08-14.

Norris, P. (2001). *Digital divide, civic engagement, information poverty, and the Internet world-wide.* Cambridge, UK: Cambridge University Press.

Poster, M. (1997). *Cyberdemocracy: Internet and the public sphere.* New York: Routlage.

Puzzanghera, J. (20 January 2014). 85 richest people own as much as bottom half of population, report says. *Los Angeles Times.* Retrieved 2014-01-22.

Reisch, R. (2010). *After-shock.* New York: Alfred A, Knopf.

Rosen, Ch. (2009). In the beginning was the word. *Wilson Quarterly.* XXXIII (4), Autumn, p. 48-53.

Rousseau, J.J. (1754-1755). *Discourse on the origin of inequality.* Holland: Marc-Michel Rey.

Stiglitz, J.E. (2012). The *price of inequality: how today's divided society endangers our future.* New York: W.W. Norton & Company.

Targowski, A. (1990). *The strategy and architecture of information management systems.* Hershey, PA: Idea Group Publishing.

Targowski, A. (2013). *Harnessing the power of wisdom.* New York: NOVA Science Publishers.

Thoma, M. (2012). "Economic inequality and political power." *Economistsview. typedpad.com.* Retrieved 2014-1-30.

United Nations (2009). "Trafficking in organs, tissues and cells and trafficking in human beings for the purpose of the removal of organs" (PDF). *United Nations.* Retrieved 2014-01-15.

Warschauer, M. (2003). *Technology and social inclusion.* Cambridge, MA: the MIT Press.

Wiseman, P. (September 10, 2013). *"Richest 1 percent earn biggest share since '20s".* AP News. Retrieved 2013-08-10.

Part III. Civilizing Virtual Infrastructure

In: Virtual Civilization in the 21st Century
Editor: Andrew Targowski

ISBN: 978-1-63463-261-4
© 2015 Nova Science Publishers, Inc.

Chapter 6

VIRTUAL AND AUGMENTED REALITY TECHNOLOGY DEVELOPMENT

William Tepfenhart[*]
Monmouth University, NJ, US

ABSTRACT

The main *purpose* of this chapter is to give an insight into where the technologies for Virtual and Augmented Reality originated in a manner that suggests where the technologies will head in the future. The *methodology* is rooted in an historical approach of establishing connections from one generation of technology to the next. Our *findings* show that the development of these technologies have evolved in a relatively straight-forward cycle of invention, refinement, increase in speed and decrease in size. Among the *practical implications* are the recognition that the computer is only playing a modern roll in what is occurring, that the transition of technology from laboratory to commercial world is slow, and that there is still a lot of room for improvement in the technologies. Part of the *social implication* out of this study includes the observation that while virtual reality remains somewhat separate from daily life, that augmented reality has become so ingrained that it will become difficult to distinguish the augmentation from the reality. The *originality* of this work includes the explorations of how ideas emerge, connect, and evolve to form new ways of seeing the world around us.

INTRODUCTION

A young boy on the verge of manhood is led into a dark cave by a tribal elder carrying a burning torch. Nervous and afraid of what he is about to experience, the young boy follows the tribal elder, the torch wavering and sputtering while barely lighting the surroundings. The

---

[*] wtepfenhart@monmouth.com

darkness is close. The only sounds are those of their footfalls and dripping water. The only smell is that of the burning torch. The still air is damp and cold upon his skin. The day to day world is left behind for a strange disquieting place. Suddenly, in front of the boy there is a herd of bison. In the light of the guttering torch, the animals, painted upon the cave wall, appear to move.

At a moment of time lost in history, a young boy was introduced to an artificial reality. Admittedly, it is a primitive one created with daps of paint upon a cave wall and the weak light of a burning torch. It is possible that the experience was enhanced with a drum simulating hoof beats and men hidden in the dark of the cave making angry snorting sounds. Yet one could argue that this is the original technological root enabling what has evolved into computer generated virtual realities.

Figure 6.1. Painting of a bison in the cave of Altamira.

In "The Master Key: An Electrical Fairy Tale," L. Frank Baum wrote (Baum, 1901):

"On the other hand," continued the Demon, "some people with fierce countenances are kindly by nature, and many who appear to be evil are in reality honorable and trustworthy. Therefore, that you may judge all your fellow-creatures truly, and know upon whom to depend, I give you the Character Marker. It consists of this pair of spectacles. While you wear them every one you meet will be marked upon the forehead with a letter indicating his or her character. The good will bear the letter 'G,' the evil the letter 'E.' The wise will be marked with a 'W' and the foolish with an 'F.' The kind will show a 'K' upon their foreheads and the cruel a letter 'C.' Thus you may determine by a single look the true natures of all those you encounter."

From a literary perspective, the concept of using a letter to denote a person's character is identical to the scarlet 'A' worn by Hester Prynne in Nathaniel Hawthorne's, "Scarlet Letter". From a technological perspective, there is a huge difference – the scarlet 'A' is a physical piece of cloth sewn onto Hester Prynne's clothes while the Character Marker is a device that overlays information on the real world in a manner that is only available to Rob Joslyn, the wearer of the device. Published in 1901, L Frank Baum's passage predicts the emergence of a technology based on electricity enabling the experience of an enhanced reality.

There is a difference in the artificial reality experienced by the boy in the cave and the enhanced reality experienced by Rob Joslyn. In virtual reality, the individual experiences an artificial world separate from his or her physical surroundings. More formally, Merriam-Webster defines virtual reality as (Merriam-Webster, Incorporated, 2014):

> an artificial environment which is experienced through sensory stimuli (as sights and sounds) provided by a computer and in which one's actions partially determine what happens in the environment

Michael Heim identified seven different elements to virtual reality: simulation, interaction, artificiality, immersion, telepresence, full-body immersion, and network communication (Heim, 1994).

In an augmented reality, the individual experiences his or her physical surroundings with additional information made accessible to them. More formally, Merriam-Webster defines augmented reality as (Merriam-Webster, Incorporated, 2014):

> an enhanced version of reality created by the use of technology to overlay digital information on an image of something being viewed through a device (as a smartphone camera)

From a user perspective, the difference from an artificial reality is that of a fake reality versus an improved reality.

The dictionary definition for virtual reality explicitly mentions the use of computers as the underlying technology while the definition for augmented reality alludes to the use of computers (digital information). This is a very incomplete view of the technologies that underlie virtual reality and augmented reality systems. Hardware and software technologies are the warp and woof on the loom by which the tapestries of virtual and augmented realities are realized.

It would be nice if it was possible to provide a standardized list of hardware and software by which one could create a system providing an individual with a virtual reality or an augmented reality experience. Unfortunately, the technologies used to create virtual and augmented realities are not yet stable and any list of products would undoubtedly be out of date before this book is actually published. What is considered current state of the art is just the most recent point in a history of technological evolution and innovation.

A HISTORY OF VIRTUAL REALITY TECHNOLOGY

It is tempting to begin a history of virtual reality technology with the introduction of computers, but this would miss the fact that the computer is just a recent technology for creating artificial realities. Much of what is accomplished using a computer today was at one time accomplished using mechanical means.

The first known flight simulator was Antoinette Barrel Trainer built in 1909 as a means of training pilots how to fly the Antoinette airplane (Moroney & Lilenthal, 2009). It basically provided simulation with interaction and artificiality. As can be seen in the photograph, it was a half barrel with a seat for the pilot and two controls, one for pitch and one for roll. The idea was for the pilot to keep the long bar in front of him aligned with the horizon while men operated levers controlling the base to affect the orientation of the barrel.

In 1931, Edwin A. Link received a patent on a training device which he called "Combination training device for student aviators and entertainment apparatus" (Link, 1931).

The Link Trainer was a giant leap forwards from previous generations of flight simulators and was used by thousands of pilots. It simulated blind flight such as what a pilot would experience at night or in storms. Organ bellows and a motor provided the means for the trainer, mounted on a pedestal, to pitch, roll, dive and climb as the student "flew" it. A rather humorous story is told about the realism experienced by the pilots (US Air Force):

> "The trainers were realistic enough that a humorous but unlikely story circulated that one student, told by his instructor that he had run out of fuel on a night flight, broke his ankle when he leaped from the trainer as though parachuting to safety."

This is the level of fidelity that one actually wants to obtain in a virtual reality and it was obtained through purely mechanical means.

Figure 6.2. Antoinette Barrel Trainer (PD-1923) (Pantoine, 2006).

In 1934, Miles and Vincent, (Miles & Vincent, 1934), developed a simulation system for instructing drivers (Caird & Horrey, 2011). It was a fairly high fidelity system that included visual feedback based on driver actions and vibrations that varied according to speed. One of the key contributions of this system was that it utilized miniature models which were projected onto a screen in front of the driver. The driver was not forced to follow a fixed path since the projector could move through the miniature model world as controlled by the driver's actions.

Figure 6.3. Link Trainer.

The use of miniature models as a mechanism for providing the individual with a visual representation of the artificial world and the kind of mechanical elements of the Link Trainer for providing the user with motion effects were incorporated into a variety of training simulators. Improvements in both areas were made in attempts to improve the fidelity of the experience, but a significant improvement had to wait upon the development of the computer.

On June 5, 1943, a contract was signed between the US Army and University of Pennsylvania's Moore School of Electrical Engineering to construct an electric general purpose computer for the purpose of calculating artillery firing tables (Goldstine & Goldstine, 1946). The product was called ENIAC and construction was announced on February 14, 1946. It was not a small machine, as described in the online version of the Encyclopedia Britannica (Freiberger, 2014):

> It occupied the 50-by-30-foot (15-by-9-metre) basement of the Moore School, where its 40 panels were arranged, U-shaped, along three walls. Each of the units was about 2 feet wide by 2 feet deep by 8 feet high (0.6 metre by 0.6 metre by 2.4 metres). With approximately 18,000 vacuum tubes, 70,000 resistors, 10,000 capacitors, 6,000 switches, and 1,500 relays,

It would not be considered programmable by today's standards, since it required rewiring the machine in order to prepare it to solve a new problem.

The technical issues to overcome before the computer would be fit for use in generating virtual realities were significant. There were no higher level programming languages to ease the development of software. This forced people to code at the assembly language level, something that was difficult to do and error prone. There weren't any I/O devices that were appropriate for immersive interaction with the computer. No one knew how to compute flat images, much less three dimensional images. No one knew how to create or model artificial worlds. Finally, computers were horrendously slow by today's standards despite their massive size.

In 1949, Short Code was invented by John Mauchly. This was the first higher level programming language and ran about fifty times slower than machine code because it was interpreted rather than translated into machine code (Malik, 1996). Alick Glennie developed Autocode in the early 1952 which included a compiler to translate it into machine code (Malik, 1996). A succession of programming languages followed, the most notable of which are: FORTRAN (1957), LISP (1958), and COBOL (1959). Ole-Johan Dahl and Kristen Nygaard wrote Simula in the 1960s as a programming language for simulation of discrete event systems (Dahl & Nygaard, 1967).

Another major technical hurdle that had to be overcome had to do with displaying images. It wasn't until 1951, when the Whirlwind I computer demonstrated the ability to generate and display images on a large oscilloscope in real time (Carlson, 2003). It solved two problems: one of having a graphical display and one of having a way of rendering images. It used vector graphics which is based on geometric primitives such as points, lines, curves, and shapes. The Whirlwind I computer ultimately led to the Semi-Automatic Ground Environment (SAGE) air defense system which allowed operators to track air traffic in real time.

In February 1962, a decade after the Whirlwind I demonstrated a real time graphical interface, Steve Russell led a team that created the first computer game, Spacewar!, with animated graphics (Wilson, 1991). This ran on a PDP-1 and used a CRT for the computer display. While not very visually appealing by today's standards, the importance of this game is the fact that it is a computer game – the outcome is determined as a result of the interaction between the user and the computer.

The first computer image generation systems for simulation became available for the space program in the 1960s (Rolfe & Staples, 1977). They initially used a patterned 'ground plane' image. Later, they were able to generate three dimensional images.

In 1968, Ivan Sutherland created the first head-mounted display (Sutherland, 1969). It was affectionately known as the Sword of Damocles because it was so heavy that it had to be mounted from the ceiling and had a rather formable appearance. It was partially transparent so the device has claim to being applicable to both virtual reality and augmented reality. The realism is very primitive with graphics comprising the virtual environment made of wireframe rooms.

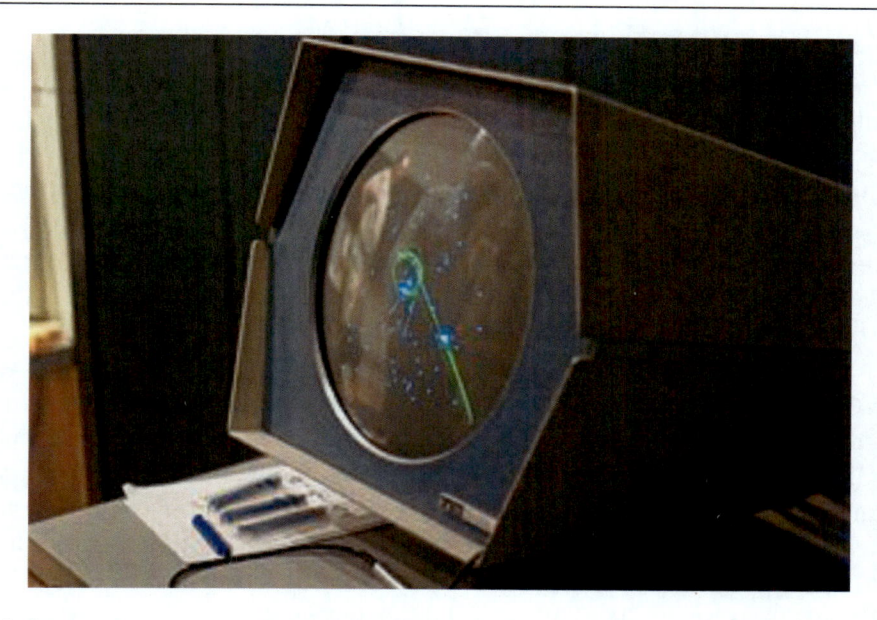

Figure 6.4. Spacewar! running on the Computer History Museum's PDP-1. [This image was originally posted to Flickr by Joi at http://flickr.com/photos/35034362831@N01/494431001] (Ito, 2007).

William Crowther, in 1976, released a game called "Colossal Cave Adventure" (Jerz, 2007). This text based game allowed players to type in two word commands to navigate through a cave. It incorporated elements of magic, humor, simple combat, and basic puzzles. One of the key elements of this game was the incorporation of an artificial world with its own rules and forms with which the user interacted. Some could call it interactive fiction. While it wasn't the first game of this genre, this game was exceptionally influential and inspired the development of a large number of adventure games.

In 1977, the Sayre Glove was created by the Electronic Visualization Laboratory (Sturman & Zeltzer, 1994). This glove was the first 'wired glove' or 'cyberglove' that served as human-computer interface. It allowed hand gestures to be interpreted by the computer.

In 1978 Roy Trubshaw started working on a multi-user adventure game that he named MUD (Multi-User Dungeon) (Kelly & Rheingold, 1980). This program is significant in that it opened the door for multiple players to simultaneously interact within the artificial world that had been constructed.

In 1980, Roberta and Ken Williams released Mystery House which was the first computer game for a virtual world to incorporate major graphics in it (Fatt, 2007). The graphics were primitive wire frames, but the images were keyed to the locations within the game world.

While working 23 years for the Air Force, Thomas Furness developed and evaluated visually-coupled systems and virtual interface concepts to improve the communication of information and control functions to the pilot. In 1986, he organized the Super Cockpit program, for the Air Force (Furness, 1986). He developed a cockpit in the form of a helmet that the pilot wears that coupled the 3D processing capabilities of a human to the machine.

The first computer generated image flight simulator that was for commercial use was the Vital II developed by McDonnell-Douglas in 1971. This was a 'night only' simulator that used a calligraphic, or stroke, approach for the simulation of light points (Rolfe & Staples, 1977).

One could call the Vital II simulator environment a virtual reality since the person sat in a realistic cockpit, the physical surroundings moved as appropriate for the pilot actions, and the visual scene was fully computer generated. Of course the purest would argue that the physical cockpit, the mechanical elements for movement, and the fact that only a fraction of the visual information to the pilot was computer generated fails to meet the full demands of being virtual.

None the less, by the 1980s all of the basic elements necessary to create virtual realities existed and were coming together. On the hardware side, computers were fast enough to compute 3D scenes and input/output devices (goggles and gloves) that could track the position and movements of the user's body had been developed. On the software side, the algorithms to generate complex 3D images and the ability to create artificial worlds had been developed.

For the next thirty years, the technological development of virtual reality systems of this type has been one of incremental improvements of the various components.

With a head mounted display, wired gloves, a powerful computer, and the appropriate software one could experience a 3D virtual world. Bulky helmet displays are being streamlined and/or being replaced by lightweight goggles. Equipment like the Wii, the Connect, and the Leap controller can take the place of the wired gloves. A camera and computer vision software can analyze gestures, body position, and movement of an individual. Computers are becoming ever more powerful.

In 1991, a second approach to virtual reality was launched. Thomas DeFanti, Carolina Cruz-Neira, and Daniel Sandin built the first room-sized virtual reality system which they called the Cave Automated Virtual Environment (CAVE) (DeFanti, Sandin, & Cruz-Neira, 1993).

Rear projection screen televisions showed scenes on three of the four walls in a room and an overhead projector placed an image on the floor. Individuals inside the room wore special shuttered glasses that synchronized with the projected images and contained sensors that allowed computers to track where people were looking.

Interaction with the system employed control wands which allowed people to move objects in the display.

A HISTORY OF AUGMENTED REALITY TECHNOLOGY

It would be entirely reasonable to expect that the history of technologies supporting augmented reality systems would be identical to that of technologies supporting virtual reality systems. They require computers powerful enough to provide the necessary computational capabilities, appropriate I/O devices, and software to augment reality. However, the purpose for augmented reality systems places constraints on the technologies that are slightly different than those for virtual realities. In particular, augmented reality systems require portability, connectivity, environmental awareness, power, and information resources. Augmented reality systems should travel with the user.

A history of the technologies for augmented reality systems is much more complicated than that for virtual reality. The reason is that there are a number of different goals with regard to digitally enhancing the experience of reality. In the world of television, there are animated weather maps, overlays on sports broadcasts, and closed captioning. For pilots and drivers, there are systems to support decision making with heads up displays, and navigation aids. For tourists, there are systems to provide guided tours with background information about items on display. For doctors, there are systems to provide real time medical information about a patient.

Having a static information resource that can travel with a person was a problem solved a long time ago with the invention of paper and its predecessors – animal skins, tree bark, clay tablets, papyrus, parchment, and other materials. The oldest known maps are a map on a silver vase dated to 11,000-12,000 B.C., the Valcamonica Valley map preserved on the wall of a building dated to approximately 6000 B.C, or the map of Babylon preserved on clay tablets from about 2300 B.C (Witaker, n.d.).

Bi Sheng invented the movable type press sometime between the years 1041 and 1048 (Tsein, 1985). While his invention didn't have the broad impact of the printing press by Johannes Gutenberg (Lechene, 2014), it was the first press that allowed mass replication of printed material for broad distribution. Presses allowed the wide distribution of printed leaflets, pamphlets, and books. The first printed tour pamphlet has been lost to history, but there had to be one that provided a description of a display with some index that allowed a tourist to read it while looking at the item on display.

In 1875, Bell developed his first version of the telephone and received a patent for it on March 7, 1876 (Bellis, 2014). In 1894, the Italian inventor Guglielmo Marconi built the first complete, commercially successful wireless telegraphy system, i.e., radio (Klooster, 2009). In 1918, the telephone and the radio merged when the German railroad system tested wireless telephony on military trains (Duetches Telephone Museum, n.d.).

The film industry developed a succession of specialized techniques for creating special effects in movies. It started, in the 1880s, with a simple approach of 'In-camera Matte', in which part of the film was blocked out from being exposed and then later exposed to a second image using a second matte to cover the previously exposed film (Fry & Fourzon, 1977). RKO, in the 1930, introduced the 'Travelling Matte,' which was used for special effects like wipes in which one scene was replaced by another (Fry & Fourzon, 1977). In 1940, the blue screen technique was introduced by Larry Butler.

The ability to store, retrieve, and manipulate information on demand without human intervention required the computer. If any understatement could be made about the ENAIC, it is that it wasn't portable. In 1966, Texas Instruments developed the first hand held calculator, code named the 'Cal Tech.' It provided four arithmetic functions and used a visual output that displayed 12 digits (Texas Instruments, 2008). It was a breakthrough in the sense that it was the first electronic computing device that was portable.

It wasn't until 1973, that mobile telephony had been developed to the point where it was hand portable. Until that time, mobile phones had to be installed in cars or other vehicles. The phone developed by Motorola weighed 1.1 kg, provided a talk time of 30 minutes, and took 10 hours to recharge (Cooper, 1973).

In the mid-1970s, building off of Sutherland's early work in head mounted displays, a helmet mounted targeting system was incorporated into a Mirage jet by the South African Air Force (Helmet mounted display, n.d.). It was basically a head mounted targeting system to aid in targeting heat seeking missiles. It was an augmented reality system in the sense that it overlaid targeting information in real time on the real world.

At this point in time, it could be argued that specialized augmented reality systems had become a reality. They were comprised of head mounted displays connected to computers in an embedded environment. The systems were special purpose in that they provided one class of information to the user. They were embedded in the sense that the augmented reality was only available within a specialized platform.

It wasn't until 1981 that a portable computer, the Osborne I, was available in the commercial marketplace. With a small 5 inch screen and dual floppy drives it came packaged in a hard case complete with keyboard. Weighting in at a lightweight 23.5 pounds, it could be carried from one place to another. There was no independent power supply which meant that it had to be set up next to an electrical outlet.

Figure 6.5. Psion Digital Assistant.

In 1980 Psion defined what a PDA was, but it wasn't until 1984 that they launched their first Digital Assistant (Jaap, 2014). It looked a lot like a calculator and ran off a 9 volt battery. It came with a card database, diary, calculator, and clock as standard programs. One could purchase DataPaks that provided additional functionality: finance, math, spreadsheet, games, and travel. It was programmable and provided much of the functionality of a computer, but it was truly portable and could be used on the go.

The PDA was very close to being an appropriate platform for an augmented reality device, but it didn't have dynamic access to an information resource (one had to have the appropriate DataPak), and it didn't have any awareness of location.

Alpha compositing, a digital method for transforming regions of a digital image transparent was invented in 1970s by Alvy Ray Smith. In the 1980s, the film industry started using alpha compositing to implement digital mattes and blue-screening processes (Porter & Duff, 1984). Live action digital compositing led to 1st&10 introducing the computer generated first down line on live television broadcast of football games in 1998 (Brannan, n.d.).

In 1984, the US Army fielded the Apache helicopter. One of the key systems of it was a head mounted display that visually coupled the aviator and the helicopter.

It used a monocular display to provide the pilot with information. It could track the head movements of the pilot, and use the head position to orient an IR sensor (Rash & Martin, 1988).

In 1978, the first experimental GPS satellite was launched. This was the first step in making accurate global location services widely available. It wasn't until 1993 that the initial operational capability was achieved with full operational capability officially recognized in 1995 (Hegarty & Chatre, 2008). This allowed devices to determine location anywhere on the globe.

In the 1990's the second generation of mobile phone services appeared. This used a digital network to transmit information and allowed access to digital media content.

Getting access to information was now a matter of reaching out and bringing it to the user without being tied to a wired system.

In 1992, IBM developed the first smartphone, named Simon. It was introduced to the world in 1993 (Buxton, 2014). It was an 18 ounce brick that combined the functionality of a cell phone with a PDA. In 1999, smart phones were released in Japan by NTT Docomo (Rose, 2004).

The Microsoft Mobile operating system for smartphones was developed in 2002 (Microsoft, 2002). In 2003, the Blackberry smartphone was released (Blackberry, 2009). Apple released the iPhone in 2007 (Honan, 2007). In 2008, the Android phone entered the market place (German, 2011).

The first-ever GPS navigation system for a production vehicle, GM's GuideStar system, was released in 1995 (Lendino, 2012).

This system was pretty limited with 2D map graphics, few catalogued points of interest, and an absence of text-to-speech. Since that time, GPS navigation has incorporated a number of features: text-to-speech, voice activation, time to destination, road conditions, points of interest, and alternate route planning.

In 1999, mobile phone manufacturer Benefon launched the first commercially-available GPS phone. By 2004, Qualcomm developed and tested "assisted GPS" technology allowing phones to use cellular signal in combination with GPS signal to locate the user to within feet of their actual location (Qualcomm, 2004).

Between 1995 and the present, more than forty companies entered into display glass arena (Optical head-mounted display, 2014). More than 11 technological approaches have been pursued. In 2014, Google began marketing Google Glass.

This product is a wearable computer with an optical display built into a pair of glasses. It features a touchpad, a camera, voice activation, Bluetooth, and Wi Fi (Google, 2014).

With Google Glass and similar products entering into the market, the Character Marker of L. Frank Baum is about to become a reality.

THE FUTURE OF VIRTUAL REALITY AND AUGMENTED REALITY TECHNOLOGY

CONCLUSION

It is sometimes said that today's science fiction will become tomorrow's reality. The Holodeck of Star Trek, the ultimate in Virtual Reality, is still fiction. A physical artificial reality based on holographic displays with transported matter, replicated matter, tractor beams, and shaped force fields seems out of reach. That doesn't mean that progress in that direction isn't being made. The US Army has developed an Omni-directional treadmill that allows one to walk in any direction without actually moving (Crowell III, Faughn, Tran, & Wiley, 2006). A 3-D holographic movie that can play in near real-time has been created at the University of Arizona (Discovery Communications, 2013). Even force fields aren't out of the question with scientists exploring the concept of using space shields to protect space craft (Rincon, 2007). There remains a lot of work to be done before the Holodeck is a reality.

In many ways, augmented reality is becoming reality. The computer generated first down line is taken as just part of the television broadcast rather than a special effect. The dynamic weather map on the news broadcast is expected rather than exceptional. What is the difference between a dashboard with physical dials in a car and a heads up display that is computer generated? There just isn't that much difference. Already people take GPS navigation programs as just another part of a car like a turn signal lever or a seatbelt. High end cars have avoidance software that will stop a car if a collision is imminent (Danielson, 2008).

There are a lot of new technologies in the lab and on the horizon that will increase the ease with which digital information will be made available. Wearable computers, such as the Arduino Lilypad, allow sensors and displays to be sown onto clothes (Arduino, 2014). With products like the Lilypad, clothes can become host to a computer.

There is also considerable interest in developing electronic wallpaper, basically computer displays that are thin and large enough to be used as wallpaper in the home (Malter, 2014).

Changing the appearance of a room could become as simple as changing what image is to be displayed on the wall.

It will be interesting to see what will be the next technological revolution in making virtual and augmented realities a reality.

REFERENCES

Arduino. (2014). *Arduino Lilypad*. Retrieved April 23, 2014, from Arduino: http://arduino.cc/en/Main/arduinoBoardLilyPad

Baum, L. F. (1901). *The master key: An electrical fairy tale, founded upon the mysteries of electricity and the optimism of its devotees.* Indianapolis, Indiana: Bowen-Merrill.

Bellis, M. (2014). *First telephone patent*. Retrieved April 23, 2014, from About.com: http://inventors.about.com/od/tstartinventions/ss/Telephone Patent.htm

Blackberry. (2009). *A short history of the blackberry*. Retrieved April 23, 2014, from Blackberry: http://www.bbscnw.com/a-short-history-of-the-blackberry.php

Brannan, S. (n.d.). *How the first-down line works*. Retrieved April 23, 2014, from HowStuffWorks: http://www.howstuffworks.com/first-down-line.htm

Buxton, B. (2014). *Detail*. Retrieved April 23, 2014, from Buxton Collection: http://research.microsoft.com/en-us/um/people/bibuxton/buxtoncollection/detail.aspx?id=40

Caird, J. K., & Horrey, W. J. (2011). Twelve practical and useful questions about driving simulation. In D. L. Fisher, M. Rizzo, J. Caird, & J. D. Lee, *Handbook of driving simulation for engineering, medicine, and psychology* (pp. 5-2 - 5-3). CRC Press.

Carlson, W. (2003). *Section 2: Emergence of computer graphics*. Retrieved April 23, 2014, from https://design.osu.edu/carlson/history/lesson2.html

Cooper, M. (1973). *US Patent No. 3,906,166*.

Cornet, B. (2006, December 20). *File: Psion organizer 2*. Retrieved April 23, 2014, from Wikimedia Commons: http://commons.wikimedia. org/wiki/File:Psion_Organiser_2.gif

Crowell III, H. P., Faughn, J. A., Tran, P. K., & Wiley, P. W. (2006). *Improvements in the omni-directional treadmill: summary report and recommendations for future development.* Army Research Laboratory. Retrieved April 23, 2014, from http://www.dtic.mil/dtic/tr/fulltext/u2/a456606.pdf

Dahl, O.-J., & Nygaard, K. (1967). *Simula*. Oslo: Norsk Regnesentral.

Danielson, C. (2008, November 12). *Mercedes-Benz TecDay special feature: PRE-SAFE and PRE-SAFE Break*. Retrieved April 23, 2014, from eMercedesBenz.com: http://www.emercedesbenz.com/Nov08/12_001507_Mercedes_Benz_TecDay_Special_Feature_PRE_SAFE_And_PRE_SAFE_Brake.html

DeFanti, T. A., Sandin, D. J., & Cruz-Neira, C. (1993). A 'Room' with a 'View'. *Spectrum (IEEE)*, 30-33, 39.

Discovery Communications. (2013, February 11). *New hologram tech sets 3D in motion*. Retrieved April 23, 2014, from Discovery News: http://news.discovery.com/tech/holographic-3d-tv.htm

Duetches Telephone Museum. (n.d.). *1900*. Retrieved April 23, 2014, from Duetches Telephone Museum: http://www.deutsches-telefon-museum.eu/1900.htm

Fatt, B. (2007). *Feature: The 52 most important video games of all time.* Retrieved April 23, 2014, from GamePro.com: http://web. archive.org/web/20070520142756/http://www.gamepro.com/gamepro/international/games/features/110028.shtml

Freiberger, P. A. (2014). *ENAIC*. Retrieved April 23, 2014, from Encylopaedia Britannica: http://www.britannica.com/EBchecked/topic/183842/ENIAC

Fry, R., & Fourzon, P. (1977). *The saga of special effects: The complete history of cinematic illusion, from Edison's kinetoscope to dynamation, sensurround...and beyond.* Prentice-Hall.

Furness, F. A. (1986). The super cockpit and human factors challenges. *Proceedings of Human Factors Society 30th Annual Meeting.* Retrieved April 23, 2014, from http://www.hitl.washington.edu/publications/m-86-1/

German, K. (2011, August 2). *A brief history of Android phones*. Retrieved April 23, 2014, from CNET: http://www.cnet.com/news/a-brief-history-of-android-phones/

Goldstine, H. H., & Goldstine, A. (1946, July). The Electronic Numerical Integrator and Computer (ENIAC). *Mathematical tables and other aids to computation, 2*(15), pp. 97-110.

Google. (2014). *Google glass*. Retrieved April 23, 2014, from Google Glass: http://www.google.com/glass/start/

Hegarty, C. J., & Chatre, E. (2008, December). Evolution of the global navigation satellite system. *Proceedings of the IEEE*, pp. 1902-1917.

Heim, M. (1994). *The metaphysics of virtual reality.* Oxford University Press, USA.

Helmet mounted display. (n.d.). Retrieved April 23, 2014, from Wikipedia: http://en.wikipedia.org/wiki/Helmet-mounted_display

Hockman, D. (1987, April). Bruce Artwick's Flight Simulator/ You've come a long way, baby! *Computer Gaming World*, p. 32.

Honan, M. (2007, January 9). *Apple unveils iPhone*. Retrieved April 23, 2014, from Macworld: http://www.macworld.com/article/1054769/iphone.html

Ito, J. (2007, May). *Starwar running on PDP-1*. Retrieved April 23, 2014, from Flickr: https://www.flickr.com/photos/35034362831@N01/ 494431001

Jaap. (2014, April). *Psion Organizer I Manual*. Retrieved April 23, 2014, from Jaap's Scratch Pad: http://www.jaapsch.net/psion/p1manorg.htm

Jerz, D. G. (2007). Somewhere nearby is Colossal Cave: Examining Will Crowther's original "Adventure" in code and in Kentucky. *Digital Humanities Quarterly, 1*(2). Retrieved April 23, 2014, from Digital Humanities Quarterly: http://www.digitalhumanities.org/dhq/vol/001/2/000009/000009.html

Kelly, K., & Rheingold, H. (1980). The dragon ate my homework. *Wired*.

Klooster, J. W. (2009). *Icons of invention: The makers of the modern world from Gutenberg to Gates.* Santa Clara, California: ABC-CLIO Limited.

Lechene, R. (2014, March 12). *The invention of typography (1450?).* Retrieved April 23, 2014, from Encyclopaedia Brittanicca: http://www. britannica.com/EBchecked/topic/477017/printing/36836/The-invention-of-typography-Gutenberg-1450

Lendino, J. (2012, April 16). *The history of car GPS navigation*. Retrieved April 23, 2014, from PC Magazine: http://www.pcmag.com/article2/0,2817,2402758,00.asp

Link, E. A. (1931). *United States of America Patent No. US1825462 A*.

Malik, M. A. (1996, December). Evolution of the high level programming languages: A critical perspective. *ACM SIGPLAN Notices, 33*(12), p. 74.

Malter, J. (2014). *Your digital wallpaper of the future*. Retrieved April 23, 2014, from CNN Money: http://money.cnn.com/video/technology/2012/07/30/t-microsoft-digital-wallpaper.cnnmoney/

Merriam-Webster, Incorporated. (2014). *Merriam-Webster Dictionary*. Retrieved April 23, 2014, from Merriam-Webster: http://www.merriam-webster.com/dictionary/

Microsoft. (2002, June 8). *Mobile phones*. Retrieved April 23, 2014, from Microsoft: http://web.archive.org/web/20020608124628/www.microsoft.com/mobile/phones/smartphone/integrated.asp

Miles, G. H., & Vincent, D. F. (1934). The Institute's tests for motor drivers. *The Human Factor, VIII*(7-8), 245-257.

Moroney, W. F., & Lilenthal, M. G. (2009). Human factors in simulation and training: An wverview. In D. A. Vincenzi, J. A. Wise, M. Mouloua, & P. A. Hancock, *Human factors in simulation and training* (pp. 18-19). Boca Raton, FL: CRC Press.

Optical head-mounted display. (2014). Retrieved April 23, 2014, from Wikipedia: http://en.wikipedia.org/wiki/Optical_head-mounted_display

Pantoine. (2006). *File:Antoinette tonno.jpg*. Retrieved April 23, 2014, from WikiMedia Commons: http://commons.wikimedia.org/wiki/File: Antoinette_tonno.jpg

Porter, T., & Duff, T. (1984). Compositing digital images. *Computer Graphics, 18*(3), pp. 253-259.

Qualcomm. (2004). *gpsOne position location technology*. Retrieved April 23, 2014, from Qualcomm CDMA Technologies: https://www.cdg.org/technology/applications/files/gpsone_cdma.pdf

Ramessos. (2008, December). *WikiMedia Commons*. Retrieved April 23, 2014, from http://en.wikipedia.org/wiki/File:AltamiraBison.jpg

Rash, C. E., & Martin, J. S. (1988). *Impact of the U.S. Army's AH-64 helmet mounted display on future aviation helmet design*. Fort Rucket, Alabama: United States Army Aeromedical Research Laboratory.

Rincon, P. (2007, April 18). *Space Shield to block radiation*. Retrieved April 23, 2014, from BBC World News: http://news.bbc.co.uk/2/hi/science/nature/6567709.stm

Rolfe, J. M., & Staples, K. J. (1977). *Cambridge Areospace Series: Flight Simulation*. Cambridge, UK: Cambridge University Press.

Rose, F. (2004). *Wired 9.09: Pocket Monster*. Retrieved April 23, 2014, from Wired: http://archive.wired.com/wired/archive/9.09/docomo_pr.html

Speer, T. (2007, March 7). *File:Link-trainer-ts.jpg*. Retrieved April 23, 2014, from WikiMedia Commons: http://commons.wikimedia.org/wiki/File:Link-trainer-ts.jpg

Sturman, D. J., & Zeltzer, D. (1994, January). A survey of glove-based input. *IEEE Computer Graphics and Applications, 14*(1), pp. 30-39.

Sutherland, I. E. (1969). A head-mounted three-dimensional display. *Proceedings of AFIPS 68*, pp. 757-764.

Swaine, M. R. (2013, 9 23). *ENIAC*. Retrieved April 23, 2014, from Encylopaedia Britannica: http://www.britannica.com/EBchecked/topic/183842/ENIAC

Texas Instruments. (2008). *Texas Instruments - 1967 electronic handheld calculator invented.* Retrieved April 23, 2014, from Texas Instruments: http://www.ti.com/corp/docs/company/history/timeline/eps/1960/docs/67-handheld_calc_invented.htm

Tsein, T.-H. (1985). Part One, vol 5. In J. Needham, *Science and civilisation in China; Paper and printing* (pp. 201-202). Cambridge: Cambridge University Press.

Twig Com Ltd. (n.d.). *twig safety and GPS tracking.* Retrieved April 23, 2014, from twig Care amd Control: http://twigworld.com/pages/en/company.php

US Air Force. (n.d.). *Fact sheet link trainer.* Retrieved April 23, 2014, from National Museum of USAF: http://www.nationalmuseum.af.mil/factsheets/factsheet_print.asp?fsID=3371

Wilson, J. L. (1991). A history of computer games. *Computer Gaming World*, 16-26.

Witaker, A. (n.d.). *Ancient cartography.* Retrieved April 23, 2014, from Ancient Wisdom: http://www.ancient-wisdom.co.uk/cartography.htm#prehistoric

In: Virtual Civilization in the 21st Century
Editor: Andrew Targowski

ISBN: 978-1-63463-261-4
© 2015 Nova Science Publishers, Inc.

Chapter 7

VIRTUALITY AND REALITY OF CIVILIZATION

Andrew Targowski[*]
Western Michigan University, US
President Emeritus of the International Society
For the Comparative Study of Civilizations (2007-2013)

ABSTRACT

The *purpose* of this investigation is to define the central contents and issues of the relations between virtuality and reality in the context of civilizational development.

The *methodology* is based on an interdisciplinary big-picture view of a Civilization.

Among the *findings* are that virtuality is a new layer of human evolution. *Practical implications:* The author recommends it is important to spend more time in reality than in virtuality in order to secure a healthy life. *Social implications:*

It is useless to oppose virtuality since it will not disappear as long as computers and their networks are in use.

Originality: This investigation, by providing an interdisciplinary and civilizational approach defined the 10 Rules of Virtuality, which should be applied by society.

INTRODUCTION

The purpose of this investigation is to define the functional relations between the real and virtual worlds. Their analysis should offer key advantages and disadvantages of the virtual world's offering for the real world. Particularly the qualitative assessment of these functional applications should provide, at least at the ball park level, their impact upon the real world.

---

[*] andrew.targowski@wmich.edu

This investigation will be provided within the broad context of the anthropological and civilizational development of humans. The broad and popular phenomenon among the young generation of practicing the application of virtuality at the dawn of the 21st century will be analyzed in answering a question: why do people want to escape from the real world into the artificial world, like the virtual world?

In such a manner post-modern stages of human development will be recognized. The result of this investigation will be a characterization of the concept "virtuality rules," which should be applied by the educated users of the new emerging landscape as they are the new rules for people living in the virtual world at the dawn of the 21st century.

THE 6000 YEARS OF REAL CIVILIZATION PRACTICE

The growth of humanity can be studied from many points of view, including such criteria as climatic conditions, the adoption of tools, productive methods of family structures. To this author's mind, the most significant criterion is the evolution of the information-communication system (INFOCO), which engineered the rise of prehistoric man, taking conscious dominance of his own existence.

The first human, Australopithecus (two-legged, with large brain and tools), took form around 3-5 million years ago in Southeast Africa. The use of tools straightened man so that 1.6 million years ago our ancestors were already moving about in an upright position. Around 120,000 years ago, from the moment when a group of about 200 to 500 people left Southeast Africa (Kenya and Tanzania) and set out for Central Asia, para-social man was formed. Around 50 to 70 thousand years ago a stable population was organized in this region. The European line is somewhat younger - only about 40 thousand years old - and its emergence is attributable to the curiosity of mobile man.

At this time, biological evolution also gave birth to cultural evolution, which gave rise to the language of inter-human communication, which formed *homo novus*.[1] Thus para-social man became speaking man, a milestone that can be dated around sixty thousand years ago. We are, altogether, the 2400th generation of speaking man, that is to say, man using the organized system, INFOCO-1 (*INFOrmation - COmmunication system*).

With the formation of INFOCO-1, mankind started to blossom socially and culturally. During the next 50,000 years, human civilization was born at the rivers Tigris and Euphrates in the near East. Ancient Civilization lasted four thousand years and, following the birth of Christ became modern civilization. This has lasted 2,000 years and now, before our eyes, it is turning into the third millennium.

The development of information and knowledge played a determining role in the development of contemporary civilization, particularly in the Western version.

Christianity is nothing less than modern ideology, which emanated superstitions and magic as well as the Cesarean system (god-man). The Christian religion is a form of

---

[1] Homo novus or Modern man in English.

emotional involvement and of information, communicated in an organized method among people, motivating its followers to a meaningful life, supported by a defined system of values, parenthetically speaking, binding Christians to our contemporary times.

Already in ancient imperial Egypt, religion was organized within an information system of papyrus, that is, a written language in the INFOCO-2 system.

Yet writing did not make a decisive difference to social communication, since it was known only to a handful of priests. The Christian religion, on the other hand, was organized in books, hand-written and copied by monks. The vital turn in human communication occurred with the invention of the printing press by Guttenberg in 1454.

From that point, the distribution of information among readers began to accelerate.

Print type can be called, metaphorically, the first "computing" device, which organized and started to unite Europe and determined her primacy in the world in the first half of the second millennium.

In the second half, primacy was assumed by Euro-America, situated around the Atlantic Ocean.

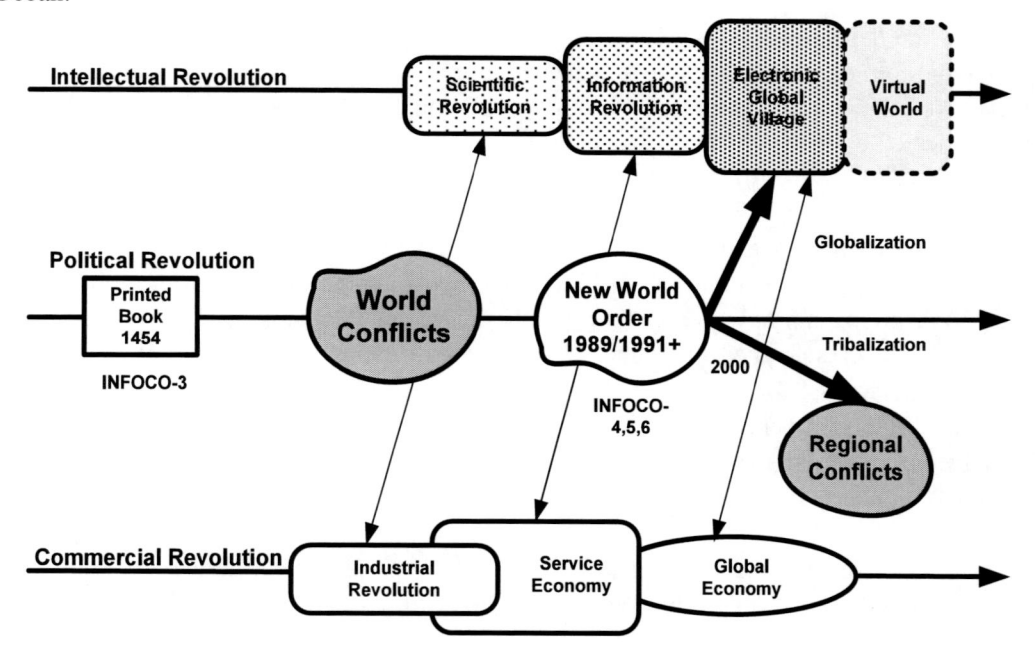

Figure 7.1. The Revolutions-oriented Development of Civilization till the 21st Century.

As illustrated in Figure 7.1., "computer arrangement", producing the printed book (INFOCO-3), initiated three interdependent revolutions in the development of Western Civilization:

- The intellectual revolution, which gave rise to the exact sciences in the sixteenth century which, in turn, produced the contemporary computer, around 1961 (Univac 1) and telecommunication networks in the 1990's.

- The political revolution, which led to the Great English Revolution in 1644-49 which created the parliamentary monarchy; the American Revolution (1776-1788), which gave rise to the republican democracy; and the French Revolution (1789) which introduced the republican system into Europe (however briefly). In the 20th century there prevailed a period of total confrontation of democratic ideology versus militarism and totalitarianism in two World Wars and the Cold War which ended with the fall of Communism and with peace.
- The trade revolution, beginning with the formation of the first private business enterprise (The Dutch East India Trade Company, 1610, dependent on its owners' shares) gave rise to the invention of the steam engine (1769), electricity (1800-1821), industry (the 19th and 20th centuries), the railway (1829), electric power (1866), the private automobile (1908), the airplane (1903), modern airlines (the 1960's), electronic computers (1946), the Internet (1962-1983) and consequently, led into the age of service and global economies in the 21st century, as well virtual reality.

The interdependence of the above-named three revolutions is self-evident. The political revolution commissioned modern armaments from business and industry, which created a market for innovation; that is, it activated an intellectual revolution. This, in turn, influenced the course of both the political and business revolutions, an influence that has been and continues to be conveyed by information and communication. In the second half of the twentieth century this conveyance gave way to automation and networking, thanks to computers (INFOCO-4) and their telecommunication networks (INFOCO-5).

As a result of the refining of all three revolutions, human civilization has branched out into two divisions: a billion people living in the Electronic Global Village (EGV) and having a so-called "access to the computers" and 4.5 billion people living in "tribal" conditions without that access. EGV dwellers have at their disposal highly complicated computer networks, which influence their lives in much the same revolutionary way as did spoken language sixty thousand years ago.

What influence this will have on mankind's bio-social development, it is too early to tell - we can only speculate.

As a consequence of language, people began to immigrate (particularly in the 19th century) in organized fashion, in search of greater living space and better living conditions, resulting in the rise of Asia, Europe, Australia and America. The computer network, on the other hand, produces the reverse effect: thanks to telecommunication, man does not have to move physically from place to place. The EGV dweller can satisfy his curiosity and his search for better living options by navigating the ocean of computerized information available, for instance, on the Internet.

Does a person with the computerized system INFOCO have a better chance of survival than someone from a tribal organization? Will the non-organized and non-informed tribal man perish as did *homo Neanderthal*, who disappeared around 30,000 years ago when confronted with *homo Cro-Magnon* who, arriving from Asia, operated in symbolic language (INFOCO-1) and even created art in the form of cave murals (recently uncovered in France)?

As it happened, Neanderthal man (the first European), who indeed possessed a brain size of 1700 c.c. and yet communicated by barking like a dog, had no subsequent influence in the development of contemporary man.[2] Evidently, it has been the INFOCO system that has had deciding influence on man's greater progress and better organization.

From an optimistic viewpoint, it is *homo electronicus* who has more opportunities for development than *homo tributus*; viewed pessimistically, the greater chance for survival belongs to primitive man, i.e. *homo tributus*.

Now, at the down of the 21st century, we find ourselves at the same kind of turning point as the world did 50,000 years ago, when human language arose and 500+ years ago when print was invented and *homo librus was born*. Since then, the deciding factor in human evolution has been INFOCO, whose various changes are illustrated in Table 7.1. The change in the paradigm, during 2000 decades from informational to network communication, is a more brutal change than the introduction of print 500+ years ago. Certainly, writing and hand-made books were already known before the appearance of print. The significance of the printed book lies in the fact that instead of reaching only tens or hundreds of readers, information began to reach thousands and in the twentieth century, hundreds of millions to a few billion. Of course, the greatest readership has been enjoyed by popular bestsellers rather than by books offering knowledge.

Info-communication that utilizes computers (INFOCO-4) and computer networks (INFOCO-5) universalizes information and knowledge instantly among several billion readers who evolved into *homo electronicus*. It is impossible to say at this point what result and influence this massive spread of information and knowledge will have on human development.

We can guess that man will be more aware of his limitations and possibilities. After the development of the Internet in the public sphere (since 1983)[3] the online communities, virtual groups, and social networks have been developing, which populated cyberspace as the infrastructure for the virtual world.

The group of applications which develop and operate cyberspace form ONFOCO-6 as the next step in the evolution of human communication. To know how to live in the virtual world homo electronicus will have to evolve into *homo hybridus*, who is skillful in engaging the virtual world for the good sake of the real world.

THE REASONS OF ESCAPING FROM REAL CIVILIZATION TO VIRTUAL CIVILIZATION

Civilized, developed nations have perhaps peaked in development at the dawn of the 21st century. Since the discovery of theoretical science in the 16th century and through the next 500 years, people from Western Civilization have achieved a good level of living.

---

[2] The resent research suggests that *homo Neanderthal* to certain degree interbred with *homo Cro Magnon*.
[3] The packet-switching network ARPANET has been developing since 1962 as a classified system, which was broken into the Milinet and Internet in 1983.

Table 7.1. The Evolution of the INFOCO System

INFOCO	Sense Organ	Humankind	Brain Size	Structure of Consciousness	Paradigm
Stimuli-Response	Nose	*Hominid* 10 M–6 M	500 cc	Archaic	Instinct Communication
Sound	Ear	*Australopithecine* 6 M.–2.5 M.	500 cc	Archaic	Sound Communication
Variety of Sounds	Ear	*Homo habilis* 2,5m.–1,8m.	750 cc	Archaic	Hand Communication
Intelligence (fire)	Brain	*Homo erectus* 1,8m.–200K	800 cc–1100 cc	Archaic Spaceless Timeless	Survival Communication
Wisdom	Brain	*Homo sapiens* 200K–50K	1750 cc–1350 cc	Magical 1D Timeless	Migration Communication
Language	Mouse	*Homo novus#* (*verbalis*) 50K–4K BC	1350 cc	Mythical 2D Natural Tempos	Symbol Communication INFOCO-1
Civilized Language	Mouth	*Homo tributus* (*scriba*) 4K BC–1452 AD	1350 cc	Mythical 2D Organized Tempos	Social Communication Writing INFOCO-2
Print, Records	Eye	*Homo libris* 1454–2000+	1350 cc	Mental 3D Spacial Abstract Time	Information Communication INFOCO-3
Computer Networks	Online	*Homo Electronicus* 1950s+---	1350 cc–1500 cc	Mental 3D Spacial Free Abstract Time Real Time	Networked Communication INFOCO-4 INFOCO-5
Virtual World	Cyberspace	*Homo hybridus* 2000+---	1350 cc–1500 cc Virtual memory	Integral 4D Real Space Virtual Space Time Free Virtual Time	Virtuality vs Reality INFOCO-6

\# Homo novus or Modern man in English.

Compare this to the year 1000 when the average life span was 25 years; today it is 78 in Western Civilization. This means that contemporary people in Western Civilization live 3 times longer today than 1000 years ago. Furthermore, their income increased during that time (1000-1998) 13-fold from $443 to $21,470 and the population rose 5.6-fold (Maddisson 2001). Nevertheless, out of 7 billion people in 2014, only 2 billion live at such a high level of being; the remaining 5 billion struggle with every day survival. Simply speaking there is not enough strategic resources for 5 billion people which could support such a high level of living, even assuming that they could reach the same level of education and civilizational infrastructure as has Western Civilization.

Moreover, there is a rapidly rising level of inequality among people in Western Civilization. Unopposed Capitalism by Communism (after the Polish Revolution in 1978) was so liberal that it has allowed for the development of "turbo-Capitalism" or undemocratic Capitalism which stratified Western Society into the "haves" (i.e. the top 1%) and the "have nots" (the other 99%). As a result of this situation, Western Civilization has entered into a deep civilizational crises triggered by the relations among 16 crises, such as: the over-communication crisis, super-capacity crisis, global business crisis, religion crisis, population crisis, ecological crisis, strategic resources depletion crises, food crisis, technology crisis, science crisis, public administration crisis, war crisis, media crisis, political crisis, culture and trust crisis, education crisis (Targowski 2013).

These 16 crises form The Great Crisis of Civilization in the 21st century which stems from the mutual interaction of 16 major crises; however, it is chiefly caused by the crisis of ideas and morality, which leads to a political, social and economic crisis. Contrary to the widespread belief that the morally declining political class is to be blamed for the crisis, it is science that is most at fault: it is unable to develop an economic theory for open globalization and it is unable to channel the progress of business and technology for the service of society, which, in turn, creates the domino effect of subsequent crises.

Getting out of this Great Crisis may take many years, possibly several generations, for which there may not be sufficient time on account of the negative dynamics of the Civilization Death Triangle (a synergy of the bombs of population, ecology and resources), whose symptoms can already be felt and which may be intensified around mid-21st century.

The future of civilization lies in the transformation of the present chaotic and suicidal civilization into a wise civilization. Is this possible? Many people from Western Civilization doubt whether this crisis can be overcome by people, who therefore seek help from virtual life, where well-being is easy and not costly. On the other hand many people from other civilizations travel to Virtual Civilization hoping that they may find some hope and relief from the misery of their daily life.

THE REASONS TO ENTER VIRTUAL CIVILIZATION

The Virtual Life Is a Very Easy Way to Avoid Real Life Problems[17]

What makes people go virtual? People eat and sleep with their cell phones. Why does virtual communication become a substitute for real love? The explanation is rather simple: Real life is much more complicated. For some people it is extremely hard to live and communicate with other real people, to find a common language with them, to love and to be loved, to get married and to have real children. Through virtual communication the idea of commitment is meaningless. This game becomes a form of reality in which it is very comfortable to live. It is a way to avoid problems, at least for a little while. As a rule, a "virtual person" is absolutely different from a "real person" although they are one and the same individual. If two virtual friends decide to meet each other in real life, they become very disappointed, as a general rule. When people meet in real life, they always evaluate each other; they are very cautious to each other in the beginning (Pridorogin 2013).

Nowadays many people (mostly young ones) are so disconnected from the physical world that they do not need to "risk" entering into reality. They can purchase of any kind of good or service they want, and can do it in any identity they choose. The online web is a place where such people spend most of their life. Life in the real world becomes so complex and politically disappointing that it looks as if people are losing interest in the real world and spending more time in the virtual world. All of this is despite the fact that it is a fake world (informational defined), and it has a superficial impact upon our lives, not only with respect to the electronic way we access information but the way we act later (being "informed") in reality.

Jon Rafman, who explores the impact of digital technology on the individual and society at large, said that sometimes virtual reality (Second Life) can seem more real than regular reality because people are free to act without outside factors (societal norms, history and culture) influencing them. They are free to do whatever they want, and this, for them, is more real because there are no inhibitions. Also online information is thought to be more credible than others.

People are now better informed by the virtual world about the real world, and as a result there is a growing disconnect with the real world and the importance of physically experiencing something. Since it looks as though people can find their utopias in virtuality, it has become quite enough for them.

Today, some people are so engaged in the virtual world that they have lost physical contact with old friends from early years of life, and they now communicate with them electronically mostly through a Skype, or sometime e-face-to-face, but without physical contact.

With the problems of everyday life in reality, some people dream about colonizing other planets. This is, however, not a feasible project in the near future; therefore, people want to create another planet under a form which is available today: namely, the virtual world.

---

[17] Pridorogin (2013).

Motives for forming a virtual planet/life are never-ending and vary from one person to another, but as one observer[18] pointed out, there are three main reasons individuals enters a virtual reality:

- People love playing games: Whether it's a card game or a computer game, we love games. Games are an outlet to create something or do something we cannot do in actual reality. Whether it is being a murderer in the game of Clue or maneuvering a Warthog in Halo to find an opponent, people enjoy games. Games allow us to become something without the natural consequences of reality.
- Living in a world on your computer protects people, you and others. It protects others from your facial expressions that often times express more emotion than your words. It protects you from being rejected or teased. Living a life on your own computer screen protects peoples' emotional stability. Living a life on your private computer saves the embarrassment of sweaty hands or shifty eyes.
- Comparing: we all do it. There are things we may not particularly like about ourselves in normal life. Perhaps some of us are not as tall as we would like to be or not as athletic or creative. But having a second life in the virtual world can change that completely. According to Brad Paisley (an American singer-songwriter and musician) you can be so much cooler online.

A Virtual Life Can Trigger Social Change

Electronic democratic thinkers have either focused on the individual and the state, disregarding the collaborative nature of public life organized within and between groups/communities, or they argue that e-communication can increase the level of debate (Noveck 2005). In groups/communities it is possible to elaborate a policy which one cannot accomplish alone.[19] Online community groups, to certain degree, are equivalent to formal organizations or corporations in the real world. Today, telematic technology enables more effective forms of collective action of virtual members of online groups in the real world.

The wisdom of crowds (Surowiecki 2004) can be used in the virtual networks of people, organized in groups. It can rebuild the contemporary legal institutions which ignore the wishes of voters after elections. As practice shows, the legal institution is structured to mainly support capital and powerful politicians.

Based on Surowiecki's book, Oinas-Kukkonen (2008) captures the wisdom of the crowds (groups) approach with the following eight conjectures:

---

[18] Virtuallivingproject— https://sites.google.com/site/virtuallivingproject/why-- accessed 1-23-2014
[19] Groups include groups of groups as well as groups of individuals. So, for example, a group of law reviews can together impose a length policy for article submissions. See *New Article Length Policy* at http://www.harvardlawreview.org/manuscript.shtml#length (Noveck 2005).

- It is possible to describe how people in a group think as a whole.
- In some cases, groups are remarkably intelligent and are often smarter than the smartest people in them.
- The three conditions for a group to be intelligent are diversity, independence, and decentralization.
- The best decisions are a product of disagreement and contest.
- Too much communication can make the group as a whole less intelligent.
- Information aggregation functionality is needed.
- The right information needs to be delivered to the right people in the right place, at the right time, and in the right way.
- There is no need to chase the expert.

However, emotional factors, such as a feeling of belonging, can lead to peer pressure, herd instinct, and in extreme cases collective hysteria, resulting in chaos and bad decisions. Connected in online groups, ordinary people no longer need to rely on a politician to make decisions. They can exercise meaningful power themselves about national, state and local — indeed global — issues. For example, seniors apply networked computers to police the conditions of urban land use.[20] The real world listens to their suggestions; if not, they may face problems in the next election.

The mobile phone "smart mob" (Rheingold 2002) allows groups to self–organize a political protest or campaign, such as the one in 2003 that elected the President of South Korea Roh Moo–hyun, who wouldn't be a president if it weren't for smart mobs that organized the vote campaign. Text messages flashed to the cell phones of almost 800,000 people urging them to go to the polls and vote for Roh. Half a million visitors logged on to his main Web site every day to donate money or obtain campaign updates.[21] In the end, Roh Moo–hyun was elected the president of South Korea.

The online group/community Meetups[22] have no offices, secretaries, water coolers or other appurtenances of formal organizations, yet they have just as much of an effect. Meetups merely facilitates the formation of online communities like the following examples: Parents come online together to decide on a policy in their children's school or an online group of scientists collaborate to overthrow an age–old publishing model and distribute their research collectively online.[23]

---

[20] The City Scan Project of the Connecticut Policy and Economic Council (CPEC), at http://www.cpec.org (last accessed 15 September 2004).

[21] available at http://www.sap.info/index.php4.

[22] Meetup is an online social networking portal that facilitates offline group meetings in various localities around the world. Meetup allows members to find and join groups unified by a common interest, such as politics, books, games, movies, health, pets, careers or hobbies. Users enter their postal code or their city and the topic they want to meet about, and the website helps them arrange a place and time to meet. Topic listings are also available for users who only enter a location. Meetup receives revenue by charging Organizer Dues to administrators of groups, currently at $12 to $19 per month depending on the payment plan.

[23] The Public Library of Science is a non–profit organization of scientists and physicians committed to making scientific and medical literature freely available. For more information, see http://www.plos.org (last visited 5 November 2004).

A Virtual Learning Environment Can Help Learning

A virtual learning environment (VLE), or learning platform, is an e-learning education system based on the web that models conventional in-person education by providing equivalent virtual access to classes, class content, tests, homework, grades, assessments, and other external resources such as academic or museum website links. It is also a social space where students and teachers can interact through threaded discussions or chat. It typically uses Web 2.0[24] tools for 2-way interaction, and includes a content management system.

Virtual learning environments are the basic components of contemporary distance learning, but can also be integrated with a physical learning environment (Dillenbourg 2000) which may be referred to as blended learning.

Virtual learning can take place synchronously or asynchronously. In synchronous systems, participants meet in "real time", and teachers conduct live classes in virtual classrooms. Students can communicate through a microphone, chat rights, or by writing on the board. In asynchronous learning, which is sometimes called "self-paced" learning, students are expected to complete lessons and assignments independently through the system. Asynchronous courses have deadlines just as synchronous courses do, but each student is learning at his own pace.

A virtual learning environment can also include students and teachers "meeting" online through a synchronous web-based application. The teacher is able to present lessons through video, PowerPoint, or chatting. The students are able to talk with other students and the teacher, as well as collaborate with each other, answer questions, or pose questions. They can use the tools available through the application to virtually raise their hand, send messages, or answer questions on the screen given by the teacher or student presenter (Wikipedia).

There are several advantages and disadvantages with regards to motivation in virtual learning.

For many students, virtual learning is the most convenient way to pursue a degree in higher education. A lot of these students are attracted to a flexible, self-paced method of education to attain their degree. It is important to note that many of these students could be working their way through college, supporting themselves or battling with a serious illness (Webster, U. 2013). To these students, it would be extremely difficult to find time to fit college in their schedule. Thus, these students are more likely and more motivated to enroll in a virtual learning class. Moreover, in asynchronous virtual learning classes, students are free to log on and complete work any time they wish. They can work on and complete their assignments at the times when they think most cogently, whether it be early in the morning or late at night (Cull, Reed & Kirk 2010).

However, many teachers have a harder time keeping their students engaged in an e-learning class. A disengaged student is usually an unmotivated student, and an engaged

---

[24] Web 2.0 describes web sites that use technology beyond the static pages of earlier web sites. A Web 2.0 site may allow users to interact and collaborate with each other in a social media dialogue as creators of user-generated content in a virtual community, in contrast to websites where people are limited to the passive viewing of content. Examples of Web 2.0 include social networking sites, blogs, wikis, folksonomies, video sharing sites, hosted services, web applications, and so forth.

student is motivated (Dennen & Bonk 2007). One reason why students are more likely to be disengaged is that the lack of face-to-face contact makes it difficult for teachers to read their students' nonverbal cues, (Cull, Reed, & Kirk 2010), including confusion, boredom or frustration. These cues are helpful to a teacher in deciding whether to speed up, introduce new material, slow down or explain a concept in a different way. If a student is confused, bored or frustrated, he or she is unlikely to be motivated to succeed in that class.

Other advantages and disadvantages are as follows:

- Key advantages of virtual learning include:
  - Improved open access to education, including access to full degree programs (Ahmad 2010)
  - Better integration for non-full-time students, particularly in continuing education(Ahmad 2010)
  - Improved interactions between students and instructors (Dalsgaard 2006)
  - Provision of tools to enable students to independently solve problems (Dalsgaard 2006)
  - Acquisition of technological skills through practice with tools and computers.
  - No age-based restrictions on difficulty level, i.e. students can go at their own pace
- Key disadvantages of virtual learning, that have been found to make learning less effective than traditional class room settings, include:
  - Ease of cheating
  - Bias towards tech-savvy students over non-technical students
  - Teachers' lack of knowledge and experience to manage virtual teacher-student interaction (Illinois University (2008)
  - Lack of social interaction between teacher and students (Elearning-companion.com.2013)
  - Lack of direct and immediate feedback from teachers (Elearning-companion.com.2013)
  - Asynchronic communication hinders fast exchange of questions (Elearning-companion.com.2013)
  - Danger of procrastination (Elearning-companion.com.2013)

The virtual learning system is recommended strongly by education administrators since it lowers costs of operating real world facilities and instructors in smaller classes. Despite some good benefits, such as broader access to education by working people, its major disadvantage is minimal possibility of learning skills of socializing with other students and professors. Learning only the content of knowledge does not provide a good education.

If the enthusiasm for "magic" e-technology prevail, Virtual Civilization will produce virtual graduates who will not know how to act in the real world.

A Virtual Community Can Help Innovating Solutions

One of the first applications of virtuality at the end of the 20th century was virtual reality applied (VR) in engineering projects by teams dispersed in distant locations. An engineering object could be simulated and interactively "touched" electronically by team members sitting in different locations. This technology cut the travelling costs and has become very popular ever since in engineering labs. The advantages of such a solution are obvious.

Another early application of VR was a tele-conference with two screens, where one showed a document or picture of a discussed solution and the second screen showed the participants of that tele-conference. A conference moderator can control time and the methods of speaking or sending a contributing solution in writing. This kind of a solution is widely applied for brain-storming sessions, since in a relatively short time one can reach some desirable solutions.

However, a face-to-face brain-storming-session has the advantage of seeing the body language of the participants which has an intuitive impact upon how an innovation can be developed.

THE VIRTUAL CIVILIZATION POTENTIAL

Brain Activity Responses Differ for Virtuality and Reality

Researchers in many countries are investigating how virtual reality works with respect to the brain. In their experiments, despite the increase in processing power and graphics capabilities, virtual reality systems just do not live up to the real world: People can always tell the difference. To find out why, researchers, in a new effort, turned to rats and observed their hippocampus—the part of the brain that has been identified as building and controlling cognitive maps.

The hippocampus has what are known as neural "place" cells. Researchers believe these are building blocks that are used to assemble cognitive maps—they become most active when a rat is introduced to a new environment or situation. Once a mental map has been created, rats use them to recognize where they are. To find out if the place cells respond differently to virtual reality, the researchers created a virtual reality environment that was nearly identical to one that existed in the real world—including a treadmill type ball to allow for simulating movement. They then attached probes to the brains of several test rats and measured place cell activity as the rats were exposed to both the virtual environment and the real one.

A team of scientists from the University of California has found that one part of the brain in rats responds differently to virtual reality than to the real world. In their paper published in the journal *Science*, the group describes the results of the brain experiments they ran with the rats. They found that "place" cells in the rats' hippocampus did not light up as much when immersed in a virtual reality experiment as they did when the rats were engaging with the real world. The researchers found that the level of place cell activity that occurred was dramatically different between the two environments. For the real world runs, approximately 45 percent of the rats' place cells fired, compared to just 22 percent for the virtual reality runs.

These results were not a surprise to the team as previous research has suggested that place cell activity is incited by at least three types of cues: visual, self-motion and proximal. Virtual reality in its current state isn't capable of generating the sensation of a breeze kicking up, the smell of bacon frying or the way the ground responds beneath the feet—all of these are part of proximal awareness. In order for virtual reality to become truly immersive, the research suggests, proximal cues must be added to the virtual experience (Yirka 2013). The described experiment on rats proved what is intuitively felt: The human brain does not respond to virtuality as well as to reality. In other words, living in virtuality only limits the quality of human existence. Furthermore, having been intensified in the dawn of the 21st century, e-mobile communication has become a concern because smart phones exercise a negative impact on the health and mental development of teenagers. This can happen not only because electromagnetic waves may trigger some illnesses, but in the long-term, the brain and memory can shrink and eventually intellectual capabilities can become limited. If this kind unhealthy communication is not improved, humans may experience regressive evolution.

Humans once were developing fully communicative language (about 50,000 years ago); its vocabulary has been growing ever since and in order to memorize it, the brain and memory are exercised. But modern, e-mobile communication among young people applies short messages, almost a code instead full blown sentences and even words.

Most of all, cell phones attract teenagers with games and sms messaging. There has been a special block language developed for short messages sent though cellular phones in order to save time pressing buttons which use as many symbols as possible.

> A 13-year-old schoolgirl from the UK surprised her teacher several years ago, when she had written a short composition about her summer holidays in the sms language. Here is what the girl wrote: "My smmr hols wr CWOT. B4, we used 2go2 NY 2C my bro, his GF & thr 3 : kids FTF. ILNY, it's a gr8 plc." Secret agents would have to spend hours to decipher the message, although it seems to be absolutely readable for any modern teenager: "My summer holidays were a complete waste of time. Before, we used to go to New York to see my brother, his girlfriend and their three screaming kids face to face. I love New York. It's a great place" (Pridogorin 2013).

This news was just a nice joke for teenagers. When they asked Russian schoolchildren if they would like to write a short composition in the sms language, they said that they would gladly do it shortening the words: less time and fewer mistakes. Teachers did not like the idea, though, because Russian grammatical literacy among schoolchildren leaves much to be desired (Pridogorin 2013).

Cellular operators sensed a profit opportunity and introduced the sms service immediately. An sms sent to a certain number takes a person into a virtual city. At first, there were just a couple of chatrooms where people talked: there were love and sex, but it was all virtual. Now there are marriage registration offices too. Two people can submit their applications there and their marriage will be registered. They hold sms-weddings and give birth to sms-children in sms-maternity hospitals.[25] In this manner people escape from the reality, where they were disappointed for some reasons and expect that virtuality will bring them, if not happiness, perhaps some sort of satisfaction even if it is only an illusion. One cannot exclude that this kind of illusion can became a new kind of addiction to virtuality, although it may be healthier than alcohol and narcotics.

The Good Impact of Virtuality upon Daily Life

Today changes between virtual and actual experience are happening all the time. Therefore, one should stop questioning this new landscape and start learning from it. Some research on these interrelations has been done at the Virtual Human Interaction Lab at Stanford where studies have been conducted to see how physical behaviors in virtual reality flow into the real world. The lab is designed with surround sound, eight cameras for optical tracking down to a quarter-inch and, under the carpet, a haptic floor (producing vibrations) loaded with 16 subwoofers. When you put on the head-mounted display and chop down a virtual redwood, you feel the forest shudder under foot.

What is interesting is what happens just after a subject has exorcised their inner lumberjack and takes off the head gear. Experiments have shown that, thanks to exposure to "virtual" tree-chopping, the subjects actually use fewer paper towels to pick up a water spill. And 24 hours later, these subjects show greater intent to recycle.

In another Stanford study, participants were given a digital, movable three-dimensional image used to represent somebody in cyberspace more attractive than themselves. Afterward they were directed to a "real world" study, ostensibly about online dating. Asked to choose photos of the people they'd like to meet, participants picked more attractive potential partners: men and women who were, let's be honest, out of their actual league. Philip Rosedale, the founder of Second Life (the online virtual world launched in 2003 that now logs $660 million in transactions and more than $75 million in revenue a year), wasn't surprised. Perceptions online and off are porous: Users who find someone's avatar physically attractive, he said, tend to hold the same view when they meet the real person. In Second Life, almost everyone is hot. "They're all impossibly beautiful. And still, somewhat less homogenous," says Mr. Rosedale. "We struggle to make ourselves quirkier in the real world." Virtual experience helps to free us, the way any new sexual, social or artistic experience might, and not just from conventionality. It's increasingly used to treat post-traumatic stress disorder, alcoholism and phobias. It has also been shown to help autistic people socialize.[26]

---

[25] http://english.pravda.ru/health/20-10-2003/3920-virtual-0/
[26] The Wall Street Journal. http://online.wsj.com/news/articles/SB10001424053111903285704576556932506260962. Accessed 9-12-2013

A Virtual Life Is Easier Than Real Life, but It Is Really No Life at All[27]

Supposing that entering the virtual world through computer games is not harmful, playing and sitting a few hours at home by one's self can lead to isolation and sooner than later to depression. Furthermore, interactive computer games can be addictive as are all kinds of remedies such as medications, drugs and liquor. Some people are so involved in the virtuality of games that they only speak about them and prefer to stay at home rather than to meet people outside of their game hubs. The miserable truth is that these players of virtuality have become imprisoned to the very technology that was intended to liberate us.

Experienced users of social networks know that one click is never sufficient to make a connection. People enter the virtual world but they cannot leave it quickly. Very soon, virtual life can become desirable to the real one since it is easier to talk to people who are far away and it requires little commitment.

It is necessary to understand that the word "social networking" is not a truthful reflection of this kind of operation nor is it even the intention of their sponsors. In fact, the "social" component should be replaced by "marketing." A prompt e-message is no substitute for calling someone to have an appropriate conversation face-to-face. Seeing someone's "picture" will never be a worthy substitute of meeting up with somebody, resulting in sustaining a real, friendly connection.

Unfortunately, due to peer pressure, it is very difficult to not be active in this virtual world. Therefore, many people are members of these social networks, where they exchange over 100 messages per day of pseudo communication. Perhaps very soon, virtual reality will be that only place where friends will meet, since in reality they will be absent.

THE REALATIONSHIPS BETWEEN VIRTUAL AND REAL WORLDS

Social Networks As Big Data Collections

The Internet became widespread at the turn of the 20th century. However, keeping personal records is not regulated by international rules or an appropriate treaty. There are some government-level, General Inspectors for the Protection of Personal Data, but their role is very limited, and the practice is so rich that officials are helpless. In the USA, the biggest computer-using country, there is no such agency. Worse, its establishment would be considered unnecessary and even bad for business. What will happen if the government turns against the people? It could be far worse.

The biggest systems of personal data storage are American social networks such as Facebook, Twitter, LinkedIn and others (see Figure 7.2.). In all, these networks have recorded personal data and user profiles of at least 1.4 billion people. These networks are great sources for intelligence services, business suppliers and employers who check the profiles of the

---

[27] Kite (2009).

people they are about to hire. This kind of data determines the success or failure of millions of people. Worse still, this data is often untrue, and inferences made upon them are fraught with error. The worst of all is that most users do not realize these possibilities. Such is also the case with the way big search engines, such as Google, Yahoo or Bing, operate; the operation is based on user profiles so that their information needs can be best satisfied.

Figure 7.2. Social Networks as Big Data about People (Photo: Public domain).

Businesses use the opportunity to sell user profiles to marketing firms which care about business sale strategies. These companies also make available the profiles of users who cause trouble to some governments. This is the case with Google, which signed a contract with the government of China to supply information on users who are under the government's watch as a condition of the company's business operations in the country., Under fire in the USA, Google sought to alter the agreement to save face. At the beginning of 2013, Google's president visited North Korea and Myanmar, ruled by totalitarian regimes. These dictatorships know what conditions to set to allow Google to do business in their countries. The company must know what kind of conditions these will be.

The recent decade has seen the development of new Big Data technology, which is about the processing of a huge amount of data collected by businesses during transactions and buyers (also potential) visiting online stores, selected by a number of detectors in smart devices, such as cameras or phone calls (smartphones). The idea is to create some characteristics of human behavior and use the data in marketing. This is how geno-metric maps are created for a majority of clients, that is, most of the people living on Earth. This is coupled with the development of intelligent application software, which can stimulate all kinds of impressions on these people, without asking them for permission, of course.

Before our very eyes a new society is emerging: that is, a data rather than information society. In such a society, the power apparatus as well as strong organizations, but also crazy "specialists" (like all kinds of fanatics), will create a new modality of everyday life, with people being spied on by various telecommunications technologies. Even now, the concept of Big Brother (see Figure 7.3) is being reified on a scale that did not even occur to Orwell in 1949 when he published his novel *1984*.

Although Orwell attributes the emergence of Big Brother to a totalitarian system, the contemporary creation of Big Brother is being formed in democracies thanks to telecommunication technologies and the appetite for client data (such as Big Data—Figure 7.4.) in big business, and among politicians determined to stay in power for as long as possible. This is also how liberal capitalism is being transformed into turbo-capitalism with all the consequences since "speed" is more important than wisdom in action. The absurdity of over-information is preparing to rule the world.

Figure 7.3. Big Brother Watches You (Photo: Public domain).

Figure 7.4. Big Data about Peoples' Activities (Photo: Public domain).

An example of a vast database with personal profiles is the Big Data collected by the Acxion Corporation in Little Rock, Arkansas. It has data on about 500 million consumers with 1500 different kinds of data. It has collected data on most US consumers. It is maintained on 23,000 servers by 6,200 employees. It has sales offices in America, Asia and Europe. Its annual turnover is $1.13 billion and it generates an annual profit of $77.26 million.[28] Another company like this is Experian, employing 17,000 employees who specialize in business analysis services not only in finances but also in Big Data. Whoever wishes to do so can buy information about any consumer's activity in the world. What they will do with the data is the buyer's secret. Firms such as Walmart and Amazon have huge databases about people. If someone thinks that these are protected, they are wrong and WikiLeaks has made the databases available.

---

[28] https://en.wikipedia.org/wiki/Acxiom, accessed 4/12/2013.

Business (interested in ever higher efficiency of marketing) and politicians feel that society will be against the collection of this type of data. Therefore the World Economic Forum that meets yearly in Davos prepared a report (World Economic Forum) in 2013 in which it recommended that an individual have a right to privacy regarding their personal data, but that it should also be possible for businesses to collect and use their data. They think that there is no "bad" data; as a Microsoft representative put it "there are only wrong uses of data." It reminds one of the current discussion in the USA about gun control. The very influential National Rifle Association maintains that it is not weapons that kill – it is humans, and it is the fault of the government that it does not arrest all gangsters. In fact, the situation is even worse, as those who are arrested are then released by indulgent judges to have a second chance: a chance for what? The NRA wants almost every citizen to have a gun and to be able to defend him or herself against gangsters and the government. Thanks to the Constitution and this policy, after 1945, twice the number of have people have died in the U.S. (1.5 million) from gun violence than in all wars the country has waged since the early 20th century.[29]

A representative of a major health insurance company, Kaiser Permanente (USA) - claims that the company has a database of its 9 million clients and that the precise data on their health and behavior allow the company to assess the quality of treatment. He is delighted with the possibility of collecting data from the client's phone calls. He goes on to say that the Golden Age of Medicine is approaching, but it can be stopped by the desire to keep the personal data of patients private. Alas, he fails to mention that the company can refuse to cover the costs of treatment of the insured person if its "data" indicates "undesirable" behavior by the insured. The delight about the role Big Data does can and does play is growing in American society, as evinced by the article "The Rise of Big Data, How It's Changing the Way We Think About the World," published in the prestigious journal Foreign Affairs.[30]

The trend of elaborating personal profiles in the 21st century is on the rise and no legal acts are in view that could counteract storing and expanding these highly advanced personal data files. As can be inferred from the German experience in carrying out the Holocaust in World War II [killing about 4 million civilians due to a very precise data on citizens in occupied countries, kept on IBM punched cards (Targowski 2014)], this kind of record-keeping is highly dangerous for humans as it may end up in the loss of job, not being hired (even though if for the right reasons, a number of crimes could be prevented), and other wrongs or persecutions, if not outright death.

The moment the Internet became widespread at the beginning of the 21st century is very difficult to precisely establish. The Internet serves individual users just fine. But in the service of public administration it is a Trojan Horse which can benefit democracies but also authoritarian regimes, especially totalitarian ones.

---

[29] The 2013 *Newsletter of the International Society for the Comparative Study of Civilizations*, 4 www.mich.edu/iscsc.
[30] *Foreign Affairs*. vol. 92(3), 2013, pp. 28-40.

Democracies are against any control of free speech in the Internet but undemocratic states control it. Thus, the democracies enable the expansion of information chaos which, however, in the long run can turn representational democracy into politically chaotic direct democracy.

Authoritarian, authoritarian-adaptive, totalitarian and pseudo-totalitarian regimes such as China effectually control free speech on the Internet. It would seem one cannot control the Internet just as one cannot nail jelly to the wall. In China, however, it was enough to employ 100,000 specialists[31] for computer network censorship in the Chinese Administration of Computer Network and Information Systems Security. These workers have enabled the design and launch of the Great Firewall, which allows the government to successfully control Internet Use. In this way, China is pursuing precise information about its "troubled" citizens, which most probably is rather ominous for them.

In December, 2012, the UN organized a conference on Internet control. The US and European democracies opposed controlling the net, but Russia, China and 87 other countries[32] were in favor of internet censorship, which indirectly leads to "segregation, isolation and elimination (deportation) and upholding the detachment between the tribe in power and the others" who lower the political "hygiene" in those countries.

To preserve the history of these type of actions by authoritarian or totalitarian powers, it to ought to be enough to be reminded that the first dictatorship that realized the dangerous role of networks for the elites in power was the People's Republic of Poland, which subjected the designer of its INFOSTRADA network (under construction in Poland in 1972-1974—Figure 7.5, Targowski 2009) to segregation, isolation and then deportation to Mexico; he was later to make his way to the USA. In this country, INFOSTRADA was translated into the Information Superhighway at the end of the 20th century and became synonymous with the New Economy.

For as long as there is not another World War, despite the development of many elaborate systems organizing computerized personal data recording, the plight of the people seems safe. How long will such a state of affairs last? It all depends on how long the Earth's resources will sustain eight or ten billion people around 2050. If these resources run out, large-scale conflicts and wars for resources will begin. But if these do not come about, the size of the population will have to be reduced anyway. And then the systems of personal data filing will prove very helpful.

Fake Identity, Honesty, Deception, and Governance Problems

Virtual social networks, at their beginning stage (the dawn of the 21st century), looked as a dreamed solution to fix a majority of social problems through better communication and enabling problem/issues solutions for the common good. Unfortunately, the virtual world is not free of crimes committed in the real world. Even worse, not only did it copy almost all sorts of crimes experienced in reality, but perhaps it has actually increased the portfolio of

---

[31] "A Giant Cage," *The Economist,* April 6, 2013, p.6.
[32] "To Each Their Own," *The Economist,* April 6, 2013, p. 14.

new crimes and further intensified some of them due to the global reach of computer networks.

New opportunities are provided by social media sites which generate revenue with targeted advertising, based on personal information. As such, they encourage registered users to provide as much information as possible. With limited government oversight, industry standards or incentives to educate users on security, privacy and identity protection, users are exposed to identity theft and fraud. Additionally, these platforms have a ton of confidential user information, and are likely vulnerable to outside (or inside) attack. On the marketing front, Google recently patented an algorithm to rate an individual's influence within social media. Once publicized, it will likely encourage greater participation by active users in order to boost their "influence score."

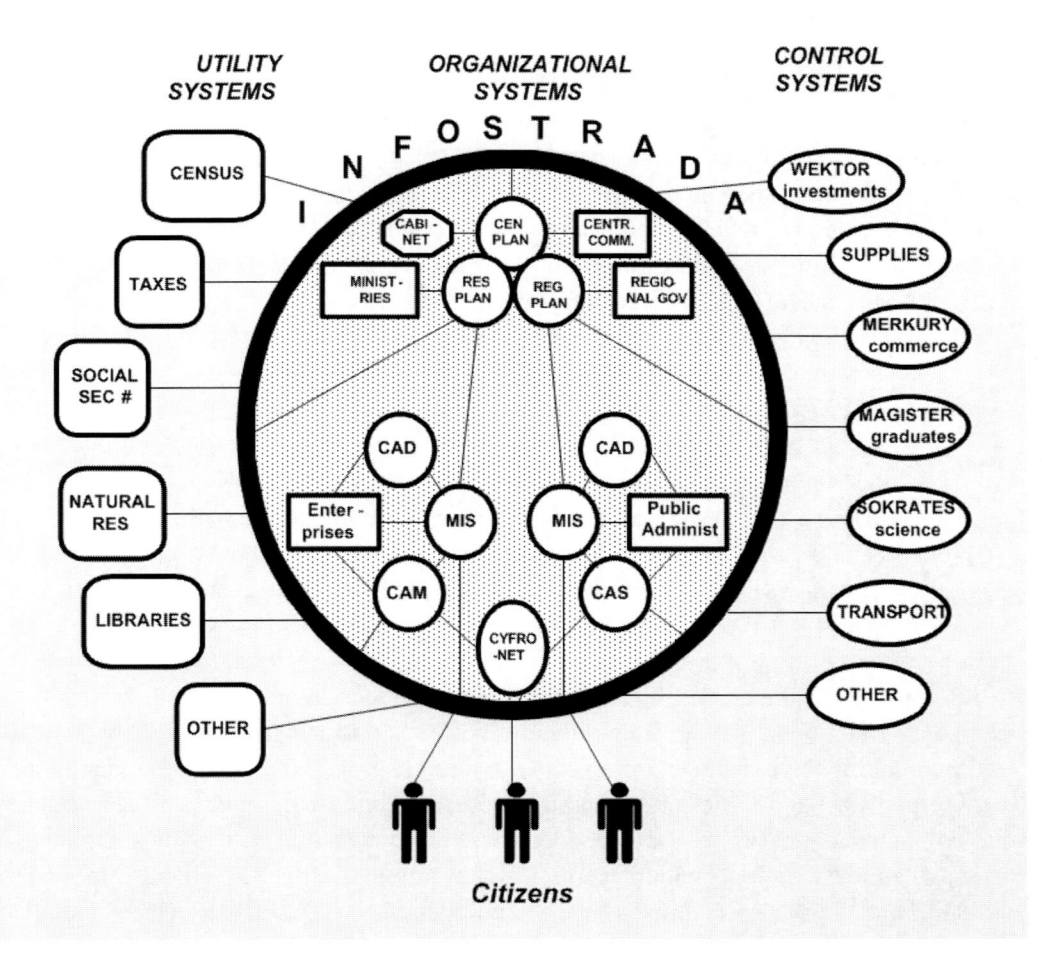

Figure 7.5. INFOSTRADA was an Enemy of the Totalitarian Regime in Poland (1972). (Targowski 2009:237).

With the increased global use of social media, there are more opportunities than ever before to steal identities or perpetrate fraud online. For example, status updates posted on Twitter, Facebook and many other social media sites can be used by criminals. If someone posts that they will be out of town on vacation, that person has opened him or herself up for burglary. If someone mentions that they are away on business for a weekend, that person may leave their family open to assault or robbery. When it comes to stalking or stealing an identity, the use of photo and video-sharing sites like Flickr and YouTube provide deeper insights into an individual, their family and friends, their house, favorite hobbies and interests.

The following profile elements can be used to steal or misappropriate someone's identity: full name (particularly your middle name), date of birth (often required), home town, relationship status, school locations and graduation dates, pet names, other affiliations, interests and hobbies. Below are just a few examples of how this information can be used to compromise someone's identity:[33]

- GPS-enabled phones sharing someone's location can reveal sensitive information like a home address, work address and the places one visits.
- Ninety-five percent of Facebook profiles have at least one application, many of which are not reviewed and can be used for malicious and criminal purposes.
- False profiles can be used to fuel resume fraud or defamation of character. A Canadian reporter recently was defamed via a false profile that included misleading posts, poorly considered group memberships and intellectually inconsistent political positions.
- An American soldier abroad in Iraq discovered his bank account was repeatedly being accessed online and drained. A security expert was able to replicate access with nothing more than his name, e-mail and Facebook profile.
- A massive data breach affected up to 100 million shoppers of the Target chain in December 2013 whose e-mail addresses and phone numbers can be in wrongful possessions. If the thieves are able to get ahold of these customers' social security numbers, it is possible that they can open credit lines on these customers' names.

Because of all the crimes capable of being committed due to identity theft, many virtual users create fake identities to protect themselves or just to misguide others about who they are, particularly in debating controversial issues. But in communication among people, identity plays a key role in understanding and evaluating a communicational interaction. If one communicating party has a fake identity or even worse if both parties are fake inter-actors, then the whole communication is fake and untruthful. In contrast to reality, in virtuality one physical person may have several identities, which creates chaos and a lack of responsibility between the communicating parties. This does not lead to a better understanding among people but to wider miscommunication and pseudo communication.

---

[33]http://www.eonetwork.org/knowledgebase/specialfeatures/pages/social-media-networks-facilitate-identity-theft-fraud.aspx, Accessed 1-23-2014.

This kind of virtual communication as it is practiced raises the issue of honesty and deception of virtual communicators. Also the issue of vulgar language is widely seen in the virtual world, particularly in all sorts of blogs. Such a level of vulgarity in the virtual is not observed in the real world.

These kinds of problems with virtual communities can be resolve by appropriate governance rules. As more and more interactions occur in online communities there must be governances established that regulate how they function, barriers to entry, and codes of conduct. A good example of a well governed virtual community is the WELL in San Francisco, perhaps the oldest such community in the world. Created in 1985 The WELL was one of the first online communities to evolve and is still going strong today. The Well is a "non-anonymous community site" and requires members to reveal their "real names" to other members (WELL Community Guidelines). Based on mutual respect and cooperation, The WELL's governing principle is "You Own Your Own Words," or "YOYOW" (WELL Community Guidelines). The community consists of various conferences that are headed by volunteers known as Hosts. Some conferences are private, but many are open to whoever would like to participate. The WELL has a Member Agreement and Host Agreement that outline the behavior expected from members and hosts. For example, members are asked not to use profanity or other inappropriate language and to only post an item in one place on The WELL, among other things. The Member Agreement also provides members with suggestions for courses of action they can take should they feel that the host of a conference has unfairly censored them:

- Email the host and discuss the deletion privately.
- Start a topic to discuss the deletion publicly.
- If your comment was deleted as "off-topic," start a topic where your comment will not be considered off-topic.
- Re-post a new version of your deleted comment in another conference.
- Re-post a new version of your deleted comment on your Web page, and point to it from within WELL conferences.
- Alter your approach in the conference.

Hosts are given a variety of powers and responsibilities. WELL management stays out of the resolution of social issues, giving the Hosts the ability to exercise their powers at their own discretion. Hosts are "exemplary citizens of the online community," those who are known for helping other users and sharing their knowledge on various subjects, and have been entrusted with responsibility for a conference (WELL Host Agreement). The duties of a host include "keeping the conference running smoothly, managing it in consistency with the WELL's technical needs and limitations, ensuring that users can find information as easily as possible and helping maintain an open and useful conversational environment in the conference" (WELL Host Agreement). While Hosts are given the power to "hide or scribble any responses, freeze, retire or kill any topics, and install or modify menu information and banners within the conference," WELL management asks them to use their powers sparingly and responsibly (WELL Host Agreement).[34]

WELL is one of the best examples of governance in a virtual community. In virtual practice one can expect and find very often that its governance will remind one of governance in the real world. This means that it can be safe from the power game, mismanagement, a lack of professionalism and dedication, and so forth.

CAN TELEDEMOCRACY REVITALIZE REPRESENTATIVE DEMOCRACY WHICH WE PRACTICE POORLY?

Since the real, developed world is full of problems and crises, there is some hope that virtual society can perhaps revitalize sustainable democracy. The main tool of this rescue strategy is the omnipotent Internet.

The dissemination of the Internet is boosting Teledemocracy (Arterton 1987), as best illustrated by social networks such as Facebook and Twitter. These virtual people tend to have a real impact on "real" society.

Take the Anti-Counterfeiting Trade Agreement (ACTA) on online plagiarism and libel: The agreement secured the rights of harmed parties along similar lines of regulation in the real world. Internet users protested against limiting freedom on the Internet, with the Polish and other European governments rejecting it, meaning the EU rejected it too. ACTA was turned down as the politicians feared their voters' response. True, some ACTA provisions are unenforceable, such as one regarding punishing server owners for the dissemination of false information. This hypothetical owner is practically unable to successfully control and possibly prevent this flow, which takes place in cycles that last merely seconds, and which can affect millions (or more) of such data flows daily.

On 12 May, 2012, the American government proposed Preventing Real Online Threats to Economic Creativity and Theft of Intellectual Property Act – PIPA – referred to by the acronym PROTECT. A similar bill was proposed in the Congress by the Republican representative Lamara Smith of Texas, on 25 October, 2011. The bill was met with vociferous protests from Internet users, as expressed by the dimming of Wikipedia and 7,000 other portals. Google collected 7 million signatures protesting the ratification of SOPA.

Internet users threatened to boycott firms that supported SOPA. The opponents of the solution proposed their own bill – Online Protection and Enforcement of Digital Trade Act. This was put forward to Congress by two Democratic politicians – Senator Ron Wyden from Oregon and Representative Darrell Issa of California in December, 2011.

Google and Facebook drafted a bill called OPEN, with the film and music industries supporting bills on the lines of SOPA and PIPA; however, the White House warned that this type of regulation might destroy the Internet architecture. As a result of widespread protests, the US Congress backed off from any regulation of the publication of and trading in digital

---

[34]http://www-cs-faculty.stanford.edu/~eroberts/cs201/projects/2004-05/online-governance/governance-structures/the-well.html. Accessed 1-23-2014.

information/image until a broad consensus is reached among the general public regarding such regulation.

In the 1990s the US Electronic Frontier Foundation (FFF) protested against the Communications Decency Act for the sake of total freedom on the Internet. Indeed, some passages in the act were questioned by the US Supreme Court. Today, all social groups are present in the Internet and guard the freedom of speech. The culture of the Internet resembles the counter-culture of the 1960s. However, if no other international treaty is signed that protects copyrights on the Internet, sooner or later art will disappear; without art, civilization will be boring. Today's civilization is so exciting thanks to advanced human creativity.

China has the least doubts regarding freedom on the Internet. The country sows the construction of the Great Firewall of China to prevent its people from reading politically inconvenient websites. The project employs 30,000 to 50,000 specialists in Internet censorship.

Political parties are being formed to guard freedom on the Internet: Sweden has seen the coming into existence of the Pirate Bay Party, with *Piratenpartei* having been set up in Germany in the 2011 elections; it got 8.9% of the vote in the Berlin region and 15 seats in the Parliament of Berlin. This party argues in favor of free city transportation services and the right to vote for foreign residents' in Germany.

In 2010 Wiki Leaks published thousands of classified documents by various governments on the Internet; this was to break the secrecy occurring in government activity. This has caused indignation on the part of not only governments but the "traditional-minded" citizens. The parties and groupings that advocate freedom on the Internet do not so much fight for what people ought to do; rather, they seek to enable people to use their limitless resourcefulness.

Rather than improve the many attempts at regulating the issue, these were trashed in the name of the alleged "freedom." But isn't civilization about restricting the idealistic freedom of man? Isn't a civilized man someone who behaves fairly and respects other people? Internet users believe that man can do anything as freedom is the supreme value. Freedom is indeed great, but a wise civilization must impose some limitations on ethics in the form of historically adopted norms of behavior.

If the imagination is allowed to run loose and if virtual communities realize how powerful they are, one can expect them turning into virtual states with their own parliaments, governments and citizens, having their own rights and passports. Without the huge costs of TV commercials, within hours, they will be able to mobilize their virtual citizens to elect real parliamentarians, who will secure the implementation of goals and interests of a virtual state in a real country.

In this way direct democracy will have replaced the indirect representative democracy, whose goal is to filter radical ideas and projects: that is, and the prevention of chaos. It is true that contemporary democracy is representative, but during the elections only; after that all mind is paid to the business of lobbyists rather than voters. Internet users are aware of this fact. Will their system be better, though? One might doubt this is so.

The 21st century exercise of the potential of community networks demonstrates that Teledemocracy leads to a direct democracy and plebiscites. F. Christopher Arterton's deliberations from 1987, concluding that tele-democracy might introduce some improvements in elections, such as raising poll turnout if the choice offered is worth bothering to vote, presents a highly idealistic position, proposed at the very beginnings of tele-democracy. The practice of the subsequent 25 years has denied Arterton's optimism.

The reality of the 2012 US presidential elections proved that the value of the options put forth before the voters were shaped by the never-ending plebiscites, quite often taking the form of repeated opinion polls. Each time polls provided opinion on the values offered and the voter supported changed, the options proposed were changed or eliminated. The chances are that the next elections will be decided by the virtual communities and farmed out to the real community of voters to cast a (commissioned) real vote in real polling stations.

Freedom as seen by today's Internet users – "tele-democrats" – leads to a pseudo-democracy, the debasement of culture and social chaos. In consequence, it may also lead to the collapse of civilization as we know it, which we appreciate and which we can be proud of. It is worth reminding ourselves that "freedom is not free."[35]

The New Architecture of Civilization at the Dawn of the 21st Century

The new architecture of civilization contains the old component which is the real world and the new component which is the virtual world. The relations between the former and latter are depicted in Figure 7.6. These relations are established by the new functions which the virtual world is providing for the real world.

The virtual functions serving the real world are in their early development at the dawn of the 21st century. Their values and disservice are assessed in Table 7.2. Today these virtual functions are the subject of fascination and early warnings. These functions have existed for a short time--about 25 years (regarding mostly online communities)-- which need to be expanded to a century or more in order to judge how well they will serve the real world. But as of today, the virtual world's functions contributes quite negatively [64% are disserving in a static (without frequency of applying each function) assessment-Table 7.2] to the real world. The functions such as social communicating, Big Data collecting, mis-communicating, and escaping are particularly harmful to the real world. Since these functions also have some positive impact upon the real world, their differential (but static) negative impact upon the real world is mitigated and assessed at the level of 22%.

---

[35] "Freedom Is Not Free" was first coined by retired U.S. Air Force Colonel, Walter Hitchcock, of the New Mexico Military Institute. The idiom expresses gratitude for the service of members of the military, implicitly stating that the freedoms enjoyed by many citizens in many democracies are only possible through the voluntary risks taken and sacrifices made by those in the military. The saying is often used to convey respect specifically to those who gave their lives in defense of freedom. "Freedom Is Not Free" is engraved into a wall at the Korean War Veterans Memorial, Washington, D.C.

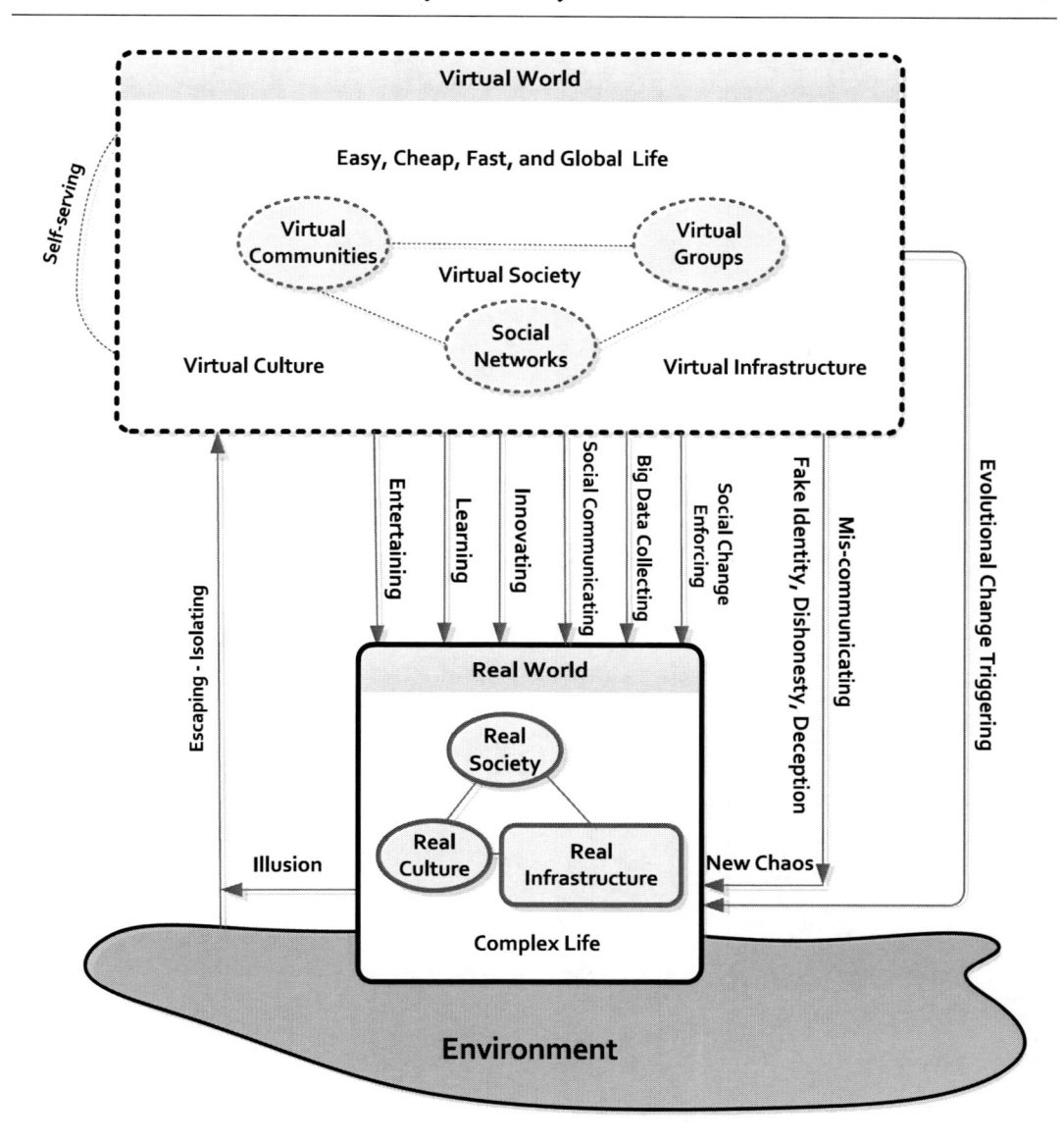

Figure 7.6. The Impact of Functions Served by the Virtual World upon the Real World and vice versa.

On the other hand, virtual functions such as innovating, social change enforcing and eventual evolutionary change contribute positively and can contribute much more to the well-being of the real world.

Table 7.2. The Qualitative Assessment of Virtual Functions Serving the Real World at the Dawn of the 21st Century (in the Likert's Scale 1 to 5)

	VIRTUAL SERVING FUNCTION	FUNCTION'S VALUE	FUNCTION'S DISSERVICE	DIFFERENTIAL BALANCE	IMPACT "3"/45 (9x5=45)	IMPACT "4"/45 (9x5=45)
0	1	2	3	4	5	6
1	Entertaining (computer games)	+3	-4	-1	-0.08	-0.02
2	Learning	+2	-3	-1	-0.06	-0.02
3	Innovating	+5	-1	+4	-0.02	**+0.08**
4	Social communicating	+2	-5	-3	-0.10	-0.06
5	Big Data collecting	+2	-5	-3	-0.10	-0.06
6	Social change triggering	+4	-2	+2	-0.04	**+0.04**
7	Mis-communicating	0	-5	-5	-0.10	-0.10
8	Escaping	0	-4	-4	-0.08	-0.08
9	Evolutional change triggering	+4	-3	+1	-0.06	**+0.02**
	TOTAL	+22	-32	-10	-0.64	-0.22

Source: Expert's judgment by the author.

THE RULES OF THE VIRTUALITY

In the light of the above reflections, one can define the following rules of virtuality:[1]

1. The use of virtual functions (applications) should take place depending on the real world's needs to improve its modus operandi today and in the future.
2. The knowledge and skills of applying virtual functions (applications) are higher among younger generations than among older generations; however, this does not mean that the results of the younger generation's applied virtuality will give it a lasting advantage; on the contrary, it can be disadvantageous due to the addictive manner of its application by former generations.
3. Virtual functions (applications) should enhance the real world's quality rather than act as a substitute, and supposedly better, solution.
4. There should be a positive balance with respect to spending more time in reality than in virtuality.
5. There should be a positive balance with respect to spending more time in the local community than in global one.
6. To secure a positive impact of virtuality upon reality, the former's developments and operations should be publically controlled similarly as is the case in reality.
7. Crimes and misbehaviors in virtual society should be judged by the real society with the application of the latter's laws.
8. For someone to be a conscious user of virtuality, the real society has to provide appropriate education for its members about virtuality's complex issues and technology.
9. To sustain the right use of the virtuality, the real society should provide appropriate virtuality-caused health care.
10. To secure well-being of the real world it is necessary to monitor the impact of the virtuality upon reality, at all levels of the real world.

These rules of the virtuality are at the beginning of their applications nowadays. It is now the right time to think about how to apply them in the real world today as well locally as globally.

CAN VIRTUAL CIVILIZATION LAST?

What Is the True Value of Being Virtual?

The true value of being virtual lies in the possibility that someone can enhance his other real world. This may only happen if someone is aware of the advantages and disadvantages of

---

[1] The first rules of virtuality were defined by Steve Woolgar in 2002 in his book *Virtual Society? Technology, Cyberbole, Reality*. Oxford: Oxford University Press.

virtuality. Eventually, someone must minimize the disadvantages of the virtuality and maximize its advantages. For example, if someone thinks that virtual education will make a completely educated person, they are wrong. Learning only content knowledge with minimal real social skills (F2F) which are provided only by reality is not enough to be knowledgeable, wise, or a skillful graduate of a school or college.

From Virtual to Real World

Several companies, including those which promote digitalization, like Hewett-Packard and Yahoo discourage their employees from working at home. To secure face-to-face communication and socialization, Google provides free cafeterias, laundry, haircuts, massages, swimming pools and cafés for its workers. When Steve Jobs planned Pixar's office for highly computer-intensive professionals, he originally wanted one unconventional placed bathroom for the entire building so that people would have to run into one another and accidentally exchange ideas. Furthermore, he knew that people communicate more efficiently when they have to pee (Stein 2009).

These examples perhaps illustrate the double standard which high-tech companies promote: Any form of computerization for their customers, including virtualization (like Google Virtual Library), while, for themselves, they try to protect good quality work in "real space."

The Virtuality as the Next Link in Humans' Evolution

Mankind has developed the past few million years. The latest major development occurred about 200,000 years ago with the branching off of *homo sapiens*. The term refers to a human who thinks and is wise (or rather smart). As it is defined in Table 6.1., *homo novus* first evolved into *homo tributus*, and subsequently into *homo libris* and at the end of the 20th century evolved into *homo electronicus*. At the 21st century good computer users (*homo electronicus*) will evolve into *homo hybridus* who are developing their structure of consciousness in integral 4D (4th D is virtual) where real and virtual space and real and virtual time are free. In other words *homo hybridus* can be anytime, anywhere, whether in reality, virtuality, or both. The primary sense organ is cyberspace, a collective intelligence—a meeting of minds on the Internet – that can validate the contribution of the individual (Lévy 1997). Furthermore, the individual can apply "collective intelligence" for their own benefit as well.

Nowadays, the development and use of collective intelligence is in *status nascendi*. Its broad and profound applications through centuries or millennia eventually should develop the next level of humans, perhaps *homo hybridus cognitous sapiens* (real/virtual man who is knowledgeable and wise).

Although, these considerations look very interesting and even promising, developmental regression is possible also. This could happen should social communication eliminate the traditional language vocabulary and substitute it by short codes, graphic icons and pictures.

What to Do in the Times of Virtual Civilization Development

Virtuality will not disappear as long as computers and their networks are in use. Therefore it is not wise to criticize the development of virtuality; rather, one should join the crowd learning and practicing virtuality. However, it is also recommended that we be aware of disadvantages and advantages of this new landscape.

CONCLUSION

1. A virtual life is easier than real life, but it is really no life at all (Kite 2009) since relationships between people who never see, touch, smell, or hear each other cannot be truly supportive, intimate, truthful and lasting.
2. Communication and co-ordination in the virtual world is easy, cheap, fast, and global; therefore, it is a new and lasting tool that will impact social identity, governance, community and society at large.
3. The virtual world became a new landscape of social life in the 21st century as a parallel to life lived in Real Civilization.
4. The use of virtual functions (applications) should take place depending on the real world's needs to improve its modus operandi today and in the future.
5. To secure a positive impact of virtuality upon reality, the former's developments and operations should be publically controlled similarly as is done in reality.
6. Crime and misbehavior in virtual society's should be judged by the real society with the application of the latter's laws.
7. Virtuality will not disappear as long as computers and their networks are in use.

REFERENCES

Ahmad, Z. (2010). Virtual Education System (Current Myth & Future Reality in Pakistan). Ssrn.com. Accessed 10-9-2013.

Arterton, F.Ch. (1987). Teledemocracy, can technology protect democracy? Newburry Park, CA: Sage Publications.

Cull, S., Reed, D., &Kirk, K (2010). "Student motivation and engagement in online courses". Serc.carlton.edu. Accessed 1-21- 2013.

Dennen, V. P., & Bonk, C. J. (2007). Bonk and Dennen-b.pdf " We'll leave the light on for you: Keeping learners motivated in online courses". Coursesites.com. Retrieved 9-12-2013.

Dillenbourg (2000). P. Virtual learning environments (PDF). EUN Conference 2000: Learning in the new millennium: Building new education strategies for schools. http://tecfa.unige.ch/tecfa/publicat/dil-papers-2/Dil.7.5.18.pdf, Accessed 1-24-2014.

Dalsgaard, Ch. (2006). Social software: E-learning beyond learning management systems". eurodl.org. University of Aarhus. Accessed 3-5-2013.

Elearning-companion.com. (2013). The Disadvantages of Online Learning. 12 February 2013. Accessed 9-12-2013.

Illinois University (2008). Strengths and Weakness of Online Education. Illinois University. 2 May. 2008.www.ion.uillinois.edu/resources/tutorials/overview/. Accessed 2-25-2009.

Kite, M. (2009). A virtual life is easier than real life, but it is really no life at all The Telegraph. Accessed 1-23-2014.

Lévy, P. (1997). Collective intelligence, mankind's emerging world in cyberspace. New York, London: Planum Trade.

Maddison, A. (2001). The world economy, a millennial perspective. Paris: OECD.

Noveck, B. S. (2005). A democracy of group. Journal of the Internet. 10(11).

Oinas-Kukkonen, Harri (2008). Network analysis and crowds of people as sources of new organisational knowledge. In: A. Koohang et al. (Eds): Knowledge Management: Theoretical Foundation. Informing Science Press, Santa Rosa, CA, US, pp. 173-189.

Pridogorin, I. (2013). Virtual Reality versus Real Life. Pravda.ru. http://english.pravda.ru/health/20-10-2003/3920-virtual-0/, Accessed 1-23-2014.

Rheingold, H. (2002). Smart mobs.

Stain. J. (2014). Work from home please! Time 2014-12-09. p. 62.

Surowiecki, J. (2005). The wisdom of crowds: why the many are smarter than the few and how collective wisdom shapes business, economies, societies and nations. New York: Doubleday.

Targowski, A. (2009). Information Technology and Wisdom Development. Hershey & New York: IGI Global.

Targowski, A. (2013). Sixteen related crises and the limits of civilization in the 21st century. Comparative Civilizations Review. No. 69:23-32, Fall.

Targowski, A. (2014). The deadly impact of informatics upon the holocaust. Mustang, OK: Tate Publishing.

World Economic Forum. (2013). Unlocking the Value of Personal Data: From Collection to Usage, (Geneva: The World Economic Forum, March, 2013).

Webster, U (18 May 2013). Online education offers a flexible experience. Webster.edu. Accessed 9-11- 2013.

Yirka, B. (May 3, 2013). Brain Activity Responses Different For Virtuality versus the Reality. http://phys.org/news/2013-05-brain-response-virtual-reality-real.html. Accessed 1-25-2014.

Part IV. The Future of Virtual Civilization

In: Virtual Civilization in the 21st Century
Editor: Andrew Targowski

ISBN: 978-1-63463-261-4
© 2015 Nova Science Publishers, Inc.

Chapter 8

THE FUTURE OF VIRTUAL CIVILIZATION

Andrew Targowski[*]
Western Michigan University, US
President Emeritus of the International Society
For the Comparative Study of Civilizations (2007-2013)

ABSTRACT

The *purpose* of this investigation is to define the future of the Virtualization Wave and Virtual Civilization. The *methodology* is based on an interdisciplinary big-picture view of Virtual Civilization's elements of development and their interdependency. Among the *findings* are: Virtuality triggers the Virtualization Wave as well as Virtual Civilization whose mission has been defined. *Practical implications:* The future of the Virtualization Wave and Virtual Civilization is not only to support the communications among young peers but also eventually to control the public policy of real civilization and to secure the common good in real societies. *Social implication:* The quest for the common good by the Virtual Society can successfully solve problems in real society but it can also create political chaos in real civilizations. *Originality:* This investigation, by providing an interdisciplinary and civilizational approach at the big-picture level defines several crucial repercussions of the Virtual Wave and Virtual Civilization, which are evolving during our time and which could be a golden solution to assure the well-being of humanity. Also an *a la* science fiction prediction is provided which assumes that if social networks can transform from being market-based to citizens-owned, virtual nations can be born as well as a global virtual nation.

---
[*] andrew.targowski@wmich.edu.

INTRODUCTION TO THE QUANTUM SOCIETY

The purpose of this investigation is to define the future of the Virtualization Wave and Virtual Civilization, since virtuality functions at these two realms of civilization.

The Virtualization Wave, as with all civilization waves, impacts other waves. While Virtual Civilization is the new layer of real civilization, the future of the former depends upon the future of the latter; therefore, both will be investigated in close relations to each other. This is the first time in the history of civilization that humans have developed "cyberspace," which is invisible but at the same time very active, involving peoples' attention and practice.

This reminds us of contemporary quantum computing, which computes at the level of sub-particles, where the same sub-particle can be at the same time in two different states such ones as "O" and "1."

Does this imply that today society has entered the stage of a quantum society? At the same time is it at the real state ("1") and also at the virtual state ("0")?

The Virtualization Wave's impact upon other waves will be evaluated in the scope of a mission and perhaps optimistically. It is assumed that there will be a new world elite composed of about 100 million young, educated people who skilfully communicate across borders and practice the value of unlimited freedom supported by collective intelligence.

This should lead to truthful and meaningful social solutions. However, it does not have to end with positive solutions, since populist democracy in theory is worse than the current practice of representative democracy. On the other hand, the latter is in strong crisis today, since "legally" acting lobbyists can buy any solution they wish.

Therefore, Virtual Society may at least claim that it is truthfully going for the common good.

Since virtuality also operates at the level of Virtual Civilization, its future will be evaluated within the framework of the future of real civilization.

THE ROLE OF TECHNOLOGY IN CIVILIZATION DEVELOPMENT

The role of technology in the development of a civilization is well presented in William McGaughey's book, *Electronic Civilization* (2001). His book shows how civilization has moved from print to electronic culture, and that its ideals have changed from the classic "truth, beauty, and good" to an elusive element called rhythm (the energy and control of the individual and of human society); and how self-consciousness (concentrating on ourselves), the enemy of rhythm, underlines the complexity of modern life. We who live today can feel the strong presence of technology in our *modus operandi*; hence, technology can be considered as one of the world-systems. Neil Postman (1993) even insists that we live in *technopoly*, which surrounds culture and technology. This idea is supported by the statement that "distance is dead" (Cairncross 1997), since geography, borders and time zones are becoming irrelevant to the way we conduct our business and personal lives; this is due to the info-communication revolution, which allows us to travel less to achieve the same results.

Since 2010, there have been about 300 million computers installed and 10 billion chips embedded in smart products (more than there are people on the Earth), which has led to the emergence of the Global Digital Nervous System. Lévy (1997) even perceives this trend as the birth of "collective intelligence" which will develop a new world for Mankind, based on cyberspace. This new world is being planned to work as a computing utility, where computing power could be as simple as tapping electricity from a socket. Sensor networks have already begun to track everything from weather to inventory, stirring fears of government and corporate intrusion. The broad application of mobile devices, cellular phones and wireless devices leads to an individual being able to be connected anywhere and anytime (Wi Fi).

Furthermore, marrying electronics and biology promises new devices that could transform millions of lives. Right now, most bio-artificial organs are meant as temporary solutions until the patient receives a human organ. Ultimately, scientists want to "grow" living tissue that will eliminate the need for a transplant. These new technologies will force us to change our approach toward how we define life, culture, and civilization. What is gained and what is lost by being digital is answered by the Krokers (1997) in their fascinating book under a very meaningful title *"Digital Delirium."* Grossman (1995) thinks that we are even building an Electronic Republic, where democracy is being redefined by info-communication processes.

Therefore, the role of technology cannot be ignored during the discussion on civilization. One of the first people to understood this relationship well was Lewis Mumford (1966) who, in his book *"Technics and Human Development"*, goes back to the origins of human culture and does not accept the view that man's rise was the result of his command of tools and conquest of nature. The author demonstrates how tools did not and could not develop far without a series of more significant inventions that were invovled in ritual, language, and social organization. Mumford and McLuhan (1962), both great philosophers of technology did not live to see the Info-Communication Revolution (late 1990s), and could not extend their findings about the role of electronic info-communication processes in civilization. The modern role of technology is marked in the World-System Model of Production in Figure 8.1.

Civilization has been growing gradually along with the cultural and industrial development of Man as *homo sapiens* for the last 200,000 years. About 40,000-50,000 years ago, humans underwent a very important genetic mutation, when the DRD4 gene was developed that encodes the dopamine neurotransmitter. It is this neurotransmitter which is responsible for human personality traits (Ding et al.). In such a way, humans became more intellectually alert, and as a result developed increasing capacities for leadership and socializing. Fortunately, the climate changes that occurred around 40,000-30,000 BC helped humans create their more developed societies, allowing them to migrate across continents and form the beginnings of infrastructure. About 10,000 BC people became farmers, animal breeders, and pottery makers. When the Ice Age ended in 9,000 BC, the warmer climate was friendlier for humans and their civilizing processes. In years between 8,000–6,000 BC, sheep, pigs, cattle and other livestock were domesticated and more people were settling in the

Euphrates and Tigris river valley, called Mesopotamia (contemporary Iraq). About 7,500 BC villages were growing in nearby Anatolia (contemporary Turkey).

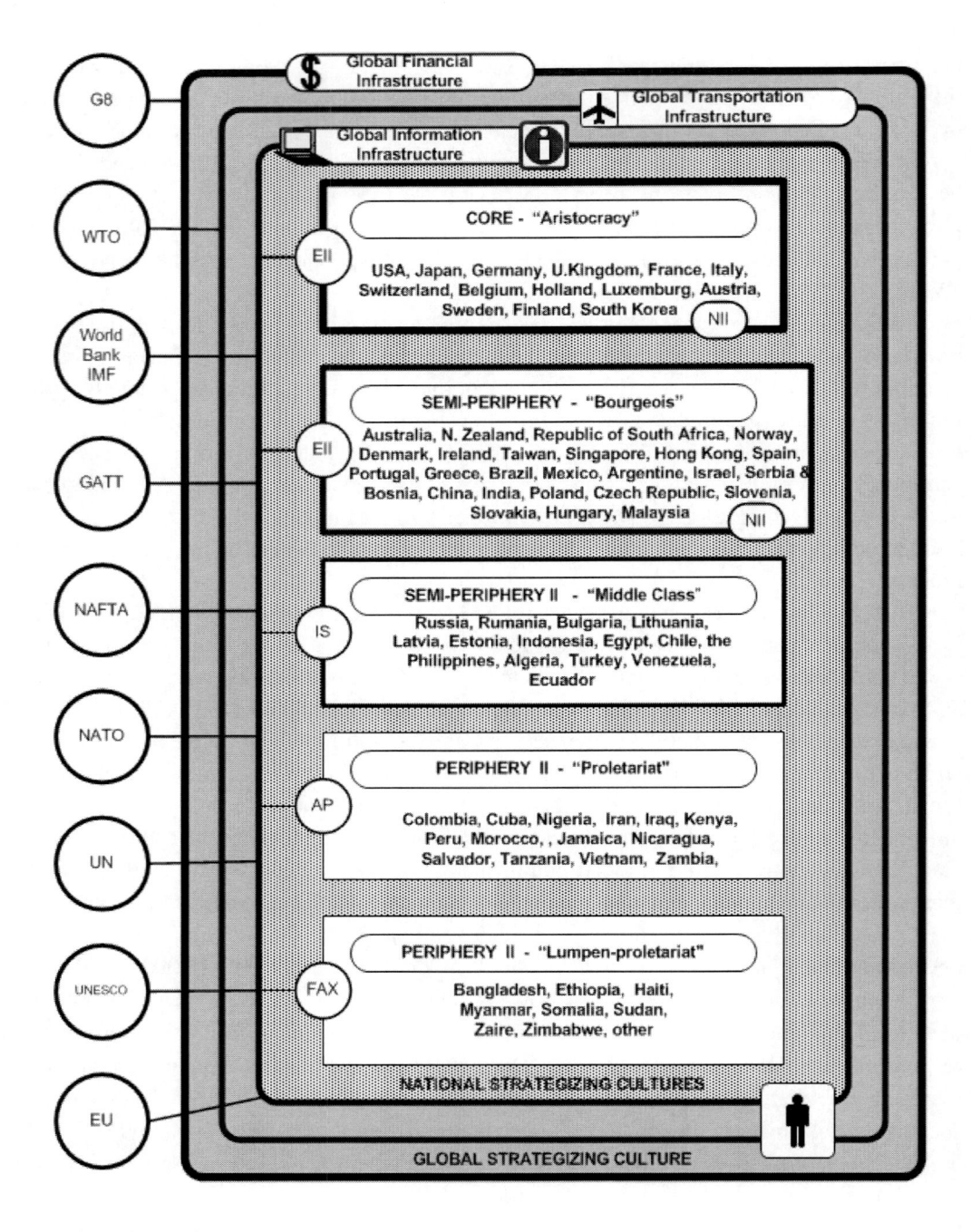

Figure 8.1. The World-System of Production (21st Century) (EII-Enterprise Information Infrastructure, NII-National Information Infrastructure, IS-Information Systems, AP- Computer Applications).

Growing populations required more food and more productive farms, which led to the development of irrigation systems (which was the first advanced technology) and work specialization. Work specialization and other kinds of non-farming tasks led in 5,000 BC to the rise of elites, who were living in towns and worshiped in temples. Eventually around 4,000 BC, city-states were formed in the Mesopotamian Valley; one of those was Uruk, with several thousand inhabitants who knew crafts, architecture and writing. These city-states were united under power holding dynasties and led to the creation of the Mesopotamia Civilization, the first historic civilization. According to Toynbee (1995) there were about 26 different civilizations, which nowadays form eight civilizations; Chinese, Japanese, Western, Eastern, Islamic, Buddhists, Hindu, and African. All these civilizations interact within the emerging Global Civilization.

According to Toynbee (1934-1961) civilization is a "tool" used by societies in response to the challenges they faced. The first civilizations coped with the challenges created by the nature (for example by heat, cold, famine or floods), and later, those created by culture (for example by the power game, social mobility and so forth). In the 21st century, after the impressive contributions of the Industrial, Scientific, and Technological Revolutions (19 and 20th centuries), societies are facing the challenges of technical infrastructure such as mega-metropolises, climate change caused by life styles resulting rom industrialization, global information infrastructure [Internet and private GAN(s)—Global Area Networks], global passenger/cargo transportation networks, and so forth.

Since Global Civilization in the 21st century is driven by super-consumerism and business, the main "tool" in marketing and production for the masses is technology. Technology is able to increase productivity and at the same time reduce costs. Therefore information technology and its byproduct, virtuality, is a technology which will apply all means to market and sell more. To prove this statement, one can bring in an example of so called social networks which are being developed by entrepreneurs to sell virtual real estate for the purpose of better marketing their business in reality.

WHY VIRTUALITY IS A WAVE AND CIVILIZATION AT THE SAME TIME?

Usually technology is a neutral tool which acts as its user wants it to. For example a rifle in good hands can be useful but in bad hands can commit a crime. The same is true with virtuality, as a tool in online shopping can help a consumer in fixing a commercial transaction. It is in this way that it functions as the Virtualization Wave. It can also enhance the operations of other civilization waves.

However, virtuality is also able to create its own society based on common values (as a religion) and operate as the next layer of the real civilization. This is done and can be done for many different purposes. For example, to enjoy independence, one can live in cyberspace based on new relations (so called social networks) or old ones to reach some common good (as some online communities), at least at a level of conceptualization and awareness.

Also, this can be done in order to agree on the common good in virtuality and later implement it in reality.

Therefore, as the Virtualization Wave, it will run as long as computer technology is used in civilization. As Virtual Civilization, it can function as long as people see it as useful in reaching their goals. But, should Virtual Civilization be regulated in order to avoid eventual societal chaos, it could be replaced by a new civilization which will become available in the future.

THE PAST AND FUTURES OF TECHNOLOGY-DRIVEN WAVES AS IMPLEMENTED

The Three Wave-like models of World Civilization offered by Toffler (1980) is here extended to the Multiple Wave-like Model, and the role of the Virtualization Wave in this model is suggested as follows:

- *Pre-wave's Settlers "Wave" (-9,000- -7,000):* This wave is still active, since people like to immigrate in search of a better life to places around the world. The Virtualization Wave can help in advising internauts where such good places may be found.
- *First Wave - Agriculture (5000 B.C. - 2000+):* We are in strife, and we must gather food in order to survive. Today, the Agriculture Wave in developed nations has reached enormous levels of productivity, where 1-2 percent of the labor force can produce food for the rest of a given population and beyond. This is mostly done by global corporations which sometimes have farms of 50,000 to 100,000 pigs or cows destroying the environment and putting small farmers out of business and work. Furthermore, this big business is able to get subsidies form the government, largely due to lobbying. To solve this problem of over productivity and environment devastation, the Virtualization Wave should force real society to return to a natural scale of healthy agriculture.
- *Second Wave - Industrialization (1880 - 2000+):* We are divided and must compete in order to rise to affluence. This wave dramatically modernized civilization in the last 160 years. In fact Western Civilization and to certain degree Japanese Civilization are so saturated in manufacturing goods and technological infrastructures that they outsource production and even research and development to developing nations. This strategy brings huge profits for global big business (thus far but not forever) but at the cost of the middle class in the source countries, which is disappearing and destabilizing the social equilibrium. This situation won't be allowed to exist for ever by the disconnected former middle class. Virtual Society may eventually organize a social revolution and regulate global economy.
- *Third Wave - Information (1980- 2000+):* We are in touch we must cooperate in order to match global competition. This wave has improved performance of the

Agricultural and Industrial Waves by introducing the application of enterprise-wide management information systems and automation and robotization of operational processes in almost every aspect of the economy and society. However, information technology is steadily inventing new applications which in general lead to a labor-free economy and unprecedented unemployment. Business and IT professionals have pushed this stage of economy for the sake of saving costs, but who will be able to afford to buy those "cheaply" made products and services? Who will pay taxes to support the common good of real society? The Virtualization Wave eventually may impact -real society to the extent of regulating the development of technology for the good of people and not to promote so called "progress."

- *Fourth Communication People Wave (2000+):* We are aware that instant e-communication optimizes our well-being. This wave promised that the Internet will create a "New Economy" and it did it. E-commerce is flourishing world-wide and has made shopping easy with a large scope of possible choices since it can be done globally. The Internet also promised to create a world family; however, and it has not yet done so. It has developed smaller communities with numerous e-relations, but they are shallow emotionally and socially, very often misleading and wrong. Cyberspace became a new medium of 24/7, nonstop entertainment/news environment addicting millions of mostly young people. Also the Internet has steadily eliminated local newspapers, transforming citizens from well-informed to poorly informed, since not every citizen has fun using electronic devises for access. Even worse, the e-commerce power houses like Amazon.com want to replace printed books by e-books which can be read on Amazon's e-readers. It is the war against human culture of writing and reading books, developed so successfully in the last 500 years. Paper can be replaced by e-paper, but the book as a cultural artifact cannot be replaced by an e-book, just as sex cannot be replaced by e-sex. Virtual Society is the product of the Virtualization Wave, and it is difficult to imagine that it can self-regulate. If this is true, this wave may destroy human culture as we have come to know it in the last 500 years, which dramatically modernized civilization, while in the previous 5,500 years of civilization, progress was steady but very slow and unrecognized during one's short life.

- *Fifth Bio-Nano Technology Wave (2000+):* We want to improve our health and the quality of life through a better understanding of the nature's frontiers. Examples of such solutions are cloning or smart drugs (bio-robots) that address human knowledge at the molecular level (Targowski and Zacher 2000). This wave may play the same role as the book played 500 years ago. It can decisively improve human health and extend the lifespan of humans. The Virtualization Wave may develop awareness of possible bad experiments which can threaten human beings. We eventually may have to stop the ability of the computer to think faster than people, appying Asimov's Law I—"do not make robots which can kill humans."

- *Sixth Globalization Wave* (1990+): We are connecting and globalizing not to be left "alone" in the world. The Internet triggered globalization and promised to narrow of the wealth gap and spread democracy. This did not happened. Businesses that are well computerized make high profits which are intercepted from stockholders by the executive class, since supposedly the executives are so good in making this profit. In fact this is done mostly by outsourcing and the Internet, which makes "distance dead." Fortune 500 CEOs make about $3,000-20,000 per hour, including stock options and other benefits. The top 25 CEOs of some hedge funds make about $1 billion per year, mostly due to the "magic" of information technology. Social media triggered the Arab Spring in 2012-2013 taking down some dictators; however, they were not able to set a democratic alternative. Even in the U.S. where democracy has more than 200 years of relatively good practice and where there is a special emphasis on freedom and privacy of individuals, the Internet has fallen into the hands of federal agencies such as the NSA, FBI, and CIA which can now control every telephone and perhaps e-mail made by a citizen, albeit supposedly to protect against terrorism. The average American citizen has surrendered their privacy to electronic magnates owning Google, Facebook, Twitter, LinkedIn and others. The Virtualization Wave if committed enough should reverse this trend of making real citizens into e-slaves.

- *Seventh Virtualization Wave* (2000+): We are increasing and sharing common knowledge to solve problems and enjoy being in communication with the rest of the world. The Virtualization Wave can easily create social chaos by civil disobedience to please the ego. It can laso create local, national, and global-wide discussion and awareness regarding how to sustain human civilization in centuries and millennia to come. Can the Virtualization Wave do this? Perhaps through creating virtual nations, the virtual global nation, and the virtual universal global nation, it will be eventually possible to develop a sort of utopia built upon the real wise civilization.
- *Eighth Communicating Things Wave* (2010+): The silent word of things is awakened just as silent movies have transformed into sound-oriented movies. The Virtuality Wave should care for surveillance-less functioning connecting things.

The wave approach towards World Civilization development must take into account the different levels of development in various countries. The leaders of this type development mostly come from Western Civilization and Japanese Civilization; however, Singapore from the Chinese Civilization is an exception to the rule. The leaders and average users of the civilization waves create civilization centers that cooperate through fast diffusion of solutions. The remaining countries form the civilization peripheries, which either slowly adapt the centers' solutions or reject them, since they do not adequately address the system of values in those countries. The latter is the case of the policy "to modernize but not Westernize" a country. A good example of this policy can be seen in Malaysia and Iran. A case of the centers' rejection is the policy of the Taliban in Afghanistan.

Of course, the Wave Model is a rather limited model which mostly emphasizes one civilizational component -- the technology-driven infrastructure. On the other hand, this model provides a good intuitive understanding of possible human development in the future (Figure 8.2).

THE FUTURES OF WORLD CIVILIZATION BEYOND 21ST CENTURY

Virtual Civilization is much more than the Virtualization Wave. It is socially active technology supporting a new human way of living. Of course it is strongly associated with the real civilization. Therefore in order to predict its future possible developments one must first perceive the future developments of real civilization.

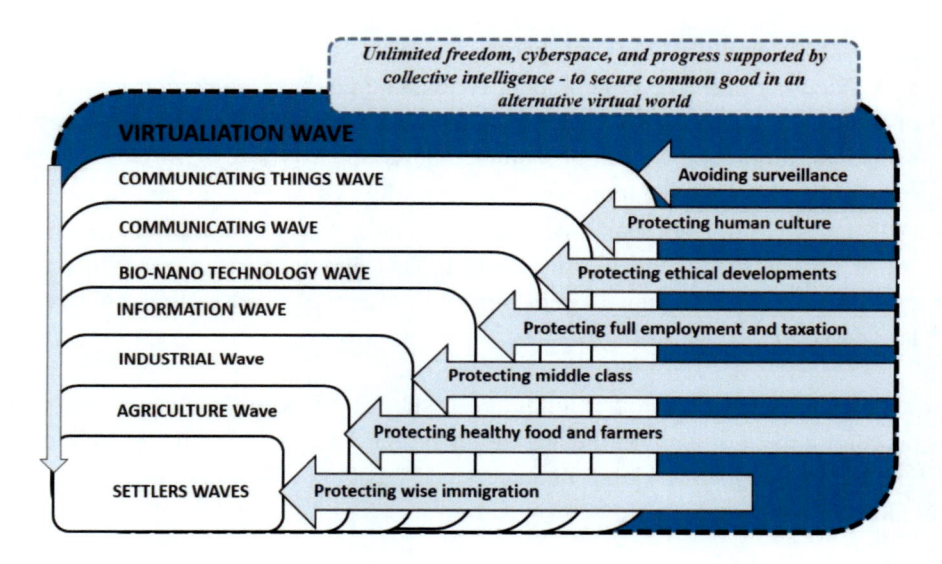

Figure 8.2. The Possible Relationships at the Level of Missions Among the Virtuality Wave and other Civilization Waves (The Optimistic Options).

The following future developments of world civilization as seen at the dawn of the 21st century are as follows:

- Future 1 – Global Civilization will develop as long as business directs politics but will collapse when the super-consumerism of the steady growing world population depletes most of the strategic resources such as energy and water. It will begin failing visibly when the population reaches 9-10 billions in about 2050. Wars for resources will take place among formerly friendly nations.
- Future 2 – Social Revolution will take place in the U.S. and Western Europe to stop the growing inequality in the Western society. This may lead to the formation of fortress nations protecting the well-being of their citizens. This revolution may take place about 2025-2030 or sooner. The role of information in sustaining political power was tested during the Polish Revolution (1980-1989) when the volume of underground press exceeded the volume of official press – the people were so well informed that the Solidarity Movement defeated the totalitarian regime. Today, in China about 100,000 computer specialists control communication within society to

protect the political status quo. For the same reason other countries with non-democratic systems do the same. But in democracy this control is impossible or at least limited, hence communication within the Virtual Society has great potential for success. Also, cyberspace is a substitute for the shop-floor level of factories, where workers could be motivated against their "oppressors." But in Western Civilization most factories have been relocated abroad, hence traditional workers have been dispersed and mostly unemployed with some difficulty to meet face-to-face. Cyberspace eliminates this inconvenience.

- Future 3 – Global Civilization is regulated in order to support international trade and information, and the flow of people helps to sustain the economic vitality of globalized nations. The commitment to regulate Global Civilization may take place after it is too late to save its best values; perhaps this will be tried as the result of a social revolution likely to occur around 2025-2030.
- Future 4 – Wise Civilization which is controlled by sustaining civilization policies such as: securing the economic vitality of citizens, environmental accountability, social responsibility, and climate control. This may take place either after a social revolution in the U.S. and Western Europe or after the collapse of Global Civilization around 2050.

In civilization practice all four futures are a subject of people's awareness today, but there is no commitment among politicians to pursue the Futures 2, 3, and 4. As it currently stands, Future 1 is the goal of global financiers and business which control governments of the main globalizing nations.

THE FUTURES OF VIRTUAL CIVILIZATION BEYOND THE 21ST CENTURY

The four futures of civilization, whether one is either pessimistic or optimistic that they will happen, require the interaction between the reality and virtuality since the former is unable to solve civilization problems. Perhaps, the virtual society will be more educated, aware, wise and altruistic and can eventually solve these problems. Figure 8.3 illustrates the roles of the virtual society in fixing civilization's modus operandi.

If Future 1 prevails then the Virtual Society increasing develop world-wide awareness about Global Civilization's super-consumerism and business-driven "productivity" in depleting strategic resources such as energy and water.

If Future 2 takes place then the Virtual Society will organize social revolution in reality (e.g. the 1% Occupy Wall Street) though common virtual intelligence and communications.

If Future 3 takes place then the Virtual Society will push for the regulation of Global Civilization in reality.

If the Future 4 takes place, it will be the result of the Virtual Civilization's collection and dissemination of the ideals of Wise Civilization in reality.

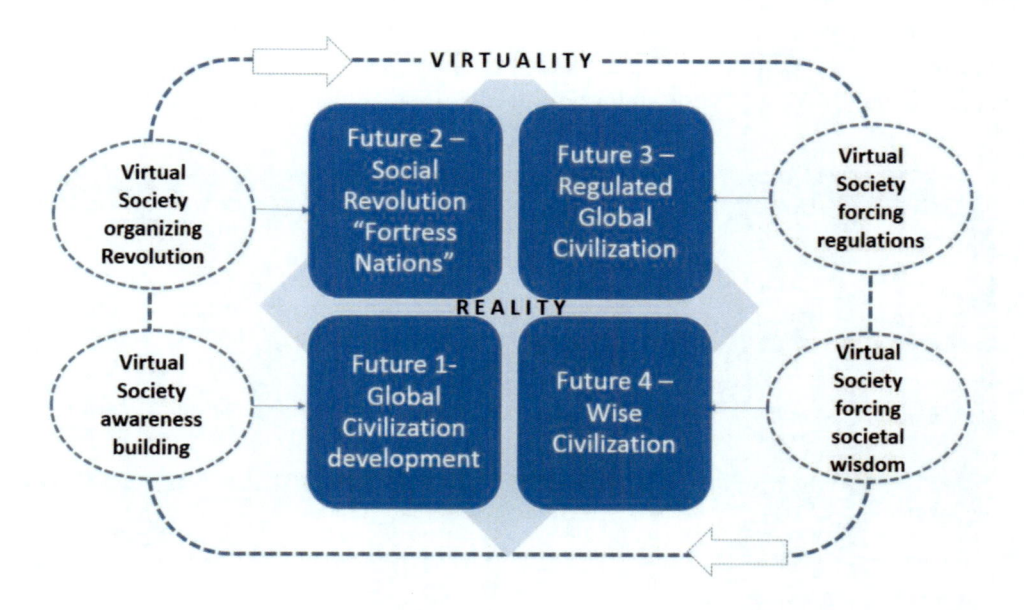

Figure 8.3. The Role of the Virtual Society in Fixing Civilization Problems.

THE SCIENCE FICTION FUTURE OF THE VIRTUALITY

The predictions of technological developments *a la* science fiction in the 20th and 21st centuries in general have been accomplished in our practice already. The race of technological progress looks as though it does not have any limits and concerns virtuality. In the 1950^s computers could be virtual, meaning a real computer could simulate a virtual one which is able to compute.

This practice is applied more often today. Later in the development of virtuality, two or more teams located in different geographical locations could electronically perceive a common object, for example a machine part and discuss its design. Nowadays, online communities with memberships in thousands have created the virtual society, but social networks with memberships in millions and even a billion plus may create a virtual nation with different boarders than the real one; a global virtual nation could even potentially be developed at the end.

This all looks like a science fiction prediction but once the political class world-wide loses touch with the reality of citizens, such social networks can evolve into virtual nations and even a global virtual nation. There is only one condition by which the marketing-oriented social networks should evolve into citizens-owned networks: in order to secure independence of thinking and acting. Is it possible that something in the virtual landscape can be organized at such a large scale and last if it is not for profit?

Figure 8.4 depicts the science fiction prediction of the future architecture of cyberspace and realspace in the context of contemporary civilizations such ones as African, Chinese, Japanese, Hindu, Buddhist, Western, Eastern, Islamic, and Global (Targowski 2014).

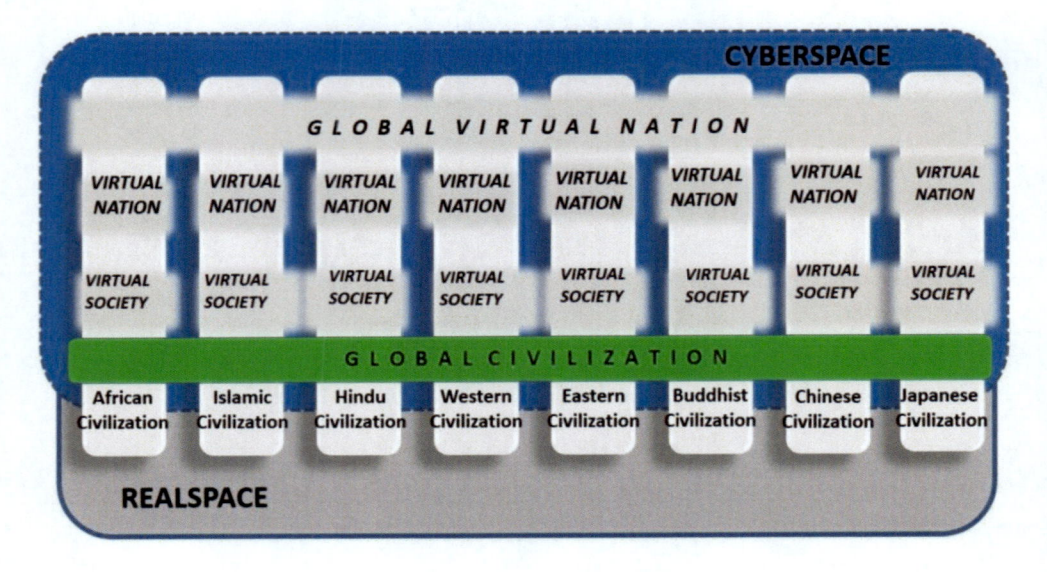

Figure 8.4. The Science Fiction Future of Virtuality Development in the Context of Contemporary Civilizations.

CONCLUSION

1. The new developments of information technology at the end of the 20th century led to the development of globalization and cyberspace as a new virtual landscape of real civilization.
2. The Globalization Wave and Global Civilization following it are strong supporters of the Virtualization Wave and Virtual Civilization following it. Due to virtuality, people can cross borders without passports and expensive travelling tickets. Because there are no borders, distance is dead in this new landscape.
3. Virtuality triggers the Virtualization Wave as the enhancement of other civilization waves, such as: Agricultural, Industrial, Information, Communication People, Bio-nano Technology, Communicating Things, and Globalization.
4. Besides the Virtualization Wave, the Virtual Society creates Virtual Civilization as a new layer of real civilization in order to function for the common good in solving civilization problems or/and enjoy world-wide relations among people for the purpose of friendship, business, scientific collaboration or/and enjoyment, and so forth.
5. Virtuality will be the future as long as computer technology is in use by humans.

6. The Virtual Society may play a decisive role in pushing politicians into the successful implementation of the futures of civilization, eventually leading to regulated globalization and wise civilization.
7. The Virtualization Wave and Virtual Civilization provide some optimistic hope for humanity in solving its sustainability-oriented problems; however, we should guard against being too optimistic as usually we tend to think unwisely that technology can solve our social problems.

REFERENCES

Braudel, F. (1993). *A history of civilizations*. New York: Penguin Books.
Braudel, F. (1992). *The wheels of commerce*. Berkley: University of California Press.
Cairnocross. (1997). *The Death of distance*. Boston: Harvard Business School Press.
Grossman (1995). *Electronic republic*. New York: Viking Penguin.
Kroker, A. and M. Kroker. (1997). *Digital delirium*. New York: St. Martin Press.
Lévy, P. (1997). *Collective Intelligence*. New York: Plenum Press.
McGaughey. W. (2001). *Rhythm and self-consciousness: new ideal for an electronic civilization*. Minneapolis: Thistlerose Publications.
McLuhan. M. (1962). *The Gutenberg galaxy*. Toronto: University of Toronto Press.
Mumford. L. (1966). *Technics and human development*. San Diego: Harcourt Brace Jovanovich
Postman. N. (1993). *Technopoly: the surrender of culture to technology*. New York: Vintage Books.
Targowski, A. and L. Zacher. (2000). The models were developed during a seminar at the Western Michigan University in March.
Targowski, A. (2009). *Information technology and societal development*. Hershey, PA & New York: IGI Publishing.
Targowski, A. (2014). *Global civilization in the 21st century*. New York: NOVA Science Publishers.
Toffler, A. (1980). *The third wave*. New York: Morrow.
Toynbee, A. (1934-1961). *A Study of history,* 12 vols. Oxford: Oxford University Press.

In: Virtual Civilization in the 21st Century
Editor: Andrew Targowski

ISBN: 978-1-63463-261-4
© 2015 Nova Science Publishers, Inc.

AFTERWORD

Andrew Targowski[*]
Western Michigan University, US
President Emeritus of the International Society
For the Comparative Study of Civilizations (2007-2013)

Virtual Civilization has transformed from the Virtual Wave into Virtual Civilization due to the advancements in info-communication technology in the 21st century, exemplified by the ability of the Internet to secure operations of virtual organizations and social networks. Therefore one can characterize the Virtual Civilization as the infrastructural character. The mission of Virtual Civilization is to control public policy of other real civilizations to secure common good in these real societies. At least such a mission has been exemplified in the practice of some virtual communities at the dawn of the 21st century.

Since at the same time in a society there is a realspace and cyberspace the society becomes a quantum society for the first time in the 6,000 years history of civilization.

Today it is still too soon to judge the impact of the Virtual Civilization upon the real ones. However, despite the positive aspects of it, like the quest for the common good, one can notice the crisis of the young generation, exemplified by a shortened attention span and the desire for constant (electronic in fact) fun comprised of long-hours of playing computer games and communicating about nothing. For example students (18-24 years old) learn less, since on average they send/answer about 100 text messages every day (Smith 2011).

It is about 5 times more than a faculty is reading/answering e-messages every day. Some eager students send twice as much messages per day (200). Hence, the Detox Digital Day was established for the first time on March 7, 2014 (Figure A.2).

The quest for the common good by virtual society may limit or even replace representative democracy by direct democracy which eventually will solve positively a few good policies, and may trigger permanent political chaos in real civilizations.

---

[*] andrew.targowski@wmich.edu.

Figure A.1. The future of walking/driving and texting 24/7, as it is the reality in the 21st century? (Photo: www.sb.cc.stonybrook.edu and www.bgwlaw.com).

The impressing many, e-communication among people from different parts of the world diminishes local interrelations and intensifies connectivity among international and/or distant, parochial cultures, which eventually separates, isolates and alienates individuals in their real living places.

At this time it is very improbable that virtual society can be regulated by real society. It means that Virtual Civilization on the one hand can be positive and on the another hand can be harmful for humanity which lives in falling civilization due to overpopulation, super-consumerism, depletion of strategic resources and environmental degradation.

Since each civilization is characterized by a religion, a religion of virtuality is one which "preaches" the value of unlimited freedom, cyberspace, and progress supported by collective intelligence - to secure common good in an alternative virtual world, since the "real" one has been going in the wrong direction during the 21st century.

Figure A.2. Digital detox retreat and analog zone. (Photo: www.likeedited.com and www.geeksugar.com).

The power of the virtuality religion is generated by *collective intelligence* which has infinite ability - since "the cyberspace is the limit" - to develop and share among virtuality members that have a strong capacity for solving problems, based on word-wide retrievable knowledge and wisdom, kept in digital format (Figure A.3).

Source: IBM Institute for Business Value.

Figure A.3. The Architecture of collective intelligence.

The liturgy of the virtuality religion applies no face-to-face communication, virtual meetings, or smart phones as the must. Virtuality religion is strongly supported by stock holders of social networks which in fact are rather of marketing than social character.

Virtuality religion is widely practiced by about 1.5 billion users in 2014, who feel that it strengthens their individual power in terms of opinion and impact upon the real world. The virtuality religion has some values such as unlimited freedom being in disagreement with the reality religion which accepts a notion that civilization limits freedom for the common good, since the nature of our planet is the limit. It will be seen whether this disagreement will lead the clash of those religions and what will be repercussions for both of them. In a broad and future sense, virtuality religion in its present formulation should be constantly enhanced and corrected to not serve only virtuality users but the real world inhabitants too.

As far as virtuality versus reality is concerned one can state that a virtual life is easier than real life, but it is really no life at all (Kite 2009). Since relationships between people who never see, touch, smell, or hear each other cannot be truly supportive, intimate, truthful and lasting. Communication and co-ordination in the virtual world is however easy, cheap, fast, and global, therefore it is a new and lasting tool to impact social identity, governance, community and the society at large. The virtual world became in the 21st century a new landscape of social life in Virtual Civilization as the parallel one to Real Civilization. The use of virtual functions (applications) should take place depending on the real world's needs to improve its modus operandi today and in the future. To secure a positive impact of the virtuality upon reality, the former's developments and operations should be publically controlled similarly as it is done in the reality. The virtual society's crime and misbehavior should be judged by the real society with the application of the latter's laws. The virtuality won't disappear as long as computers and their networks will be in use.

Figure A.4. Are they real or virtual members of the society? (Photo: www.dpadmagazin.com).

One of the consequence of the virtuality is virtual divide as one of civilization divides. Virtual divide should be combined with digital divide which both have the following impact upon people:

a. Improve reasoning of the Information Elite because they make a broad scope of information for problem solving and decision making instantly available.
b. Worsens the reasoning of Average Citizens because they do not have good knowledge/skills of handling information as the Information Elite does. They become "Datamaniacs" whose reasoning sometimes is good sometimes is bad.

The Digital and Virtual Divides of civilization lead to the dichotomy of society into developed and undeveloped citizens. To minimize this process one must develop Techno-psychology and Techno-philosophy and Regulations how to apply the society friendly ICT (Information-Communication Technology). Whether the society is able to regulate the technological change is another question. This author is rather pessimistic.

The Virtual Divide is the most socially dangerous out of all divides of civilization. It should remind us, that it is unacceptable and a situation created by it can be either strong civic unrest or even social revolution in developed nations. If the financial elite won't look better for the common good, the virtual activists may replace representative democracy with direct democracy which is able to create social chaos.

The Virtual Divide is very strong between the financial elite members and disconnected poor non-members as well as with virtual activists; it is almost impossible to minimize the gap between them today. Even now this gap is widening as the former is increasing rapidly its income and the latter is increasing its grasp of the virtual groups' communication ability for defining common goals.

Figure A.5. Will digital and virtual divide trigger class warfare? (Photo: www.dmcordell.blogspot.com and www.doomsteaddiner.net).

The new developments of information technology at the end of the 20th century led to the development of globalization and cyberspace as new virtual landscapes of real civilization. The Globalization Wave and following it Global Civilization are strong supporters of the

Virtualization Wave and following it Virtual Civilization and vice versa. Due to virtuality, people cross borders without passports and expensive travelling tickets. Because there are no borders and distance is dead in this new landscape.

Virtuality triggers the Virtualization Wave as the enhancement of yet another civilization wave, such waves include; Agricultural, Industrial, Information, Communication People, Bio-nano Technology, Communicating Things, and Globalization. Besides the Virtualization Wave, Virtual Society creates Virtual Civilization as a new layer of real civilization to function for the common good in solving civilization problems and/or enjoy world-wide relations among people for the purpose of friendship, business, scientific collaboration and/or enjoyment, and so forth. The Virtualization Wave and Virtual Society function simultaneously impacting in their ways the remaining civilization waves and real society as well.

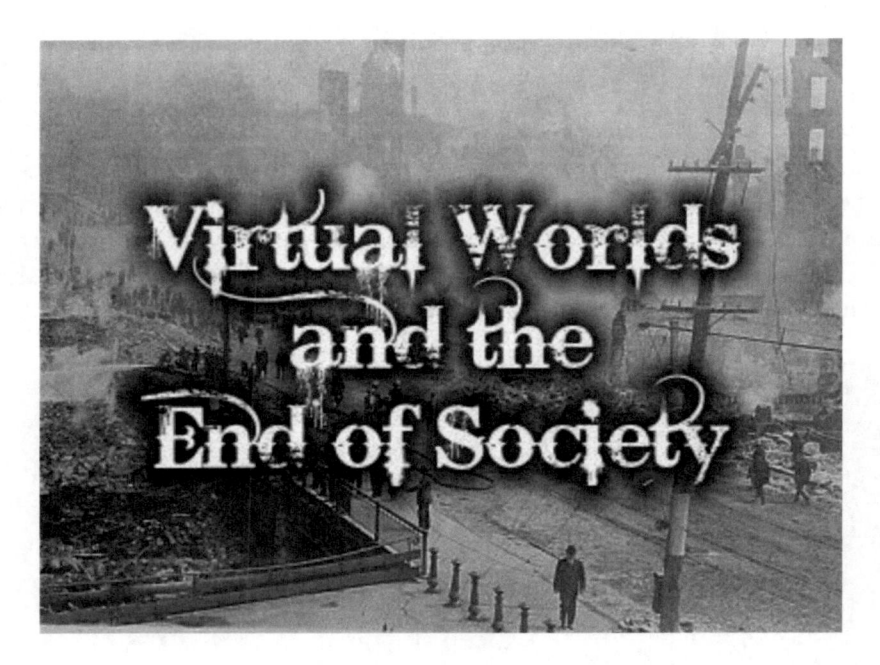

Figure A.6. Will the virtuality technology end real society as we have known it during the last 6,000 years of real civilization? (Photo: www.virtualwayfarer.com).

Virtuality has the future as long as computer technology remains in use by humans. Virtual Society may play a decisive role in pushing real politicians into successful implementation of the futures of civilization, eventually leading to regulated globalization and wise civilization.

The Virtualization Wave and Virtuality Civilization provide some optimistic hope for humanity in solving its sustainability-oriented problems but it can be too optimistic a statement as usually we used to think unwisely about technology being able to solve our social problems.

REFERENCES

Kite, M. (2009). A virtual life is easier than real life, but it is really no life at all. *The Telegraph*. Accessed 1-23-2014.

Smith, A. (2011). *Americans and text messaging*. Pew Research Center. http://pewinternet.org/Reports/2011/Cell-Phone-Texting-2011.aspx

EDITOR CONTACT INFORMATION

Dr. Andrew Targowski, Professor
Western Michigan University
5485 Saddle Club Dr
Kalamazoo, MI 49009
Tel: 269-375-6860
E-mail: Andrew.targowski@wmich.edu

INDEX

#

20th century, 5, 13, 50, 88, 97, 123, 133, 136, 139, 140, 150, 166, 173
21st century, vii, x, 4, 13, 21, 23, 24, 45, 49, 53, 75, 78, 82, 85, 86, 88, 94, 97, 99, 122, 124, 125, 127, 134, 139, 140, 146, 150, 151, 152, 159, 163, 167, 169, 170, 172
3D images, 112

A

access, vii, 14, 29, 50, 56, 58, 66, 82, 84, 85, 86, 88, 89, 97, 115, 124, 128, 131, 132, 142, 161
accountability, 164
acquisition of knowledge, 64
ACTA, 144
AD, 4, 126
adaptation, 64, 90
administrators, 130, 132
adolescents, 38, 40
adults, 76, 77
advancement, 20, 96, 98
advancements, 24, 97, 169
advertisements, 62, 88
affluence, 160
Afghanistan, 162
Africa, 4, 76, 122
age, 7, 36, 47, 53, 54, 124, 130, 132
agencies, 18, 162
aggregation, 130
agriculture, 160
Air Force, 108, 111, 114, 120, 146
alcoholism, 135

algorithm, 141
Amazon, vii, 50, 51, 83, 85, 138, 161
American Revolution, 123
American society, 47, 48, 139
American Way of Life, 51
ancestors, 100, 122
anthropology, 75
appetite, 30, 137
appointments, 35
Arab Spring, 162
arithmetic, 113
arrest, 139
Asia, 80, 122, 124, 138
Asian-Pacific region, 76
assault, 88, 142
assertiveness, 57
assessment, 93, 94, 121, 146
assets, 77
AT&T, 10
Atlantic Ocean, 123
attitudes, 58, 61, 99
augmented reality (AR), viii
authenticity, 63
authority(s), 46, 51
automation, 9, 15, 16, 87, 124, 161
autonomy, 77
avoidance, 57, 116
awareness, 21, 32, 37, 66, 92, 95, 96, 115, 134, 159, 161, 162, 164

B

background information, 113
baggage, 69
bandwidth, 92

Bangladesh, 18
banks, 48
barriers, 143
barriers to entry, 143
base, 108
basic needs, 51
beams, 116
beer, 8, 95
behaviors, 39, 56, 57, 65, 68, 70, 135
being informed, 48
beliefs, 4, 29, 46, 56
benefits, 67, 77, 132, 162
Berlin, 5, 145
Big Brother, 20, 137, 138
Big Business, 50
Big Data, 95, 136, 137, 138, 139, 146, 148
Big Digital Business, 51
Bing, 84, 137
bison, 106
Biz Stone, 50
blogger, 92
blogs, 92, 131, 143
blue screen, 113
Bluetooth, 56, 116
Bolshevik Revolution, 10
bonds, 93
bonuses, 78, 79, 80
boredom, 132
brain, 8, 13, 20, 47, 89, 122, 124, 133, 134, 152
brain size, 124
brain-storm, 133
branching, 150
Brazil, 18, 70
Britain, 18
browser, 65
Buddhist, x, 5, 46, 166
building blocks, 133
business model, 62
businesses, 48, 50, 56, 88, 92, 137, 139
buttons, 134
buyer(s), 137, 138

C

CAM, 33, 34
candidates, 20, 80
capitalism, 79, 78, 79, 80, 101, 127, 137
cascades, 97
cash, 10, 17
catalyst, 64

categorization, 82
cattle, 157
CAVE, 112
CB Simulator, 29
cell phone(s), 115, 128, 130, 134
censorship, 140, 145
Central Asia, 122
Central Europe, 80
challenges, 4, 5, 36, 118, 159
chaos, 3, 24, 73, 99, 130, 140, 142, 145, 146, 155, 160, 162, 169, 173
chat rooms, 83
chatrooms, 134
Chicago, 89
childhood, 100
children, 38, 40, 74, 128, 130, 135
China, 9, 13, 18, 20, 51, 76, 120, 137, 140, 145, 163
chopping, 135
Christian(s), 46, 122, 123
Christianity, 46, 122
Christmas, 46
CIA, 162
circulation, 9
circumcision, 74
citizens, 21, 23, 30, 36, 49, 67, 79, 80, 139, 143, 145, 146, 161, 162
City(s), 4, 8, 47, 130
civic engagement, 86, 101
Civil Rights Movement, 75
Civilization Death Triangle, 127
civilization progress, 75
civilization sustainability, xi
clarity, 4
Clash of Civilizations, 75
class warfare, 173
classes, 13, 131, 132
classification, 25
classroom, 51
clients, 13, 137, 139
climate, 157, 159, 164
climate change, 157, 159
Clinton administration, 47, 82
cloning, 161
clusters, 37
CMC, 28
CNN, 119
codes, 143
coercion, 74
cognition, 8, 64, 90, 93, 94, 96
cognitive map, 133

Index

cognitive theory, 69
Cold War, 75, 124
collaboration, 35, 39, 166, 174
collective intelligence, 21, 23, 45, 49, 53, 78, 82, 86, 150, 156, 157, 170, 171
collectivism, 57
colleges, 14, 35, 51
combined effect, 61
commerce, 39, 70, 83, 161, 167
commercial, vii, 17, 29, 35, 37, 74, 105, 112, 114, 159
commercials, 80, 145
Commission for Virtuality Faith Standards, 51
common sense, 82, 97
communication ability, 99, 173
communication technologies, 66, 70, 91
Communications Decency Act, 145
Communism, 46, 75, 79, 124, 127
community(s), 9, 14, 21, 25, 29, 31, 35, 39, 41, 51, 54, 77, 82, 83, 84, 85, 98, 100, 125, 129, 130, 131, 143, 144, 146, 151, 159, 161, 165, 172
compassion, 76
competition, 75
competitiveness, 67, 92
competitors, 93
complexity, 39, 68, 156
complications, 84
composition, 134
composting, 115
computation, 118
computer, ix, 9, 10, 13, 14, 17, 20, 21, 24, 28, 38, 39, 49, 51, 54, 61, 62, 68, 70, 82, 88, 89, 97, 105, 106, 107, 108, 109, 110, 111, 112, 113, 114, 115, 116, 117, 120, 123, 124, 125, 129, 136, 140, 141, 148, 150, 160, 161, 163, 165, 166, 169, 174
Computer, 10, 21, 29, 70, 87, 111, 118, 119, 120, 126, 140, 158
Computer networks, 21
computer self-efficacy, 62
computer systems, 82
computer technology, 160, 166, 174
computer use, 14, 150
computerization, 150
computing, 13, 83, 113, 123, 157
concept, 93
conceptualization, 159
conference, 47, 48, 133, 140, 143
configuration, 56
conflict, 75, 82, 86, 99
conformity, 59

confrontation, 99, 123
congress, 9, 46, 51, 53, 77, 80, 144
Congressional Budget Office, 77
connectivity, 24, 56, 113, 170
consciousness, 8, 9, 20, 150
consensus, 145
Constitution, 139
construct validity, 57
construction, 4, 109, 140, 145
consumers, 28, 30, 56, 60, 83, 138
consumption, 75, 76
controversial, 142
convention, 93
convergence, 54, 99
conversations, 17, 39, 58
cooperation, 57, 143
coordination, 34
correlation(s), 58
cost, 17, 67, 80, 160
creativity, 145
crimes, 20, 84, 139, 140, 142
criminals, 20, 142
crises, 127, 144, 152
crowds, 129, 152
cues, 62, 67, 132, 134
cultural differences, 56
cultural influence, 29
cultural memory, 21
cultural tradition, 49
cultural values, 57
culture, ix, 4, 7, 15, 17, 21, 25, 30, 38, 40, 50, 54, 55, 56, 57, 58, 59, 60, 61, 63, 64, 65, 67, 68, 69, 70, 71, 87, 89, 127, 128, 145, 146, 156, 157, 159, 161, 167
cures, 85
curriculum, 10, 49
customer service, 83
customers, 93, 142, 150
cyberbullying, 38
cyberculture, 58
cyberglove, 111
cyberspace, vii, viii, x, 3, 17, 20, 21, 25, 45, 47, 49, 51, 53, 54, 58, 86, 100, 125, 135, 150, 152, 156, 157, 159, 164, 166, 169, 170, 171, 173
cycles, 6, 144
Czech Republic, 67

D

dance, 8

danger, 38
Darwinism, 46
data, ix, 28, 35, 51, 59, 67, 83, 84, 90, 92, 93, 94, 95, 136, 137, 138, 139, 140, 142, 144
data collection, 35
data mining, 95
database, 70, 115, 138, 139
Davos Party, 98
decay, 4, 75
decentralization, 130
deception, 143
defamation, 142
degradation, 24, 60, 68, 75
delirium, 167
democracy, 3, 20, 24, 48, 51, 73, 75, 79, 99, 123, 140, 144, 145, 146, 151, 152, 156, 157, 161, 164, 169, 173
democrats, 146
Denmark, 66, 76
depersonalization, 88
depression, 136
depth, 30, 39
designers, 15, 67
detachment, 81, 140
developed nations, 97, 99, 127, 160, 173
developing nations, 82, 160
developmental process, 7
dichotomy, 73, 91, 99, 173
diffusion, 62, 64, 67, 162
digital culture, 55, 58, 59, 60, 61, 63, 64, 65, 67, 69
Digital Delirium, 157
digital divide, ix, 29, 66, 67, 70, 82, 85, 86, 97, 100, 172
digital format, 23, 49, 50, 53, 171
digital immigrants, 67, 71
digital library, 17
digital natives, 67, 89
digital technology, 128
Digital Trade Act, 144
digitalization, 51, 85, 88, 89, 90, 150
dimensionality, 55, 57, 68, 69
directors, 79
discrete event systems, 110
discrimination, 71, 74
diseases, 35
dispersion, 21
distance learning, 131
distribution, 76, 77, 92, 100, 113, 123
District of Columbia, 47
divergence, 89, 99, 101

diversity, 47, 130
doctors, 78, 113
domestication, 12, 87
dominance, 47, 122
donations, 37, 80
dopamine, 157
downsizing, 49
DRD4, 157
DRD4 gene, 157
dream, 128
dreaming, 8, 78, 80
drugs, 136, 161
Dutch East India Trade Company, 124
DVD, 84
dynamism, 57

E

early warning, 146
Eastern Civilization, 5, 75
e-banking, 14
eBay, vii, 83
e-book, ii, 28, 50, 161
ecology, 14, 127
e-commerce, 10, 17, 70, 83, 161
e-communication, 24, 48, 78, 129, 161, 170
economic crisis, 127
economic downturn, 79
economic growth, 11, 16, 77, 92
economic performance, 16
economic status, 97
economic theory, 127
economics, 15, 59, 89
ecosystem, 4
EDI, 83
e-documents, 84, 88
education, 9, 12, 14, 27, 28, 29, 31, 35, 37, 39, 40, 49, 51, 57, 58, 68, 74, 75, 78, 82, 90, 100, 127, 131, 132, 149, 150, 152
EGV, 124
Egypt, 8, 123
Egyptians pyramids, 74
e-information, 14, 48, 50
e-learning, 14, 131, 132
election, 20, 47, 80, 81, 130
electricity, 10, 48, 85, 107, 117, 124, 157
electromagnetic, 134
electromagnetic waves, 134
Electronic Civilization, 156
electronic communication, 91

Electronic Frontier Foundation, 145
Electronic Global Village, 124
Electronic Republic, 157
electronic way, 128
e-mail, 10, 14, 17, 82, 83, 88, 98, 142, 162
e-meetings, 49
emerging world, 25, 54, 86, 100, 152
emotion, 129
emotional stability, 129
employees, 35, 47, 138, 150
employers, 47, 136
employment, 16
empowerment, 79
End of History, 75
endorsements, 32
end-users, 56
enemies, 46, 74
energy, 31, 48, 156, 163, 164
enforcement, 4
engineering, 67, 88, 117, 133
English Language, 17
English Revolution, 123
Enlightenment Project, 75
enslavement, 87
entrepreneurs, 87, 159
environment(s), ix, x, 17, 20, 24, 38, 56, 58, 64, 66, 73, 91, 92, 107, 110, 112, 114, 131, 133, 134, 143, 160, 161
environmental awareness, 113
environmental degradation, 170
epidemic, 34
e-publications, 49
equality, 76
equilibrium, 91, 160
e-readers, 161
Eritrea, 66
e-smart executives, 49
ethics, 21, 145
ethnicity, 30, 82
euphoria, 29
Euphrates, 4, 122, 158
Europe, 10, 76, 77, 99, 123, 124, 138, 163, 164
European Union, 51
everyday life, 53, 128, 137
evidence, 39, 59, 62, 82
evil, 38, 39, 106
evolution, 4, 8, 40, 46, 55, 59, 60, 69, 75, 84, 89, 107, 121, 122, 125, 134
exchange rate, 76
exclusion, 28

exercise, 88, 130, 134, 143, 146
expertise, 35
exploitation, 74
exposure, 67, 135
expressiveness, 58, 63, 65
external environment, 69
extraction, 74
eye movement, 88

F

F2F, 91, 150
F2P, 91
Facebook, vii, 17, 18, 20, 28, 29, 30, 36, 50, 63, 65, 66, 84, 87, 89, 92, 136, 142, 144, 162
face-to-face communication, 50, 53, 62, 98, 150, 172
face-to-face interaction, 28
facial expression, 129
factories, 14, 164
faith, 47, 49, 51
fake identity, 142
families, 40
family life, 27, 28
famine, 159
farmers, 12, 157, 160
farms, 159, 160
fat, 78, 80
FBI, 162
fear(s), 78, 157
feelings, 17
femininity, 57
fidelity, 108, 109
filters, 89
financial, 29, 77, 78, 82, 99, 173
financial elite, 78, 99, 173
financial resources, 82
Finland, 66, 100
flight, 108, 112
flight simulator, 108, 112
floods, 159
fluid, 56
food, 4, 7, 8, 12, 13, 46, 88, 127, 159, 160
food production, 4, 12
football, 115
force, 10, 51, 56, 60, 74, 86, 91, 93, 116, 157, 160
forced labor, 74
formation, 4, 28, 30, 39, 92, 122, 124, 130, 163
foundations, 4, 78
France, 124
fraud, 20, 141, 142

freedom, 21, 45, 49, 51, 53, 144, 145, 146, 156, 162, 170, 172
freedom of speech, 49, 145
French Revolution, 76, 80, 123
friendship, 166, 174
Friendster, 29
funding, 80
fundraising, 37
funds, 162

G

gambling, 85
games, 24, 33, 49, 67, 78, 88, 92, 111, 115, 118, 120, 129, 130, 134, 136, 148, 169
Gates Foundation, 79
GDP, 13
genre, 111
geography, 156
Germany, 76, 145
gestures, 111, 112
Gini coefficient(s), 76
glasses, 92, 112, 116
Global Area Networks, 14, 159
Global Civilization, 20, 23, 47, 97, 159, 163, 164, 166, 173
global competition, 56, 60, 160
Global Digital Nervous System, 157
global economy, 10, 17, 91, 160
global mobility, 12
global scale, 56, 92
globalization, 27, 28, 49, 92, 95, 96, 127, 161, 166, 167, 173, 174
glue, 28, 60
goals, xi, 14, 49, 82, 99, 113, 145, 160, 173
God, 46
Google, vii, 30, 40, 50, 56, 84, 87, 89, 116, 118, 129, 137, 141, 144, 150, 162
Gordon Gekko, 46
governance, 143, 144, 151, 172
governments, 14, 18, 20, 21, 56, 59, 137, 144, 145, 164
GPS, ix, 115, 116, 119, 120, 142
grades, 131
gravity, 8
Great Crisis, 127
Great Firewall, 140, 145
Greece, 80
greed, 46, 47
group membership, 142

growing inequality, 77, 163
growth, ix, 4, 13, 51, 58, 70, 76, 77, 78, 79, 80, 82, 87, 122
Guinea, 66
gun control, 139
Guttenberg, 123

H

happiness, 135
health, 4, 13, 14, 35, 78, 130, 134, 135, 139, 149, 152, 161
health care, 4, 13, 149
health information, 35
health insurance, 139
hemisphere, 5
Henry Ford, 78
heroism, 57
Hewett-Packard, 150
high school, 97
high school diploma, 97
higher education, 131
highways, vii, viii
Hindu, x, 5, 46, 159, 166
hippocampus, 133
history, 4, 7, 10, 25, 28, 40, 41, 59, 61, 70, 75, 100, 106, 107, 108, 112, 113, 117, 118, 119, 120, 128, 140, 156, 167, 169
Hollywood, 86
hologram, 117
homes, 14
homework, 118, 131
homicide, 77
homicide rates, 77
homo sapiens, 150, 157
Homo tributus, 126
homogeneity, 65
honesty, 143
Honesty, 140
Hong Kong, 67
host, 116, 143
House, 46, 47, 57, 70, 111
House of Representatives, 46, 47
HTML, 83
hub, 34
human, vii, xi, 4, 8, 9, 10, 12, 14, 15, 28, 39, 45, 47, 55, 56, 73, 74, 75, 78, 81, 84, 87, 88, 91, 97, 101, 111, 113, 118, 121, 122, 123, 124, 125, 134, 137, 145, 150, 156, 157, 161, 162, 163, 167
human behavior, 137

human brain, 134
human cognition, 14
human development, 122, 125, 162, 167
human dimensions, 97
human existence, 134
human experience, 47
human health, 161
human interactions, 55
human trafficking, 74
humanism, 46
hunting, 4
Huntington, S., 100
hygiene, 140
hysteria, 130

I

Iceland, 66
ICT, 13, 46, 67, 68, 82, 84, 85, 86, 89, 90, 91, 92, 93, 96, 97, 99, 173
ideal(s), 10, 156, 164, 167
identification, 36, 46
identity, 25, 28, 54, 57, 58, 63, 66, 80, 128, 141, 142
ideology, 9, 21, 25, 48, 122, 123
illusion, 118, 135
image(s), ix, 88, 100, 107, 110, 111, 112, 113, 115, 117, 119, 135, 145
imagination, 8, 145
IMF, 21
imitation, 64
immersion, 107
immigrants, 14, 67, 71
improvements, 47, 48, 61, 67, 112, 146
income, 50, 74, 76, 77, 78, 82, 99, 127, 173
income distribution, 77
income inequality, 76, 77
income transfers, 77
independence, x, 130, 159, 165
India, 13, 18, 51, 76, 77, 124
individualism, 9, 57
individuals, 14, 24, 46, 48, 55, 69, 77, 85, 92, 129, 162, 170
indoctrination, 46
Indonesia, 18
Industrial Revolution, 10, 49, 75
industrialization, 159
industry(s), 17, 27, 28, 34, 35, 40, 60, 113, 115, 124, 141, 144
inequality, ix, 50, 54, 66, 67, 74, 75, 76, 77, 78, 100, 101, 127, 163

Inequality, 74, 75, 76
infancy, 29, 100
inferences, 137
INFOCO, 122, 123, 124, 125, 126
Information, v, 3, 6, 10, 11, 12, 13, 14, 15, 16, 25, 32, 33, 34, 40, 54, 55, 59, 69, 70, 71, 82, 84, 88, 90, 91, 93, 99, 126, 130, 140, 152, 158, 160, 166, 167, 173, 174
Information Ocean, 84
information processing, 9, 92
information sharing, 32, 35, 39
information technology, vii, x, 17, 47, 61, 66, 70, 159, 161, 162, 166, 173
Informatization, 87
INFOSTRADA, 21, 140, 141
infrastructure, 5, 6, 7, 17, 23, 58, 80, 125, 127, 157, 159, 162
Innovation, 92
Instagram, 30, 58, 65, 84
instinct, 47, 130
institutions, 15, 35, 70, 85, 95, 129
integration, 132
intellectual contribution, 50
intellectual property, 97
intelligence, 13, 18, 21, 23, 25, 45, 49, 53, 54, 78, 82, 86, 92, 100, 136, 150, 152, 156, 157, 164, 170, 171
interdependence, 124
interface, 61, 65, 68, 110, 111
international communication, 25
international standards, 84
international trade, 74, 164
Internet, vii, viii, 10, 12, 14, 20, 21, 24, 27, 28, 29, 36, 38, 39, 51, 55, 56, 59, 60, 64, 66, 67, 68, 69, 70, 71, 80, 82, 83, 84, 85, 86, 87, 88, 90, 91, 92, 93, 95, 97, 101, 124, 125, 136, 139, 140, 144, 145, 146, 150, 152, 159, 161, 169
Internet addiction, 38, 68
Internet dependency, 67, 68, 70
Internet of things, 56, 69, 87
interpersonal communication, 89
interpersonal relations, 28
interrelations, 24, 135, 170
intervention(s), 113, 157
inventors, 50, 92, 117
investment, 35, 36
Iran, 162
Iraq, 142, 158
IRC, 33, 34
Ireland, 67

irrigation, 74, 159
Islam, 75
Islam Civilization, 75
Islamic morality, 75
isolation, 136, 140
issues, 3, 5, 21, 22, 36, 66, 73, 85, 86, 98, 110, 121, 130, 140, 142, 143, 149
Italy, 80
iteration, 92

J

Japan, 18, 67, 115
Jew, 46
job creation, 92
Jones, St., 25, 54
journalism, 40

K

Kenya, 122
kill, 139, 143, 161
knowledge, 5, 6, 8, 13, 18, 23, 48, 49, 53, 56, 64, 66, 73, 88, 89, 90, 91, 92, 93, 94, 95, 96, 97, 98, 99, 122, 125, 132, 143, 149, 150, 152, 161, 162, 171, 173
knowledge divide, 95, 97
knowledge society, 91, 97
Korea, 9, 130

L

labor force, 97, 160
landscape(s), x, 86, 122, 135, 151, 165, 166, 172, 173, 174
language, 8, 30, 46, 47, 50, 51, 62, 67, 83, 110, 122, 123, 124, 125, 128, 133, 134, 143, 151, 157
Latin America, 76
Latvia, 67
laws, 8, 60, 74, 92, 149, 151, 172
lead, 15, 18, 28, 48, 53, 58, 73, 82, 86, 92, 99, 130, 136, 142, 146, 156, 161, 163, 172, 173
leadership, 4, 13, 48, 70, 74, 157
learners, 97, 152
learning, 9, 10, 14, 33, 51, 64, 74, 84, 100, 131, 132, 135, 151, 152
learning environment, 131, 152
learning skills, 132

leisure, 3, 14, 21, 62, 67, 84
leisure time, 14
level of education, 127
Lévy, P., 100, 152, 167
liberal democracy, 75, 79
life cycle, 4
lifetime, 9
light, 106, 112, 133, 149, 152
link trainer, 120
LinkedIn, vii, 29, 30, 50, 65, 136, 162
literacy, 88, 134
livestock, 157
living conditions, 124
lobbying, 160
local community, 149
local government, 14
love, 28, 128, 129, 134
loyalty, 34, 36

M

magazines, 49, 50
Main Street, 78
majority, 5, 21, 27, 61, 74, 78, 79, 81, 137, 140
Malaysia, 162
man, 8, 47, 87, 92, 95, 100, 122, 124, 125, 126, 145, 150, 157
management, 10, 13, 55, 95, 101, 131, 143, 152, 161
Managerial capitalism, 80
manipulation, 4
manufactured goods, 13
manufacturing, 8, 31, 160
manufacturing companies, 31
mapping, 33
market share, 49
marketing, 35, 37, 51, 53, 100, 116, 136, 137, 139, 141, 159, 165, 172
marketplace, 114
marriage, 46, 134
masculinity, 57
mass, 48, 51, 113
material resources, 75
materialism, 11
materials, 113
matter, 9, 15, 68, 69, 70, 77, 115, 116
McLuhan, M., 25
measurements, 35
mechanization, 12

media, 6, 9, 23, 27, 28, 29, 30, 31, 35, 36, 37, 38, 39, 40, 41, 49, 62, 65, 67, 69, 70, 79, 89, 92, 99, 115, 127, 131, 141, 142, 162
media richness, 62, 65, 67
medical, 113, 130
medicine, 88, 117
membership, 49, 78, 80, 82, 86, 90, 95, 97
memory, 17, 100, 126, 134
mental development, 134
Mercedes-Benz, 117
Mesopotamia, 158, 159
messages, 24, 39, 58, 62, 64, 65, 66, 82, 83, 130, 131, 134, 136, 169
metaphor, 83
methodology, 3, 45, 55, 60, 73, 105, 121, 155
Mexico, 18, 140, 146
Microsoft, 61, 115, 119, 139
middle class, 77, 80, 160
Middle East, 4, 5, 12
military, 4, 5, 65, 74, 95, 113, 146
miniature, 109
Minneapolis, 70, 167
miscommunication, 142
mission, 3, 13, 24, 155, 156, 169
mixed reality (MR), ix
mobile communication, 10, 134
mobile device, 157
mobile phone, 114, 115, 116, 130
mobile telephony, 114
models, 61, 64, 109, 131, 160, 167
modernity, 10
modifications, 51
modus operandi, 7, 81, 149, 151, 156, 164, 172
momentum, 62
monks, 8, 123
Moon, 8
moral code, 46
moral development, 74
morality, 15, 39, 74, 75, 127
Mossberger, K., 100
motivation, 98, 131, 151
MR, ix, x
MUD, 111
multimedia, 67, 83
murals, 124
music, 8, 31, 50, 144
Muslim, 46
mutation, 157
mutual respect, 143
Myanmar, 137

Myspace, 18, 29

N

narcotics, 135
national culture, 21, 55, 56, 57, 58, 59, 65, 68, 69, 70, 71
navigation system, 115
needy, 78, 81
negative consequences, 39
neglect, 20
nervous system, 9
Netherlands, 66, 67
Netizens, 90
network members, 51
networking, vii, 17, 29, 30, 32, 35, 36, 38, 39, 40, 41, 61, 62, 65, 66, 124
neural network, 85
neurotransmitter, 157
neutral, 58, 159
New Civilization, 48
New World Order, 75
Newsweek, 50
Next Link, 150
Nigeria, 18
nonverbal cues, 132
North America, 76
North Korea, 137
Norway, 66
NSA, 162

O

Obama, 81
OECD, 76, 100, 152
officials, 136
omission, 76
online communities, 14, 21, 29, 51, 82, 83, 85, 98, 125, 130, 143, 146, 159, 165
online dating, 135
online information, 128
online learning, 100
operating system, 61, 89, 115
operations, 14, 20, 24, 45, 95, 137, 149, 151, 159, 169, 172
opinion polls, 146
opportunities, 59, 125, 141, 142
optimism, 117, 146
optimization, 16, 21

organ(s), 8, 9, 74, 101, 150, 157
organizational behavior, 70
organize, 4, 21, 22, 28, 47, 130, 160, 164
originality, 55, 105
Orwell, 137
outreach, 36, 37
outsourcing, 13, 17, 162
overlap, 59
overlay, 107
overpopulation, 24, 170
oversight, 141
ownership, 74, 95

P

Pacific, 76
Pakistan, 18, 20, 151
parallel, 23, 65, 151, 172
Parliament, 145
participants, 27, 39, 88, 89, 131, 133, 135
password, 14
PDA, 115
peace, 5, 10, 124
perceived outcome, 63
Perceived usefulness, 70
permission, 137
personal accounts, 65
personal life, 48
personality, 157
personality traits, 157
physicians, 130
pigs, 157, 160
Pinterest, 30
PIPA, 144
Pirate Bay Party, 145
pitch, 108
planets, 52, 128
platform, 34, 35, 36, 49, 65, 85, 114, 115, 131
PLATO, 29, 41
playing, 24, 74, 79, 88, 105, 129, 136, 169
Poland, 20, 21, 140, 141
police, 130
policy, 21, 89, 129, 130, 139, 162
Polish Revolution, 127, 163
political crisis, 127
political participation, 80, 97
political parties, 23, 36
political power, 75, 79, 101, 163
political revolution, 123, 124
political system, 7, 27, 28, 86

politics, 14, 36, 39, 47, 48, 59, 78, 80, 81, 82, 89, 130, 163
politics divide, 80
polling, 146
pools, 150
poor, 76, 77, 78, 79, 80, 82, 86, 98, 99, 173
population, 16, 27, 58, 59, 66, 67, 68, 76, 77, 101, 122, 127, 140, 160, 163
population growth, 16
portability, 113
portable computer, 114
portfolio, 140
Portugal, 80
positive addiction, 68
positive correlation, 58
post-industrial society, 13
postmodernism, 100
post-traumatic stress disorder, 135
poverty, 21, 74, 101
PowerPoint, 131
president, vii, 3, 20, 45, 46, 48, 60, 73, 80, 81, 121, 130, 137, 155
President Obama, 60
prevention, 145
primacy, 123
principles, 25, 48, 49, 92, 93, 94
printed books, 9, 161
private information, 66
private property, 50
problem solving, 99, 173
producers, 87
profanity, 143
professional careers, 97
professionalism, 65, 69, 144
professionals, 32, 35, 95, 96, 150, 161
profit, x, 12, 18, 37, 130, 134, 138, 162, 165
programming, 13, 57, 110, 119
programming languages, 110, 119
project, 21, 57, 74, 128, 145
proliferation, 88
property rights, 74
prosperity, 97
PROTECT, 144
protected health, 35
protection, 141
pseudo-democracy, 146
psychological processes, 40
psychology, 64, 68, 91, 99, 117, 173
public administration, 16, 127, 139
public life, 82, 129

public offices, 80
public opinion, 20
public policy, 3, 24, 91, 155, 169
public service, 36
publishing, 14, 48, 130

Q

quality of life, 14, 57, 161
quantum computing, 156
quantum society, vii, 156, 169
questioning, 10, 135

R

race, 30, 39, 82, 165
radiation, 119
radio, 14, 113
railway, 124
rash, 17
ratification, 144
reaction time, 93
reactions, 63
readership, 49, 50, 125
reading, 24, 48, 83, 89, 90, 145, 161, 169
real civilization, x, xi, 3, 24, 48, 73, 88, 99, 155, 156, 159, 163, 166, 169, 173, 174
real environment, ix, 17
real estate, 159
real life, 80, 128, 151, 152, 172, 175
real time, 83, 110, 113, 114, 131
real world, 21, 48, 53, 69, 78, 80, 81, 85, 86, 93, 99, 107, 114, 121, 125, 128, 129, 130, 132, 133, 135, 140, 143, 144, 146, 147, 149, 151, 172
realism, 108, 110
reality, viii, ix, x, 9, 17, 39, 41, 45, 53, 56, 78, 81, 86, 105, 106, 107, 108, 110, 112, 113, 114, 115, 116, 117, 118, 121, 124, 128, 129, 133, 134, 135, 136, 140, 142, 146, 149, 150, 151, 152, 159, 160, 164, 165, 170, 172
reason, 28, 60, 61, 63, 68, 74, 75, 84, 90, 113, 132, 164
reasoning, 90, 95, 99, 173
recession, 93
recognition, 47, 69, 105
recommendations, 117
reconstruction, 75
regression, 151
regulations, 9, 49, 91

Reinhold, H., 54
rejection, 162
relatives, 34
reliability, 57
relief, 127
religion, ix, 4, 6, 10, 30, 45, 46, 47, 49, 50, 51, 53, 122, 123, 127, 159, 170, 171, 172
religious beliefs, 29
Renren, 30
rent, 74
replication, 71, 113
requirements, 60
RES, 32, 33
researchers, 61, 133
reserves, 16
resolution, 143
resources, 13, 14, 16, 17, 20, 24, 52, 53, 82, 90, 98, 113, 127, 131, 140, 152, 163, 164, 170
response, 4, 56, 69, 79, 144, 152, 159
restrictions, 132
retail, 31, 83
revenue, 28, 130, 135, 141
rhythm, 21, 156
rights, 60, 74, 131, 144, 145
risk(s), 65, 66, 128, 146
ROI, 36
root, 106
Rousseau, J.J., 101
rules, 5, 7, 8, 9, 47, 49, 50, 74, 77, 92, 93, 94, 95, 111, 122, 136, 143, 149
rules of virtuality, 50, 149
Russia, 18, 80, 140

S

safety, 10, 36, 108, 120
Saudi Arabia, 20
scholarship, 10
school, 14, 29, 51, 68, 85, 95, 96, 97, 130, 142, 150, 152
science, x, 8, 9, 10, 13, 46, 53, 76, 78, 88, 116, 119, 127, 155, 165, 166
science fiction, x, 78, 116, 155, 165, 166
scope, 4, 39, 74, 75, 92, 99, 156, 161, 173
SCT, 64
second generation, 115
secondary schools, 95
security, 50, 59, 98, 141, 142
segregation, 140
self-consciousness, 156, 167

self-efficacy, 61
self-expression, 58, 63, 65
self-improvement, 47
self-organization, 23
self-regulation, 54
Semantic Ladder, 93, 94, 95
Semantic Web, 84, 92
semantics, 93
Senate, 46
sensation, 134
senses, 9
sensors, 112, 116
servers, 83, 138
service provider, 29, 59
services, 4, 14, 17, 31, 36, 59, 62, 74, 83, 115, 131, 136, 138, 145, 161
sex, 134, 161
sexual exploitation, 74
sexual slavery, 74
shape, 17, 67
shareholders, 79
sheep, 157
Shinto, 46
shock, 48, 54, 101
signs, 68
silver, 113
simulation, 107, 108, 109, 110, 112, 117, 119
simulator, 112
Singapore, 162
skin, 106
Skype, 128
slavery, 74, 100
slaves, 74, 162
sleep deprivation, 38
smart mob, 130
smart phone, 53, 56, 61, 89, 115, 134, 172
SMS, 64
smuggling, 100
social behavior, 28
social capital, 77
social change, 147
social cognition, 55
Social Cognitive Theory, 64
social cohesion, 28, 77
social context, 85
social control, 28
social development, 92, 124
social group, 17, 65, 145
social identity, 151, 172
social inequality, 74, 75, 76

social influence, 61
social interactions, 65
social justice, 86
social life, 13, 29, 86, 95, 151, 172
social media, 27, 28, 30, 31, 35, 36, 37, 38, 39, 40, 41, 62, 92, 131, 141, 142
social network(s), vii, x, 10, 17, 18, 24, 27, 28, 29, 30, 31, 32, 35, 36, 37, 39, 40, 41, 49, 51, 53, 61, 62, 63, 65, 66, 85, 89, 92, 98, 125, 130, 131, 136, 140, 144, 155, 159, 165, 169, 172
social networking, 17, 27, 28, 29, 30, 31, 32, 35, 36, 37, 40, 41, 61, 62, 63, 65, 66, 89, 92, 130, 131
social norms, 58, 64
social order, 8, 74, 80, 86
social organization, 157
social phenomena, 21
social problems, 79, 140, 167, 174
social relations, 34, 86
social responsibility, 164
social security, 142
social skills, 150
social structure, 28, 30
social support, 35
socialism, 100
socialization, 17, 28, 39, 57, 150
software, 60, 67, 68, 83, 87, 107, 110, 112, 116, 137, 152
Solar Model, 27, 30, 31, 39
solidarity, 21
solution, 7, 45, 48, 50, 58, 73, 77, 93, 133, 140, 144, 149, 155, 156
SOPA, 144
SoundCloud, 84
South Africa, 114
South America, 4
South Korea, 67, 130
Southeast Africa, 122
space-time, 10
Spain, 77, 80, 99
spam, 66
specialists, 90, 98, 137, 140, 145, 163
specialization, 159
species, 75, 89
speculation, 77
speech, 48, 49, 115, 140, 145
spending, 13, 18, 34, 128, 149
Spring, 25, 54, 162
state(s), 7, 19, 20, 59, 86, 93, 107, 129, 130, 134, 140, 145, 156, 159, 172
statistics, 29, 31, 41

steam engine, 124
steel, 13
stereotypes, 56
steroids, 56
Stiglitz, J., 101
stigmatized, 28
stock, 53, 162, 172
stockholders, 162
storage, 21, 84, 92, 136
storms, 108
strategies, xi, 16, 36, 49, 82, 95, 99, 137, 152
stratification, 74
stroke, 112
structure, 4, 8, 30, 64, 150
style, xi, 47, 64, 66, 74, 91
subjective well-being, 11
succession, 110, 113
Sun, 8, 88
suppliers, 136
Supreme Court, 145
surplus, 74
surveillance, 36, 162
survival, 8, 124, 125, 127
sustainability, xi, 11, 167, 174
sustainable growth, 97
Sweden, 66, 67, 76, 145
Switzerland, 67
sympathy, 77
symptoms, 127
synthesis, 4

T

takeover, 47
talent, 13
Taliban, 162
TAM3, 61, 63
Tambini, D., 54
Tanzania, 122
target, 5
Targowski, A., 25, 54, 71, 101, 152, 167
Task Force, 51
taxes, 77, 78, 88, 161
teachers, 131, 132
team members, 133
teams, 36, 133, 165
techniques, 59, 113
technological advances, 56
technological change, 99, 173
technological developments, 7, 165

technological progress, 165
technological revolution, 117
technologies, 22, 27, 28, 58, 61, 88, 89, 93, 105, 107, 112, 113, 116, 137, 157
technology acceptance model, 71
Technopoly, 167
teenage girls, 38
teens, 38, 40
telecommunications, 9, 137
tele-democrats, 146
telephone(s), 9, 10, 48, 85, 113, 117, 162
tempo, 8
territory, 7
terrorism, 75, 162
testing, 60
text messaging, 21, 25, 175
Thanksgiving, 46
theft, 66, 141, 142
Theory of Planned Behavior, 62, 69
Third Wave, 11, 12, 47, 160
thoughts, 9, 36, 56
threats, 57
throws, 46
Tigris, 4, 122, 158
tissue, 157
Toffler, A., 25, 54, 167
Toffler, H., 25
top-down, 74
Toynbee, A., 54, 167
toys, 56
trade, 7, 74, 124
trafficking, 74, 100, 101
training, 33, 65, 108, 109, 119
traits, 68
transactions, vii, 135, 137
transformation(s), 15, 18, 56, 64, 67, 127
translation, 84
transmission, 82
transplant, 157
transportation, 4, 12, 145, 159
trauma, 9
treatment, 139
triggers, 155, 166, 174
Tumblr, 30
Turkey, 158
Turks, 10
turnout, 146
turnover, 138
tweets, 64

Index

Twitter, vii, 18, 28, 30, 36, 37, 50, 51, 63, 65, 92, 136, 142, 144, 162
typology, 78, 80, 86, 95, 97

U

UK, 101, 119, 134
unions, 79
United Nations (UN), 74, 76, 77, 101, 140
United States (USA), 18, 46, 76, 77, 80, 81, 118, 119, 136, 137, 139, 140
universe, 88
universities, 35, 40
updating, 51
urban, 6, 130
US Supreme Court, 145

V

vacuum, 109
Valuation, 30
values, 5, 6, 21, 45, 47, 51, 53, 57, 58, 70, 82, 91, 95, 123, 146, 159, 162, 164, 172
VAN, 14
variations, 55, 59, 68, 69
vector, 110
vehicles, 114
velocity, 21
video games, 67, 92, 118
videos, 17, 32, 33
Vietnam, 18
Viking, 25, 167
violence, 139
virtual America, 48
virtual civilization, 29, 30
virtual community(s), 17, 24, 25, 31, 41, 54, 131, 143, 144, 145, 146, 169
virtual country, 78
virtual divide, 21, 172, 173
virtual environment, ix, 110, 133
virtual groups, 83, 98, 99, 125, 173
Virtual Human Interaction Lab, 135
virtual learning environment, 131
virtual life, 127, 136, 151, 152, 172, 175
virtual members, 23, 129, 172
virtual organization, 10, 24, 47, 169
virtual reality, 17, 53, 105, 107, 108, 110, 112, 113, 118, 124, 128, 129, 133, 134, 135, 136
virtual rich elite, 82, 86

virtual society, vii, ix, 3, 24, 27, 28, 30, 39, 51, 59, 78, 82, 144, 149, 164, 169, 170
Virtual Wave, 17, 23, 24, 155, 169
virtual word, 51
virtuality, viii, ix, x, xi, 45, 47, 48, 49, 50, 51, 53, 82, 121, 122, 128, 133, 134, 135, 136, 142, 149, 150, 151, 156, 159, 164, 165, 166, 170, 171, 172, 174
virtuality doctrine, 49, 51
virtuality education, 51
virtuality religion, 51, 53, 171, 172
virtualization, 150
Virtualization Wave, 155, 156, 160, 161, 162, 166, 167, 174
vision, 49, 84, 112
VLE, 131
vocabulary, 47, 134, 151
vote, 20, 81, 130, 145, 146
voters, 129, 144, 145, 146
voting, 22, 36, 49, 85
VR, 133

W

W3C, 84
wages, 79
walking, 170
Wall Street, 46, 78, 99, 135, 164
Walmart, 95, 138
war, 5, 10, 50, 75, 78, 93, 127, 161
Washington, 54, 100, 146
waste, 134
water, 86, 106, 130, 135, 163, 164
wealth, 4, 6, 12, 21, 48, 74, 76, 77, 78, 82, 86, 87, 92, 98, 100, 161
wealth distribution, 76
wealth divide, 78
weapons, 9, 139
wear, 106
web, 10, 49, 61, 65, 66, 83, 84, 89, 93, 100, 118, 119, 128, 131
Web 3.0, 92
Web 4.0, 92, 100
web browser, 93
web pages, 83, 84
web service, 83
web sites, 61, 65, 66, 131
webpages, 17
websites, 40, 83, 131, 145
WELL, 29, 143, 144

well-being, ix, 3, 13, 18, 45, 73, 78, 80, 127, 147, 149, 155, 161, 163
Western Civilization, 5, 9, 17, 20, 78, 80, 97, 123, 127, 160, 162, 164
Western Europe, 163, 164
White House, 144
wholesale, 31
Wikipedia, 66, 67, 87, 92, 118, 119, 131, 144
wilderness, 13
wireless devices, 157
Wisdom, 93, 120, 126, 152
wise civilization, 127, 145, 162, 167, 174
withdrawal, 68
Wix, 83
Woolgar, St., 54
workers, 13, 16, 17, 79, 140, 150, 164
workforce, 13

working class, 79
World Bank, 76
world order, 100
World War I, 81, 139
World Wars, 124
World Wide Web, 29, 50, 83, 84
World-System of Production, 158
worldwide, 28, 83
WWW, 83, 84, 87

Y

Yahoo, vii, 30, 50, 84, 92, 137, 150
Yale University, 24
young people, 134, 161
YouTube, 30, 41, 142